DISABILITY, CULTURE, AND EQUITY SERIES

Alfredo J. Artiles and Elizabeth B. Kozleski, *Series Editors*

Condition Critical—Key Principles for Equitable and Inclusive Education
DIANA LAWRENCE-BROWN & MARA SAPON-SHEVIN

Condition Critical

Key Principles for Equitable and Inclusive Education

Diana Lawrence-Brown
Mara Sapon-Shevin

with contributions from

Subini Annamma • Laura Atkinson • David J. Connor •
Elizabeth Z. Dejewski • David Feingold • Ana Maria García •
Kathryn Henn-Reinke • JoDell Heroux • Kathleen Kotel •
Elizabeth B. Kozleski • Valerie Owen • Susan Peters •
Julie Ramirez • Maryl A. Randel • Janet Sauer •
Stacey N. Skoning • Graciela Slesaransky-Poe •
Robin M. Smith • Virginia Zeitlin

Foreword by Nirmala Erevelles

Teachers College, Columbia University
New York and London

Published by Teachers College Press, 1234 Amsterdam Avenue, New York, NY
10027

Library of Congress Cataloging-in-Publication Data

Lawrence-Brown, Diana.
   Condition critical : key principles for equitable and inclusive education /
   by Diana Lawrence-Brown, Mara Sapon-Shevin ; with Contributions by
   Janet Sauer, Graciela Slesaransky-Poe, Ana Maria García, Stacey N. Skoning,
   Kathryn Henn-Reinke,David J. Connor, Subini A. Annamma, Robin Smith,
   Elizabeth B. Kozleski, Laura Atkinson, JoDell Heroux, Susan Peters, Maryl
   Randel, Valerie Owen, Kathleen Kotel, Julie Ramirez, Virginia Zeitlin, Elizabeth
   Dejewski, & David Feingold ; foreword by Nirmala Erevelles.
      pages cm. — (Disability, equity, and culture series)
   Includes index.
   ISBN 978-0-8077-5476-4 (pbk. : alk. paper) —
   ISBN 978-0-8077-5477-1 (hardcover : alk. paper)
      1. Inclusive education. 2. Educational equalization. I. Sapon-Shevin, Mara.
   II. Title.
   LC1200.L386 2013
   371.9′046--dc23   2013029152

ISBN 978-0-8077-5476-4 (paper)
ISBN 978-0-8077-5477-1 (hardcover)
eISBN 978-0-8077-7279-9

Printed on acid-free paper
Manufactured in the United States of America

21   20   19   18   17   16   15   14   8   7   6   5   4   3   2   1

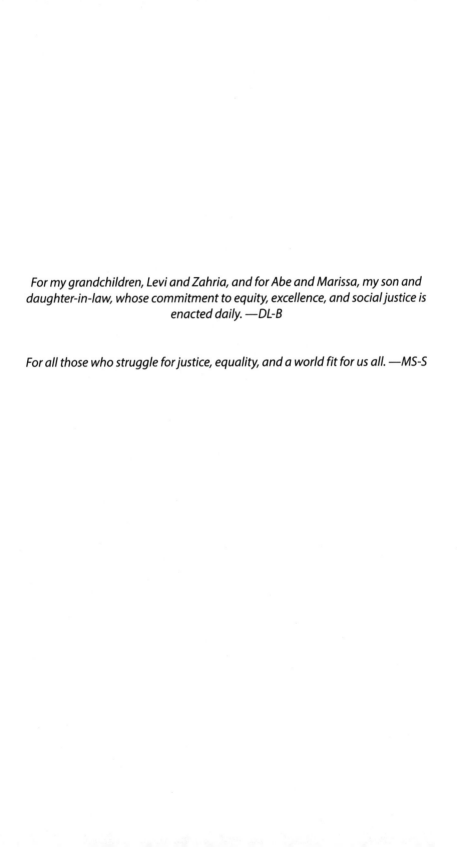

For my grandchildren, Levi and Zahria, and for Abe and Marissa, my son and daughter-in-law, whose commitment to equity, excellence, and social justice is enacted daily. —DL-B

For all those who struggle for justice, equality, and a world fit for us all. —MS-S

Contents

Foreword

I am sitting in my study, laptop propped on my lap, as I begin writing this foreword on disability, difference, and education. But it is hard to concentrate, since my mind is on other things that seem more grievous than my struggle to tap out letters on a blank screen. A televised trial about the murder of a 17-year-old African American boy, Trayvon Martin, by George Zimmerman, a 29-year-old man of White and Hispanic descent, in a gated community in Florida has mesmerized me. Zimmerman, a self-appointed neighborhood watchman for this gated community, became suspicious of Martin, who was returning to his father's girlfriend's house with Skittles and an iced tea that he had bought at the neighborhood store. Against the advice of the 911 operator, Zimmerman followed Martin for a short time, got into a scuffle with him, and allegedly shot him in self-defense.

Central to the trial is the key witness for the prosecution, Rachel Jeantel, who was on the cell phone with Martin a few minutes before the fatal shots were fired. But Jeantel's telling testimony, offered in her unique diction of teenage street slang blended with the accents of her Haitian and Dominican cultural heritage, seems to confound almost all the officers of the court, who ask her to repeat herself several times. Zimmerman's attorneys in particular assumed a tone of surprised disdain in the face of her barely concealed frustration at their attempts to make her appear untrustworthy, uncouth, uneducated, and sometimes stupid. I am unsure whether this is their strategy to cast doubt on Jeantel's credibility or their shocked recognition that the heavy-set, dark-skinned African American teenage girl, fidgeting self-consciously in the glare of television cameras and strangers' eyes, represents the embodiment of irreducible difference that their White upper-class privileged heteronormative patriarchal masculinity finds impossible to bridge.

Even before Rachel Jeantel has left the witness box, social media erupts in horror at her appearance, her accent, her language, her (lack of) sex appeal, her (lack of) intelligence, her class background, and her racial/ ethnic roots. I abruptly switch off the television only to turn it on again to sit in angry solidarity with her against this wall of public contempt that threatens to engulf this vulnerable teenager constructed as an outcast even by members of her own community. I am moved by the immense courage and poise she exhibits even when the defense lawyers as well as other officers of the court, with all their trappings of class privilege, try to silence her, even as she steadfastly refuses to let them force her to betray her friendship with her murdered friend. And yet, the chattering heads on almost all the news channels (both liberal and conservative) continue this tirade of shaming that lasts long after the other witnesses testify, the final arguments are made, and the jury comes out with the verdict of not guilty. After the verdict is read, I wipe away angry tears and try to refocus on my writing, but the images of the trial click on and off like an unending slide show in my head till it dawns on me that what I have witnessed and what I should be writing about is the way in which race, class, gender, sexuality, and disability violently intersect in social contexts of exclusion and inclusion to produce this inexplicable tragedy.

I am a teacher and, in a bid to transform this immobilizing rage into productive possibility, I try to think of the lessons to be learned about the complexities and contradictions of social justice at the intersections of social difference in a purportedly democratic society. Stepping back for a moment and looking at the broad picture of this terrible tragedy that left a 17-year-old boy dead and his friend a figure of public ridicule, I think of how different it would have been if we did not practice exclusion on the basis of difference along the lines of race, class, gender, sexuality, ethnicity, and disability. I think of how different it would have been if we as a community of conscious and critical citizens were able to, in Paulo Freire's (1985) words, "read the world" so that we could actually become agents of social transformation.

Condition Critical provides an opportunity to begin to imagine this more humane world. The introduction describes inclusion as "a fundamental way of seeing and responding to human difference for the benefit of everyone involved." Here, inclusive education is not a set of decontextualized skills used only with disabled students but rather a commitment to critical pedagogy and social justice that engages disability, race, class, gender, sexuality, and ethnicity as intersecting categories that impact student experiences in transformative ways. Here, inclusive education is conceptualized as critical pragmatism that is committed not only to the critical analysis of teachers' assumptions about education and its outcomes for marginalized students (in particular) but to the concrete ways in which teachers can organize space/time/curriculum to enable all students to be meaningfully included in diverse classrooms.

This book transforms inclusive education for children from diverse backgrounds and intersecting identities from an abstract ideal into tangible praxis. Every author reminds the reader that the uniqueness of difference does not lie in its deviance but in its embodiment of unimaginable possibilities. This is indeed a radical vision; think about the ways in which an inclusive ethos that realizes possibility in difference rather than deviance could have transformed the sequence of events that led to Martin's death. In response to the tragic events, a thought-provoking meme began appearing on social media asking how different it would have been if Zimmerman had offered Martin a ride in the rain to his destination rather than first stalking him and then shooting him. Think about how different it would have been if we had responded to Rachel Jeantel's nervous debut on prime-time television by recognizing her humanity in all its imperfect authenticity. Think about how an inclusive education could have radically transformed our dangerous stereotypes of race, class, gender, sexuality, and disability. Think about how schools characterized by structures of inclusion rather than exclusion can be life-affirming catalysts for change. This book offers an accessible way to place inclusive pedagogies at the center of transformative educational praxis.

—Nirmala Erevelles
The University of Alabama

REFERENCES

Freire, P. (1985). "Reading the world and reading the word: An interview with Paulo Freire. *Language Arts, 62*(1), 15-21.

Acknowledgments

We wish to express our gratitude to friends and colleagues who help us think better about issues of oppression, liberation, and responsive pedagogy: Bill Ayers, Lee Bell, Catherine Cornbleth, Anne Donnellan, Micah Fialka-Feldman, Anne-Claire Fisher, René Garrison, Kevin Kumashiro, Norm Kunc, Susan Mary Paige, Therese Quinn, Gillian S. Richardson, Nancy Schniedewind, Christine Sleeter, Robin M. Smith, Suzanne SooHoo, Beth Blue Swadener, and Carol Ann Tomlinson.

We are grateful to our many students at Syracuse University and St. Bonaventure University, who have helped us translate big ideas into interactive strategies.

I, Diana, am grateful to my husband, Kent, for his unfailing love, support, and encouragement.

I, Mara, am very appreciative of Peppy, who sat next to me while I wrote and edited and kept me calm in the face of computer malfunctions and brain overload.

I am also deeply appreciative of Dalia Shevin, who holds and shares a clear vision of what a world of connection and justice looks like, and Leora Sapon-Shevin, who uses her teaching gifts to help those who have been marginalized regain their places at the center of their lives.

I also express my deep gratitude to my partner, Karen, who helps me remember what is important and helps reboot my brain when it is spinning.

We would like to acknowledge the support of Susan Liddicoat, who edited this manuscript with skill and insight; series editors Alfredo Artiles and Elizabeth Kozleski; and Brian Ellerbeck from TC Press, who supported this manuscript and helped make our journey smoother.

We are grateful for the generosity of those who contributed "Ground Truth" responses, artwork, and photographs used in the book.

We also appreciate the skilled clerical support of Jennifer Craver, Maithreyee Dubé, Michelle Mondo, and Rachel Ventura, who made our tasks as authors much easier.

Critical Pedagogies, Inclusive Schooling, and Social Justice

Diana Lawrence-Brown

We can, whenever and wherever we choose, successfully teach all children whose schooling is of interest to us. We already know more than we need to do that. Whether or not we do it must finally depend on how we feel about the fact that we haven't so far.

—Ron Edmonds

What comes to mind when you read these comments from Ron Edmonds? Are there certain students, or groups of students, whose schooling has been of insufficient interest to our society? Is schooling of certain groups more important to you than other groups? How do education, effective inclusion, and social justice come together in your mind?

INCLUSIVE SCHOOLING AND SOCIAL JUSTICE

Throughout this book, we will argue that an important foundation of social justice is equity and excellence through inclusive schools and societies. As suggested by Figure I.1, society (the body) can be viewed as the foundation of our schools (the head); equity (here envisioned as the arms) supports excellence.

A strong society can, if it so chooses, devote necessary resources to provide equitable schooling for all of its pupils. But consider what happens when society's commitment to excellence is weaker for some students than for others. In Figure I.1, one arm would be less able to hold up its end; the slope would tip sideways. We can imagine the increased difficulty for the climber on the lowered side. This graphic illustration

Figure I.1: Equity and Excellence

is borne out in the form of lopsided funding, class sizes, availability of qualified teachers, expectations for students—and ultimately lopsided achievement. Our commitment to excellence has not been equitable for all of our children.

Connecting Inclusive Schooling and Critical Pedagogies

Although inclusion is often viewed in schools as being concerned primarily with students with disabilities, we use the term here much more broadly. Inclusive education is viewed here not as a form of special education but as critical pedagogy. Teaching from a critical pedagogy standpoint includes multiple perspectives such as multicultural education, disability studies, and critical pragmatism.

Diverse students are an increasing presence in today's schools, with accompanying interest and concern by educators. This is partly due to our increasingly diverse society, but also related to growing concerns with traditional segregated programs, such as remedial and special education, English language programs, tracking, gifted education, and other pull-outs. Our goal with this book is to develop a critical analysis of our educational system among current and prospective educators (teachers, administrators, and related services personnel). This book differs from others that identify as having a critical perspective in that the focus is on inclusion of students with a broad range of traditionally marginalized differences (including but not limited to disabilities, cultural/linguistic/racial background, gender, sexual orientation, and class).

School change efforts for different groups of marginalized students have operated largely in isolation from each other. However, many of these movements for inclusive practices and anti-oppressive education have much in common. For example, Ball and Harry (1993) describe the following goal of multicultural and social reconstructionist education, shared by advocates and self-advocates for a wide range of traditionally marginalized groups:

> To reform the school program so that all students experience success, social equity, and cultural pluralism . . . . [and are prepared] to use political analysis of inequities inside and outside of school and to use collective social action to redress inequality. (p. 432)

Clearly, various marginalized groups are connected not by physiological similarities (be it disability, race, gender, etc.) but by sociological similarities (in the ways they've been treated by dominant groups). Importantly, they may share a vision for a strength-based educational system based on a view of human difference as essentially valuable, not deficient. To the extent that marginalized groups share such goals, they may be most effective as collaborators.

Analyzing Outcomes and Assumptions

Political, economic, cultural, and social power imbalances connect in producing marginal educational practices and outcomes for students from traditionally marginalized groups (Darder, Baltodano, & Torres, 2009). To address such inequitable practices and outcomes, critical analysis is required among educators, recognizing and analyzing assumptions about education and people with traditionally marginalized differences (e.g., assumptions about the nature of exceptionality, socioeconomic status, culture and race, parenting, poverty, disproportionality, and religion). An important question for us is, how does the marginalized and/or privileged status of students connect with how they are treated in schools? The resulting understandings help educators make sense of and act more effectively within our educational systems.

Learning to apply a critical perspective is a challenging and often overlooked aspect of teacher and administrator preparation, which we seek to address with this book. Critical analysis can be enormously helpful in understanding experiences educating students with traditionally marginalized differences—particularly when confronted with educational practice that fails to live up to legal, ethical, and educational rhetoric. This book explores ways that damaging assumptions take hold, their impact on educational outcomes, and how they can be disrupted.

OVERVIEW OF KEY PRINCIPLES FOR EQUITABLE AND INCLUSIVE EDUCATION

The foundation for this book is provided by 12 key principles (outlined below) that we believe are important to developing and applying a critical perspective toward educating diverse students. We both recognize and reject traditional, deficit-model assumptions; instead we provide the reader with models of culturally relevant, responsive pedagogy built on acknowledging and valuing student diversity. These key principles bring together important ideas and strategies from school change efforts for different groups of marginalized students, for there is considerable overlap among practices and perspectives advocated by these groups. Thus, the principles that provide the structure for this book are drawn from the literature supporting these social justice movements as well as a variety of practical school change experiences.

Key Principle 1: *Inclusion is not primarily a special education, or even an education, issue. It is a fundamental way of seeing and responding to human difference for the benefit of everyone involved.*

We see human difference as essentially valuable, not as deficient. Our society needs the strength and vitality of varied abilities and perspectives. It is not an integrated placement by itself that is powerful, but the degree to which we value (or come to value) those placed (Kyle, 1993). Physical *integration* offers the opportunity, not a guarantee—a necessary but insufficient condition for *inclusion*.

An important consideration, then, is whether individuals from traditionally marginalized groups should be *accommodated* by or *assimilated* by the mainstream. Traditionally, supports and modifications have been provided on a pull-out basis, using a deficit model that assumes that certain students should be "put right" through a separate program as a condition for being assimilated back into the general education classroom. However, supports and services can be more effective when pushed in using a collaborative team approach.

When, for example, services such as special education, English language learning, remedial, and gifted education are integrated within the general education classroom, students formally identified as needing these varied services can receive them without the stigma and loss of classroom instructional time that contribute to concerns with pull-out models. Just as important, other students benefit from increased availability of supports, staff, and strategies that are traditionally accessible only by certain students (e.g., Lawrence-Brown, 2004; Zirkel, 2008).

Mere assimilation deprives everyone of these benefits and of strengths that emerge (in children and educators) through supporting all students. Environments that *will* not accommodate difference are not fitting for anyone.

Key Principle 2: *An important foundation of social justice is equity and excellence in education. Critical analysis is required to recognize and analyze assumptions about education and outcomes for people with traditionally marginalized differences (including but not limited to disabilities, cultural/linguistic/racial background, gender, sexual orientation, and class).*

This principle requires attention to issues of power, decision making, and voice, with careful consideration of how the local context shapes school improvement efforts. These understandings help educators make sense of and act effectively within our educational systems.

Key Principle 3: *Traditionally marginalized differences (including but not limited to disabilities, cultural/linguistic/racial background, gender, sexual orientation, and class) are best understood and responded to within a broader construct of diversity. Each of us has multiple identities that can be represented or viewed in different ways.*

It is the right of each person to choose how she or he is identified, including use of person-first language and description of individual characteristics (including but not limited to exceptionalities, racial/cultural background, gender, sexual orientation, and class).

Let us consider the example of disability. According to Smith, Gallagher, Owen, and Skrtic (2009), "Disability is best understood by listening to disabled people tell about their lives" (p. 245).

> The actual impairment a person experiences is a real and important part of daily life. This lived experience, which may include considerable challenges, generally poses considerably less restriction than what the society imposes due to assumptions of deficit and incompetence. (p. 244)

The deficit assumptions are mistaken as normal, naming people with differences as incompetent, yet disability is part of the normal spectrum of life that requires considerable competence to manage.

Other traditionally marginalized differences are also viewed from this deficit perspective, casting those so labeled as *less* when in fact *more* is required from them to survive under oppressive conditions resulting from a society that systematically privileges certain groups over others.

In addition, the *intersection of* gender, class, disability, and other identities has major implications for students' experiences and outcomes in
schools. Focusing on only one dimension "ignores complex power relationships that shape their lived experiences, and is unlikely to provide
an effective approach to combating inequity in education" (Sullivan &
King Thorius, 2010, p. 95).

***Key Principle 4:** Marginalized differences are socially constructed; how we
respond to individual differences is impacted by factors such as history, culture/
geography, race, gender, and socioeconomic status.*

For example, Americans have been conditioned to see skin color as
representing natural and biologically distinct races; however, this is not a
universal view, nor is it supported by genetic analysis. "The 'racial' worldview was invented [during the colonial period] to assign some groups to
perpetual low status" (p. 3) and rationalize poor treatment of conquered
and oppressed peoples including slaves (American Anthropological Association, 1998).

As another example, segregation of students with disabilities in the
United States more than doubled over the last century. According to the
White House Conference on Child and Health Protection (1931), the percentage of students in special classes in 1928–1929 ranged from .31% (in
Wisconsin) to 1.49% (in Minnesota). In 2010, the nationwide average was
3.3% (U.S. Office of Special Education Programs, 2012). During the same
period—perhaps unsurprisingly, given the increasingly restricted scope
of students represented in their classrooms—general educators came to
see themselves as unqualified to teach the full range of students (Tyack &
Cuban, 1995).

A related problem is disproportionality; students of color are routinely underestimated and then over-referred as having disabilities, resulting
in disproportionate labeling and placement of Black and Hispanic students in special education and other lower educational tracks, including
segregated classrooms. Poor students also are overrepresented. While this
reflects inadequate and biased testing procedures, it is also a product of a
racist and classist society that tends to view as incompetent people who
live, behave, and communicate differently than dominant groups. Merely
improving assessment is insufficient to end disproportionality if it leaves
in place the same disdain for culturally based and class-based patterns of
living and learning (Seidl, 2001).

***Key Principle 5:** There are many parallels between different civil rights
movements, including those movements representing groups that have been
discriminated against on the basis of characteristics such as disability, gender,
sexual orientation, national origin, race, and language.*

Issues of oppression, segregation, bias, stereotyping, loss of rights, and unequal opportunities apply to a wide range of societally marginalized groups (Sapon-Shevin & Zollers, 1999). Marginalized groups have not all been oppressed by the same methods, at the same times, and to the same degree. But each has been treated unjustly and can connect in mutually beneficial ways around civil rights and social justice concerns.

Disability has not always been viewed as a form of diversity, yet deficit perspectives form the foundation of traditional special education in similar ways as they have for other segregated systems. It is important to understand that by locating disability within a critical perspective toward marginalized differences more generally, the implication is *not* that other marginalized differences should be viewed as impairments—quite the contrary. Adopting this perspective does not mean advocating but *rejecting* traditional deficit-oriented perspectives that position people with differences (including but not limited to disability) as inferior, incompetent, or less than normal.

Concern that *traditional* conceptions of disability could become conflated with race in particular are valid in a social and economic system built on assumptions of inferiority of non-Whites (and people with disabilities) and in an educational system that routinely misidentifies students of color as having disabilities (Ball & Harry, 1993). It is vitally important for educators to confront the intersection of special education with race, class, and culture, including how misinterpretation of non-dominant cultural values and practices contributes to oppression of non-dominant groups, even if inadvertently (Pugach & Seidl, 1998).

Despite a similar transformative vision for our educational system, multicultural and other inclusive education movements have operated largely separately. Alterations made using these parallel strategies function primarily as add-ons, effecting little real change in schools and classrooms (Sullivan & King Thorius, 2010). Expanded advocacy for all students who have been denied equitable access to educational opportunity is a critical step in transforming a racist, classist, and ableist system (Pugach & Seidl, 1998).

Key Principle 6: *Educational services in the United States were developed and continue to be based on largely unexamined assumptions about what is beneficial for certain students (e.g., that effective education for diverse students requires a separate program) that are unsupported by outcomes research (e.g., direct comparison of outcomes from inclusive and separate programs).*

Educational rhetoric describes the purpose of special services as beneficial to students; however, the lived experience of students and educators within these systems often renders the rhetoric threadbare (e.g., Lawrence-Brown, 2000). In response, once-accepting participants may begin to reject the arguments supporting the system and begin to work for change, to bring our practices closer to our values (Freire, 2009, p. 54).

Special service categories (especially those overpopulated by students of color or who are poor) function to legitimize and maintain a system of tracking and segregation that "amounts to a denial of access to knowledge" (Seidl, 2001, p. 400) as well as a self-devised explanation for the failure of schools to serve all students well (Pugach & Seidl, 1998).

Key Principle 7: *All children are valuable members of classroom and school communities, with differing voices, strengths, abilities, and contributions. Inclusive communities embrace and expand children's sociocultural repertoires while also dealing with controversy and conflict in creative and constructive ways.*

Building communities capable of valuing all students requires supportive educators who recognize and are skilled at challenging oppression, along with collaborative relationships that are embedded in ongoing analysis of how race, culture, and class are used or misused to explain outcomes of schooling (Pugach & Seidl, 1998).

Key Principle 8: *Students learn in many different ways. In order for students to be successful, educators must be flexible in their approaches, drawing from a repertoire of methodologies that value differentiation and support individualization.*

All students benefit from a quality, inclusive education with meaningful access to the general education curriculum.

Programs and curricula must be planned from a universal design for learning (UDL) stance and only then further modified as needed. Students and educators must receive supports, supplementary aids, and services necessary for effective inclusion.

Key Principle 9: *All behavior is a form of communication, including that which is labeled as "problem behavior." Educators who understand the underlying message of the behavior (often an important need of the student) can create more effective instructional and environmental interventions (Donnellan, Mirenda, Mesaros, & Fassbender, 1984).*

It has been believed that aversive procedures are sometimes necessary; however, research has shown that a wide range of non-aversive methods are more effective in managing dangerous or disruptive behaviors (TASH, n.d.). Educators who understand how race, class, and culture influence behaviors are less likely to misinterpret them.

Key Principle 10: *Assessment methods and results are impacted by the expectations and level of respect we have for students. Unbiased and culturally sensitive processes enhance and assist in identifying students' strengths along with their needs.*

How we design and use assessments reflects how power is exercised in schools and society, and our assumptions about fairness, difference, and measurement. Effective assessment moves away from traditional functions of ranking and classifying students to using assessment to determine how well the learning design meets the needs of the learners.

Key Principle 11: *Self-determination is the right of every person to direct his or her own life; effective educators help each student identify and move toward his or her personal vision. Educators can help discover each student's vision through close observation of and interaction with that student and his or her family, rejecting the notion that some students are incapable of academic achievement, self-determination, sexuality, integrated employment, or post-secondary education (cf. TASH 2000a, TASH 2000b). Each student must have a rich repertoire of experiences to draw upon in developing his or her vision and the appropriate supports to communicate and grow toward this vision.*

For this to happen, educators must be vigilant with high expectations and efforts to counteract the debilitating impacts of stereotyping and discrimination. Responsible educators represent and advocate for marginalized students in ways that show their capabilities for contributing to schools and society.

Key Principle 12: *Effective education requires repertoires of advocacy to facilitate successful school change, including understanding factors that facilitate or hinder change efforts.*

Failures to successfully integrate individuals with societally marginalized differences into general education and community environments are indicators of a need to re-evaluate supports provided to students and educators (rather than indicators of a need for movement into more restrictive settings). Effective advocates work with the larger community to create coalitions across groups built on ongoing discussions of social justice and other shared issues and values. They understand resistance as expected and multidimensional, identifying and acting upon potential teachable moments (Darder et al., 2009; Sapon-Shevin, 2008). Successful school change requires understanding risks (e.g., for untenured educators) that may be associated with "rocking the boat" and strategies to manage these risks.

Although it is important for the law to uphold principles of inclusion and nondiscrimination, passing legislation is a poor way to change attitudes. Without understanding life conditions and experiences and unrealized strengths of people from marginalized groups, it is unlikely that they will be recognized by policymakers and the general public as fellow citizens whose abilities and perspectives have important contributions for schools, neighborhoods, and society. Decisions will then be made either out of condescension and pity or out of a grudging, skin-deep compliance with legal mandates. Assumptions of the superiority of people from privileged groups will remain unchallenged without conscientization leading to experiences that negate these assumptions (Peters & Chimedza, 2000). Effective inclusive schools can be important sites for conscientization and transformative experiences.

ORGANIZATION OF THIS BOOK

The key principles outlined above provide the framework for this book. Each of the numbered principles is taken up in depth in a correspondingly numbered chapter. The chapters are grouped into two parts. In Part I, Chapters 1–6 help educators understand and critique the status quo, and to re-envision people with traditionally marginalized differences as valuable members of a diverse society. In Part II, Chapters 7–12 demonstrate how educators can *enact* their visions of inclusive education through critical and pragmatic pedagogies that are responsive to this wide range of differences. Attention is also given to meeting the needs of highly able students within a heterogeneous, inclusive context. Specific consideration is given to school change issues, including micro-political factors (e.g., minimizing risks for untenured educators). At the end of the book, the Conclusion challenges readers to consider possible reactions of opponents to inclusive education, and to formulate their own educational visions and action plans.

We identified the need for this book based on our collective experience with inclusive education, teacher and administrator preparation, and school change efforts. Our intent is to be helpful and empowering to new and experienced educators (teachers, administrators, and other school personnel). Chapters are reader-friendly, assuming no background in critical theories and perspectives. They are enlivened with features such as the following:

- Personal experiences (e.g., narratives, cases, stories) of new and experienced educators and people with traditionally marginalized differences. These are embedded throughout the text, to help demonstrate critical analysis and illustrate other important concepts.

- Application activities that help students understand and apply the key principles. These can be used by a professor to create active and student-centered class sessions that support the key principles, or can be completed by students on their own. Application activities are marked with a shovel icon.
- Multiple intelligence connections (e.g., artwork, photos, poems, and links to online videos) that can deepen readers' understandings and enhance their efforts to construct their own critical perspectives. These are not marked separately, but are embedded in the narrative, application activities, and/or related resources.
- "Think About This" comments from the lead authors, providing a dialogic component with the contributors of the other chapters and enabling a diversity of perspectives throughout the text. "Think About This" comments are marked with a question mark icon.
- "Ground Truth" reactions to chapters, contributed by outside stakeholders such as parents and practitioners, are provided to further enable a diversity of perspectives throughout the text.
- "Related Resources" provide supplemental information and activities; they are available at www.tcpress.com (click on "Free Downloads," scroll down to this book). Also included is a list of the key principles for the book.

LEARNING TO APPLY CRITICAL ANALYSIS: A PERSONAL PERSPECTIVE

Over my years as a teacher of students with a variety of differences (with labels such as significant disabilities, gifted/talented, and/or racially/culturally diverse), I've seen brilliant successes—students who made more progress in reading and writing in one year than they had in their entire school history, violent students who reached out with tenderness to those younger and more vulnerable, students who'd been previously excluded but amazed us with their gifts and capabilities—once they were given *both* the appropriate supports *and* the opportunity to learn in the general education curriculum. (Too often, we divorce supports from opportunity to learn. In order to gain the supports, we require students to give up the general education experience.)

I've also seen many failures. I've seen students incapacitated by purported "individualized" programs offering one-size-fits-all supports. I've seen gifted students drop out of school without discovering their gifts, debilitated by others' assumptions about their deficits. I've seen students resegregated into separate programs despite their success in inclusive programs (e.g., Lawrence-Brown, 2000). I've seen an unconscionable number of students smothered by the ignorance and lack of imagination of the educators and policymakers responsible for their learning.

I taught for many years unequipped to confront and understand such breakdowns of our educational systems. As a result, I was often prepared to accept the mainstream view of the failure of these students—mostly that it was the unfortunate result of *their* characteristics (or alternatively, of their home life). Learning to apply a critical perspective to analyze characteristics of *systems*, not just students, enabled me to better understand so many circumstances that failed to live up to educational (and legal) rhetoric.

Unfortunately, I didn't learn to apply a critical perspective until I was more than 15 years into my teaching career. My students and I endured the consequences of oppressive educational systems and practices uncritically, lacking the tools to analyze those experiences. It would have been enormously helpful to me, both professionally and emotionally, had I learned these skills much sooner. More important, it would have helped my students as I became a more effective educational change agent.

We hope that this book reaches you much sooner in your professional development, and that you'll be able to use these skills not only to understand oppressive educational systems, but to help change them by developing your own critical pedagogy.

REFERENCES

American Anthropological Association. (1998). American Anthropological Association statement on "race." Retrieved from http://understandingrace.org/about/statement.html.

Ball, E. W., & Harry, B. (1993). Multicultural education and special education: Parallels, divergences, and intersections. *Educational Forum, 57*, 430–437.

Darder, A., Baltodano, M., & Torres, R. (2009). *The critical pedagogy reader, 2nd ed.* New York: Routledge.

Donnellan, A., Mirenda, P., Mesaros, R., & Fassbender, L. (1984). Analyzing the communicative functions of aberrant behavior. *Journal of the Association for Persons with Severe Handicaps, 9*, 201–212.

Freire, P. (2009). From *Pedagogy of the oppressed*. In Darder, A., Baltodano, M. & Torres, R. (Eds.), *The critical pedagogy reader, 2nd ed.* (pp. 52–60). New York: Routledge.

Kyle, J. (1993). Integration of deaf children. *European Journal of Special Needs Education, 8* (3), 201–220.

Lawrence-Brown, D. (2000). The segregation of Stephen. In Cornbleth, C. (Ed.), *Curriculum politics, policy, and practice*. Albany: State University of New York Press.

Lawrence-Brown, D. (2004). Differentiated instruction: Inclusive strategies for standards-based learning that benefit the whole class. *American Secondary Education, 32*(3), 34–62.

Peters, S., & Chimedza, R. (2000). Conscientization and the cultural politics of education: A radical minority perspective. *Comparative Education Review, 44*(3), 245–271.

Pugach, M. C., & Seidl, B. L. (1998). Responsible linkages between diversity and disability: A challenge for special education. *Teacher Education and Special Education, 21*(4), 319–333.

Sapon-Shevin, M. (2007). *Widening the circle: The power of inclusive classrooms.* Boston: Beacon.

Sapon-Shevin, M. (2008). Teachable moments for social justice. *Independent School, 67*(3), 44–47.

Sapon-Shevin, M., & Zollers, N. (1999). Multicultural and disability agendas in teacher education: Preparing teachers for diversity. *International Journal of Leadership in Education, 2*(3), 165–190.

Seidl, B. (2001). Review of the book *Advances in Special Education: Multicultural Education for Learners with Exceptionalities. Early Childhood Research Quarterly, 16(3),* 395–402.

Smith, R. M., Gallagher, D., Owen, V., & Skrtic, T. (2009). Disability studies in education: Guidelines and ethical practice for educators. In J. Andrzejewski, M. Baltodano, & L. Symcox (Eds.), *Social justice, peace, and environmental education: Transformative standards* (pp. 235–251). New York: Routlege.

Sullivan, A., & King Thorius, K. (2010). Considering intersections of difference among students identified as disabled and expanding conceptualizations of multicultural education. *Race, Gender & Class, 17*(1/2), 93-109.

TASH. (n.d.) Resolution Opposing the Use of Aversives and Restrictive Procedures. Retrieved from http://www.tash.org/IRR/resolutions/res02aversive.htm

TASH. (2000a). Resolution on Choice. Retrieved from http://www.tash.org/IRR/resolutions/res02choice.htm

TASH. (2000b). Resolution on Services and Supports in the Community. Retrieved from http://www.tash.org/IRR/resolutions/res02supports.htm

Tyack, D., & Cuban, L. (1995). *Tinkering toward Utopia.* Cambridge, MA: Harvard University Press.

U.S. Office of Special Education Programs. (2012). Table 1-15: Percentage of students ages 6 through 21 served under IDEA, Part B, as a percentage of population, by disability and state: Fall 2010. Retrieved from https://www.ideadata.org/TABLES34TH/AR_1-15.pdf

White House Conference on Child Health and Protection. (1931). *Section III, Education and training: Committee on special classes.* New York: Century.

Zirkel, S. (2008). The influence of multicultural educational practices on student outcomes and intergroup relations. *Teachers College Record, 110*(6), 1147–1181.

PART I

UNDERSTANDING AND ENVISIONING INCLUSIVE EDUCATION

CHAPTER 1

How We Respond to Differences—
And the Difference It Makes

Mara Sapon-Shevin

Key Principle 1: *Inclusion is not primarily a special education, or even an education, issue. It is a fundamental way of seeing and responding to human difference for the benefit of everyone involved.*

For many people, the word *inclusion* means including students with disabilities in typical educational settings. It is sometimes seen as an extension of the principle formerly known as "mainstreaming," or trying to bring children with disabilities back into the "mainstream" of education.

But, increasingly, people are realizing that this definition of inclusive education is extremely limiting because it fails to acknowledge that children vary in a myriad of different ways. To think about education that is inclusive and responsive to one set of differences (called disabilities) and to ignore differences of race, ethnicity, gender, sexuality, language, religion, and class doesn't create an educational system that is truly inclusive of all (Puchach, 1995; Sapon-Shevin, 2007). Modifying an art activity for Jason who has cerebral palsy and limited use of his hands is a good start—but when Jason is African American, Muslim, and lives with his mom, then sending him home with a Christmas ornament that says "For Mom and Dad" doesn't really evidence thinking about him as a student with many characteristics, identities, and educational needs.

My own personal teaching background began in special education, when I worked with a segregated class of students who had in common *only* that they had been unsuccessful in regular education—and then labeled as "learning disabled." They brought to our classroom a wide variety of educational and personal histories, and huge discrepancies in their educational needs. Charlie had been locked in a closet for four years and, at six, was tiny and fragile and emotionally volatile. Martha had recently been moved to a foster family, and her verbal skills were excellent and highly developed—and most of what she said was angry. Carlton was bright and excellent at math, but his speech was so difficult to understand that no one interacted with him and he was immensely frustrated. Terrance had been the only African American child in a White school, and when he was caught shoplifting, he was labeled learning disabled and assigned to my class. Bonnie was very dependent on others to do things for her and lacked initiative of any sort; if she dropped her pencil, it stayed on the floor until someone else picked it up. The list went on and on.

It was not helpful to me to know that they all had the label of "learning disabled." Rather, I had to get to know each child and figure out what he or she needed—and how to provide that within a shared classroom community. Their needs were not limited to some narrow range of academic challenges—learning to read and write. They also needed to learn to work together, to trust one another and me, and to be willing to try new things. I had to understand their family situations and their other needs in order to teach them successfully.

And, as I worked with my class, I became increasingly frustrated that I was asked to work in a segregated setting. I was one of two special education teachers of children 5–8 years old in a school that served 4th- to 6th-graders, so my students weren't even the same age as the typical students in the school. I had a different administrator, who came from a different district to supervise me; I didn't eat lunch with the other teachers, nor did I have bus duty, which might have seemed like a good thing, but it kept me different and isolated from the other teachers in the same ways that my students were isolated. We didn't go to school assemblies or on field trips, and the parents of our students weren't part of the Parent Teacher Organization. We were viewed as a thing apart—special education—and this simply reified that there were two kinds of children in the world: regular education students and special education students.

> **? Think About This:** It's important for new educators to understand that, unfortunately, a segregated experience is still common in special education today.

This dichotomous thinking, labeling, and academic programming resulted in an increased gap between my students and the other students in the school and decreased chances for the students with special education labels to return to the mainstream. At the end of each year, I was asked, for each student, "Is Michael ready to go back?" "Go back to what?" I would ask. "Go back to the regular classroom." I was asked to sign off that Michael would be successful in a 3rd-grade classroom without even knowing which 3rd grade that might be, who his teacher would be, how the classroom would be organized or run, or what training that new teacher would have in working with students who had educational and behavioral challenges. And so I, like many, tended to keep my kids just one more year, so that I could be more sure. But, ironically, the research shows that the longer students are out of the mainstream, the lower their chances of successful return—so different have been their educational experiences and their socialization opportunities with other students (Hibel, Farkas, & Morgan, 2010; Kintz, 2011; Taylor, 1988).

This experience made me certain that there are *not* two kinds of children: regular and special. There is either one kind of child (human) or 30,000 kinds of children, but never two. And I realized that we needed to work to make regular classrooms places that (1) welcomed all students, (2) were organized to promote community and collaboration, (3) provided instruction using all kinds of pedagogical strategies, and (4) included a curriculum that was rich, engaging, multilevel, and culturally responsive for all students.

This chapter explores the concepts that are necessary to embrace a truly inclusive definition of inclusion and to consider how our responses to differences shape our attitudes, beliefs, expectations, and school practices related to diversity:

- How we define normality and abnormality will affect how we look at human variation.
- Good inclusive education is good education. Changes and modifications made to create a classroom that embraces diversity through classroom community practices, multilevel curriculum, and inclusive pedagogical practices benefit *all* students.

NORMALITY VS. ABNORMALITY

The idea that *normality* is something other than a fixed concept with clear parameters is difficult for many to understand. Most people are raised being told that it was normal to do certain things and abnormal to do other things: Women wear dresses, but not men; singing in public is not considered appropriate; carrying a stuffed animal is acceptable if you're 6, but not if you're 16. Often the consequences of behaving abnormally include social sanction, and sometimes, worse—incarceration, acquiring a label of mental illness, electroshock therapy, death. Even if the consequences of being seen as abnormal are not as dire, they often result in limited access to resources or opportunities.

The ways in which we use normality as a way of judging and policing others' behavior are often limiting and sometimes oppressive. In order to unpack the concept of normality, it is important to understand the following:

- Normality is a social construct, and there are not clear or universal definitions or boundaries.
- People use the concept of normality to regulate others' behavior and to control the variation.
- We are all multifaceted human beings who exist and act along many continua.
- Cultural differences (big and small) radically affect our definitions of what is normal.
- Our attitudes toward difference are the big problem, rarely the differences themselves.
- Some responses to diversity are positive and enriching; others can be dangerous and even deadly.
- Expanding our understanding of normality and variation will enrich our lives, deepen our relationships, and improve our communities. Diversity is not a problem to be solved, but a natural and enriching facet of our lives.

Why Normality Is a (Dangerous) Social Construct

What does it mean to call something or someone "normal"? One meaning of *normal* is "typical"—that is, what we are most likely to see or hear. This is a meaning that is more statistical than anything else (like an average); a potato of "normal" size evokes an image of a particular dimension. We also apply the word to behavior; it is "typical" for children to cry when they are hurt; it is "typical" for people to arise in the morning and go to sleep at night. As a statistical concept (i.e., a statement of how likely something is to happen), the word *normal* is not in and of itself problematic. But we often extend the idea of typical to being right, or appropriate, or good. Therefore, things that aren't typical are wrong, inappropriate, or bad. So if it is typical for women to wear dresses but not men, then a man wearing a dress is not just atypical, but wrong, strange, or even dangerous. If it is typical to communicate using vocal verbalizations, then other forms of non-verbal communication, such as miming, signing, or facilitated communication (a way that non-speaking people communicate with a keyboard), are abnormal, and may be judged as needing to be fixed, changed, or remediated.

It becomes even more complicated when we recognize that some behaviors might be judged normal or abnormal based on a wide variety of other factors, such as age, gender, frequency, context, and status, as well as other markers. For example, a 6-year-old who carries around a stuffed animal, talks to it, and is comforted by it is considered normal, but a 36-year-old who does the same is labeled as crazy and possibly dangerous. In some countries, men holding hands in public is seen as a sign of

Activity 1.1: How Did You Learn What Was "Normal"?

Answer the following questions:

1. What messages did you get from parents and other adults about the importance of being normal? What did that mean to them? To you?
2. What, if any, were the sanctions you received if you behaved in ways that were deemed abnormal? Was there appreciation for being different? Concern about what others would say? Worries about your future? Support for marching to your own drum?
3. For each of the following areas, what messages did you get about what was normal: eating (what, where, when); sleeping (how long, when, where); clothing (choices, options); playing (what was in/appropriate, with whom)?

Share your responses with a partner and then with the whole class. Talk about how these early messages have shaped your current understanding about the concept of normality.

friendship; in other places, this is read as homosexuality and deviance and is potentially very dangerous for the hand-holders. Race, class, dis/ ability, and gender also affect how particular behaviors are interpreted and judged. It has been said that rich men are eccentric, poor men are crazy. Similarly, a person with the label of "mentally retarded" will be further marginalized by carrying a Mickey Mouse lunch pail, while a university professor who does so will likely be seen as "trendy."

Engaging in Activity 1.1 will likely lead to understandings that

1. we received early messages about what was normal and what wasn't;
2. there was variation in how much being different was either appreciated and supported or sanctioned and criticized; and
3. our ability as adults to be open, accepting, and flexible in our thinking about human variation is heavily influenced by early messages we received about normality, differences, and variations.

How Normality Is Used to Control Difference

Emma Van der Klift and Norman Kunc (1994) created a table showing some of the ways differences are responded to in society, and the consequences of each response (see Figure 1.1). They explain:

We live in a society that tells us there is only one "right" way to be. At times all of us feel measured against an unfairly strict standard: white, able bodied, young, intelligent, successful, attractive, thin and preferably male. Normalcy is a tight bell-curve, allowing little deviance without societal repercussion. Even those of us who find ourselves encompassed well within the confines of the curve feel pressure to conform to the middle, while those who fall outside its range feel that they are seen not only as deviant, but deficient.

It is puzzling that this standard of normalcy includes so few of us. We know that diversity, not uniformity, is the real societal norm. After all, the human community consists of great variety; race, gender, language, color, religion, ability and sexual orientation. People of color make up most of the world's population. Women comprise fifty one percent of the global population. Most of the world does not live in a state of affluence (p. 396).

We also have to be willing to look carefully at the ways in which some responses to difference, such as tolerance, are also highly problematic. Although *tolerating* someone is definitely better than hurting or excluding that person because of a bias you hold against him or her, it is still less than ideal and falls short as a goal. I do not want to be tolerated by my friends, or told that they will ignore my differences in the name of acceptance or friendship. This kind of thinking leads easily to responses that are best characterized as "I don't care if you're different as long as I don't have to be around it, accept it, or acknowledge it." Consider comments like the following:

- "I don't mind gay people as long as they don't flaunt their sexuality in public."

Figure 1.1. Ways in Which Society Responds to Differences

Category of Response	Consequences
MARGINALIZATION	Segregation
	Avoidance
	Aggression
REFORM	Assimilation
	Rehabilitation
TOLERANCE	Resignation
	Benevolence
VALUING (Diversity as Normal)	Equal Worth
	Mutual Benefit
	Belonging

Source: "Hell-bent on helping" by E. Van der Klift & N. Kunc, 1994, in *Creative and collaborative learning: A practical guide to empowering students and teachers*, edited by J. Thousand, R. Villa, & A. Nevin, (pp. 391–401). Baltimore: Paul Brookes. Reprinted by permission.

- "I understand that he talks that way because he has cerebral palsy, but I think it's gross and I don't want to be around him."
- "Why does she have to keep bringing up her religion all the time?"

But the consequences of how we view difference can go beyond the negative response of "marginalization" in Figure 1.1. The Anti-Defamation League uses a graphic called "The Pyramid of Hate" to discuss the escalating ways in which negative responses to difference have been played out in the world (see Figure 1.2).

The Pyramid of Hate forces us to consider where we learned how to respond to differences and the consequences of that education or lack thereof. This model is very powerful in looking at how what may seem like innocent behavior at first—jokes, name-calling, and exclusion—can quickly escalate. The bullying of today can become the hate crime of tomorrow. The recent attention to the spate of bullying suicides has provided ample evidence of the deadly consequences of intolerance and hatred toward those perceived as different.

Figure 1.2 The Pyramid of Hate

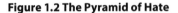
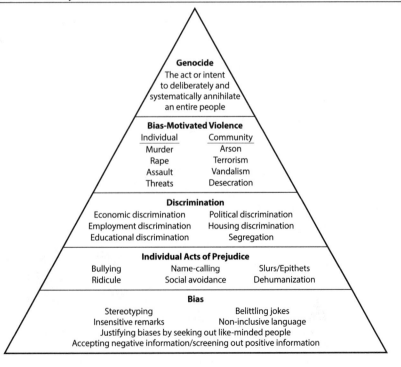

Activity 1.2: So Many Differences: How Do We Respond?

Make a list of all the differences children bring to school. Try to include not just categories like racial differences and gender, but also things like family structures, allergies, physical size, and living situations. As a small group, discuss whether each of these differences should be: Celebrated? Tolerated? Remediated? Ignored? For example, we might want to celebrate or embrace the different kinds of foods students bring to school for lunch, but if a child has no lunch, then some action should be taken. Discuss how we decide which differences we should embrace and which we should try to address more actively.

What Happens When Human Complexity Is Reduced to a Single Label?

Van der Klift and Kunc (1994) use the term *disability spread* to refer to the way that we tend to see one aspect of a disability, then generalize it and grow it, so that it becomes the whole person (see Figure 1.3). Instead of seeing people as complex human beings with lots of strengths, challenges, skills, needs, gifts, and interests, we reduce someone to "the cerebral palsy kid" or "the deaf woman." And because we often have misconceptions, stereotypes, and flat-out wrong information about the disability itself, our propensity for enlarging its meaning and impact on the person becomes even more dangerous.

Van der Klift and Kunc explain: "When disability is seen as the largest component of a person, much of what is unique and 'human' about her or him will be obscured. When needs and deficits are what we see, we only see what that person cannot do" (p. 399).

There is a clear relationship between the concept of disability spread and how we reduce other people's multiple identities (not just abilities/

Figure 1.3. Disability Spread

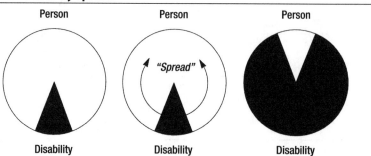

Source: Van der Klift & Kunc, 1994, reprinted with permission of Brookes Publishing.

Activity 1.3: What's in a Label?

Think about what would happen if you were forced to describe yourself using only labels and negative descriptors of who you are. Compare the following two descriptions of the same person—one negative and the other positive:

Middle-aged woman, with chronic neck and back pain

- Messy and disorganized
- Constantly seeks attention and approval
- Hyperactive and unable to sit still

Energetic and vibrant woman, always in motion

- Large variety of hobbies and pastimes
- Story and joke teller who enjoys entertaining
- Friendly and personable
- Persists in spite of aches and pains

Write two descriptions of yourself, both accurate and referencing the same behaviors, needs, and characteristics, one negatively and one positively. Discuss how you think people would respond to the two different descriptions. Discuss implications for how we describe our students.

disabilities) to single labels: "the gay man"; "the fat woman"; "the Muslim student"; "the Puerto Rican kid." Every time we reduce human variation to a single descriptor, we deny people's full humanity and increase the chances that we will respond from a place of stereotype and limited/distorted expectations. (This concept is explored more fully in Chapter 3.)

WHAT FULL INCLUSION WOULD REALLY MEAN

Narrow definitions of inclusion are often connected to similarly limited understandings about what inclusion can mean in terms of school placement and educational programming. Simply putting a diverse group of bodies into a common space does not constitute full inclusion, nor does it yield the intended benefits of this visionary goal. Physical proximity is a necessary step, but it is insufficient to build an inclusive, cooperative community or to reap the benefits of heterogeneity.

Unfortunately, many schools have claimed that they were engaging in inclusion, but failed to create an environment that valued differences or to provide sufficient supports for educators and students; they also often

Activity 1.4: What Does Inclusion Mean?

Find at least five different definitions of *inclusion*. These might come from a website, article, textbook, or experienced teacher.

Compare the definitions, and develop a word web that shows similarities and differences in language and definition, inclusion/exclusion of various populations, support provided, and so forth.

Explore the various strengths, weaknesses, and implications of different definitions.

maintained segregated programming. When educators or policymakers declare that "inclusion doesn't work," they are rarely describing a carefully designed, well-resourced, thoughtful process of including all students. Rather, they are often responding to situations in which students were (often unceremoniously) dumped into general education settings without adequate planning or support.

Inclusion Requires Radical Reconceptualization of Curriculum, Pedagogy, and School Structures

I often use the following metaphor to explain the breadth and depth of what is required by inclusion and what is possible. When teachers are engaging in dental education, they have students brush their teeth and then give them a little red tablet to chew. This tablet is called a "revealing tablet" because it shows clearly any places that have not been adequately brushed, thus alerting the brusher to areas that need more attention (Sapon-Shevin, 1996).

Activity 1.5: What Were Your School Experiences with People with Disabilities?

Talk with a partner about your own schooling experiences regarding people with disabilities:

- What kinds of contacts/relationships did each of you have, and what messages did you receive about differences?
- If either of you were identified as having a disability, what relationships did you have with students who were not so identified?
- How do those experiences shape your current understanding about what's possible?

When educators express concerns about requests to include students with disabilities, their areas of focus can function like a revealing tablet:

1. If we include a child like Marco, then we'll have to look at the school climate—our kids can be very cruel.
2. If we include a child like Terry, we'll have to rethink our curriculum—much of what we teach isn't really relevant to his life and experiences.
3. If we include a child like Carissa, then we'll have to rethink our pedagogy—whole group instruction just doesn't work for her.
4. If we include a child like Patrick, then we'll have to give our educators more training and support—they aren't really ready or prepared.

My response to these objections is "yes, yes, yes, yes." If we include a child who has some actual or perceived difference, it helps us to see all the places in our schools that need work—that need to be examined carefully in order to make them welcoming and accommodating for all students. Attending to school and classroom climate, curriculum, pedagogy, and teacher preparation and support are essential to successful inclusion. And these are things we should be doing on an ongoing basis for the benefit of *all* students. But sometimes it is only when we see a dramatic discrepancy between school as it is and the needs of a particular child that we realize that there are inadequacies, limitations, and flaws in how we do school. Attempts to include a child can function as a revealing tablet for the classroom or school, showing us clearly the areas that require more work! Sadly, rather than thanking that child or his or her parents for presenting us with a rich opportunity to examine our current practices and make them better, schools often seek to exclude or segregate the child who is different so as to remove the challenges presented.

The objections to inclusion cited above are often raised regarding students with disabilities, but they are also directed at students with other differences. The school is a hostile place for students who identify as queer, so we attempt to either regulate the students' behavior to make the difference disappear, or we advise removing the children to a school for queer youth. We realize that our curriculum isn't culturally relevant to students of color in our school, so we propose that they attend a school that focuses on diversity. These purported solutions have in common that they leave intact (and unimproved) the current classroom/school practices, policies, and procedures, to say nothing of the messages that are sent about diversity and inclusion.

There is good news, however. While the changes required for schools to be fully and genuinely inclusive are massive, it is not a zero-sum game. That is, making things better for a child with Asperger's syndrome who has limited social skills and needs friends will not make things worse for other children and, in fact, may introduce practices and changes that will benefit many more children. Implementing more culturally relevant pedagogy—even if the impulse for this originates because there are many Hispanic kids in the class, for example—will result in a richer, fuller curriculum for all. Accommodations made originally for marginalized students are generally beneficial to other students as well. Asking everyone to be the same—that is, to assimilate—deprives everyone of these benefits and of the strengths that emerge in children and educators from supporting all students. Although some highly competent, mainstream students may be able to survive or even succeed in environments that do not differentiate or attend positively to differences, these are not ideal classrooms for anyone. Good inclusive education is good education.

What Does Fully Inclusive Education Look Like?

School Climate and Culture. Inclusive education demands close attention to creating classroom and school communities that are warm and welcoming for all. I have identified six key components of such a welcoming community (Sapon-Shevin, 2010):

1. A classroom marked by *cooperation* rather than competition.
2. *Inclusion* of all students; no one has to "earn" their way into the community.
3. An atmosphere in which differences are *valued* and addressed openly.
4. A place that values the *integrity* of each person, that is, each person is valued in his or her wholeness with multiple identities.
5. A climate in which people are encouraged to display the *courage* to challenge oppression and exclusion.

 Activity 1.6: Talk It Up!

Create an ad campaign to promote inclusive education and redefine "normality." Make posters, write jingles, and film brief public service announcements that present concepts of diversity and inclusion that make it clear that you are advocating for the full and meaningful inclusion of all students in a community in which they are valued, accepted, and welcomed.

6. A setting that offers not just physical *safety*, but also emotional and relational safety for all its members; they can feel secure in their belonging.

In such a culture, differences are openly addressed and discussed; exclusion and marginalization are challenged directly. Combating racism, homophobia, classism, sexism, religious oppression, language privilege, ableism, and other forms of difference are seen as essential learning for all.

Curriculum. Curriculum in inclusive settings is rich and interactive, acknowledges multiple intelligences, and has many points of entry. Good curriculum design begins with knowing who the students are, in all their complexities, and making sure that what is taught is meaningful and culturally relevant. Good curriculum design means moving away from lock-step, skill-driven deficit models of reading and language toward more balanced approaches to language arts instruction, which includes real literature that lets children work at different skill levels. For example, a dinosaur reading unit might include books and print materials about dinosaurs at many different levels, in addition to non-print media, music, and movement activities. One teacher working in an inclusive classroom said, "Why would I want 25 copies of the same textbook?" and instead acquired many different materials (books, DVDs, songs, posters, computer software, video clips) that could be accessed by different students.

When things are narrowly designed, we end up having to retrofit the lesson or exclude some students, but when the initial design is inclusive, all students can find their place in the learning. For example, when a 5th-grade teacher did a unit on "Living Green," students were involved at various levels:

- LaDonna did research on carbon footprints and brought that information to the group.
- Matthew and Rosaria headed up a school recycling program that involved their making social connections (and practicing their social skills) with other students and teachers.
- Carlos, who used a voice-activated computer, produced an "infomercial" about saving the planet and presented it to various groups.
- Three students developed an ad campaign and used their math skills selling space in the school newsletter to local businesses.

The development of more interactive, participatory curriculum projects is also conducive to both cooperative learning approaches and the inclusion of children working at many levels and bringing various strengths and histories to the classroom.

Pedagogy. Similarly, all students benefit when teaching is not designed only for students who learn best by listening, speaking, reading, or writing. Udvari-Solner and Kluth (2007), in their book *Joyful Learning: Active and Collaborative Learning in Inclusive Classrooms*, share a collection of teaching strategies that can be used with a wide range of learners. These are not identified as "teaching strategies for students with disabilities," but simply as good teaching. What most inclusive strategies have in common is that they are engaging, interactive, and constructivist (drawing on students' prior knowledge), as well as encouraging and promoting peer support.

When students collaborate, they not only bring their own individual experiences, cultures, and strengths to their classmates' learning, but they are also positioned so that they can actively support and teach one another. Many educators report that when they implemented pedagogy that was more interactive and hands-on, many students benefited, not only the student with a putative disability. (See more on this in Chapter 8.)

Educator Support. Inclusive education also requires that educators be well prepared and well supported. Although excellent preservice education is important, it is impossible to fully prepare any educational professional for the demands of teaching a wide range of learners in inclusive classrooms. Ongoing in-service education on all aspects of curriculum, pedagogy, and school culture is imperative if educators are to feel supported. Particularly as schools implement high-stakes testing and competitive teacher-evaluation schemes, a commitment to inclusive education will demand that teachers do not feel that their commitment to inclusive, heterogeneous education will negatively affect their own evaluations and compensation.

High-quality inclusive education also demands extensive "people supports" so that educators (perhaps those labeled as "general" and those as "special") are provided collaborative planning time. Structures must also be created and maintained so that those who push into the general education classroom, such as special education teachers; physical, occupational, and speech therapists; and consultants on gifted education are true team members in educational design and instruction. Inclusion doesn't mean that one teacher has to do it all her- or himself, but rather that schools truly support collaboration and cooperation and provide evidence of the adage that "None of us is as smart as all of us."

Inclusion is not simply an organizational structure, but rather a commitment to making a place for everyone in classrooms, schools, and the world and regarding diversity as enriching and positive.

GROUND TRUTH: THE STUDENT'S VIEW

From an Interview with Micah Fialka-Feldman, Student

Micah Fialka-Feldman is a strong advocate for inclusion and a frequent keynoter at education conferences. He is currently at Syracuse University working as a teaching assistant and for a peer-support program. Micah himself has received a host of labels (including "cognitively disabled"), but none of those labels would begin to describe his warmth, caring, and deep insights about people and educational change. He reflects here on what inclusion means to him:

> Inclusion is when the students are working all together, and they are in the same classroom, and they live in the town with their friends, and they all do things all together. Inclusion could be a scary thing because people haven't done it, but they could try it and see how it goes for the whole school year.
>
> If students are segregated, they'll just know all the kids with disabilities and not have a chance to meet other students. And people who don't have disabilities won't get to meet other kids.
>
> I don't remember being in the segregated classroom but I do remember going into a separate door. All the kids with disabilities went in a separate door, and all the other kids went in a separate door. It felt weird. We went in a separate door. It would have been cool if all the kids could go in the same door with all their other friends.

He talks about why some teachers are reluctant to be inclusive:

> I think they are afraid of students and that teachers don't know if they could be in the classroom through the whole day. And they might need help. And they don't know how to help them. They're afraid that if this student does something wrong, they won't know how to tell them or help them.

He describes a positive experience of inclusion:

> I was included on the cross country team and track team, and I didn't have to try out. I could just join the team. I made a lot of friends from it. We would have races every Saturday. I felt like it was fun being on a team.

And a negative one:

> I was trying to live in the dorm [at Oakland University] and I thought that because I was paying tuition I could live there. But the school administration said, "He's not a student." But I had an ID that said I was a student. They didn't think I was a student. [Micah won his lawsuit and was able to live in the dormitory!]

Micah is confident that inclusion makes a difference for everyone:

> Sometimes people who don't know people with disabilities don't think they can do things and don't know they can go to a job. If someone doesn't know about people who are African American or gay, they might also think these things about other kinds of people—they might be thinking a different way.
>
> I think that if they grew up with an inclusive school—maybe the world would be different. And maybe people with disabilities could get jobs and be able to work and not be worried.

REFERENCES

Hibel, J., Farkas, G., & Morgan, P. L. (2010). Who is placed into special education? *Sociology of Education, 83*(4), 312–332.

Kintz, M. (2011). Ability grouping and how it is affecting American classrooms. *ESSAI, 9*(20), 56–58.

Pugach, M. C. (1995). On the failure of imagination in inclusive schooling. *Journal of Special Education, 29*(2), 212–223.

Sapon-Shevin, M. (1996). Full inclusion as disclosing tablet: Revealing the flaws in our general education system. *Theory Into Practice, 35*(1), 35–41.

Sapon-Shevin, M. (2007). *Widening the circle: The power of inclusive classrooms.* Boston: Beacon Press.

Sapon-Shevin, M. (2010). *Because we can change the world: A practical guide to building cooperative, inclusive classroom communities.* Thousand Oaks, CA: Corwin Press.

Taylor, S. J. (1988). Caught in the continuum: A critical analysis of the principle of the least restrictive environment. *Journal of the Association for the Severely Handicapped, 13*(1), 218–230.

Udvari-Solner, A., & Kluth, P. (2007). *Joyful learning: Active and collaborative learning in inclusive classrooms.* Thousand Oaks, CA: Corwin Press.

Van der Klift, E., & Kunc, N. (1994). Hell-bent on helping: Benevolence, friendship, and the politics of help. In J. Thousand, R. Villa, & A. Nevin (Eds.), *Creative and collaborative learning: A practical guide to empowering students and teachers* (pp. 391–401). Baltimore: Paul Brookes.

CHAPTER 2

Understanding Critical Perspectives—Who Benefits?

Diana Lawrence-Brown

> When I give food to the poor they call me a saint. When I ask why the poor have no food they call me a communist.
>
> —Helder Camara, Brazilian cleric, 1909-1999

Key Principle 2: *An important foundation of social justice is equity and excellence in education. Critical analysis is required to recognize and analyze assumptions about education and outcomes for people with traditionally marginalized differences (including but not limited to disabilities, cultural/ linguistic/racial background, gender, sexual orientation, and class).*

Education is considered the great equalizer. People over time and across gender, racial, national, cultural, and ability groups have sought out education as a means to greater social, economic, and personal opportunity. And while *compulsory* education has been in place for more than a century, *equitable* education remains elusive:

> Inequities in educational opportunity exist on many levels, including those of race, class, gender, language, migrant and disability status. These core inequities themselves are perpetuated in the composition of corporate executive boards and construction crews, enrollment in our institutions of higher education and confinement in our prisons, in our classrooms and in our emergency rooms, in inheritance lines and unemployment lines. Research shows, however, that from one generation to the next, equitable access to high-performing public schools can break these barriers. (Schott Foundation, 2009, p.1)

It's true that higher levels of education are a benefit to diverse groups in social, economic, and personal outcomes. Income is one example:

Activity 2.1: Explore the Relationship Between Education and Income

For more about educational levels and income among various groups, try this activity: *Educational Attainment: A Data-Driven Learning Guide*, available at http://www.icpsr.umich.edu/icpsrweb/instructors/ddlgs/guides/educationattain/sections

Higher levels of education do lead to higher earnings across race and gender groups, for example (Crissey, 2009). Understanding this relationship has contributed to decades-long efforts to equalize educational opportunity through federal action such as the following:

- *Brown v. Board of Education* (1954, banning segregation by race)
- Education for All Handicapped Children Act (1975, banning exclusion of students with disabilities from public schools)
- *Lau v. Nichols* (1974, requiring schools to either teach students from cultural/linguistic minorities in their own language or to teach them English)
- Title IX (1972, banning discrimination on the basis of sex)

Yet people from traditionally marginalized groups continue to earn considerably less in comparison to more privileged counterparts—*even when* they have the same levels of education. For example, women earn less than equally educated men (Kelly, 2005), Blacks and Hispanics earn less than equally educated Whites (Kelly, 2005), and people with disabilities earn less than those without disability labels—again, even with equal levels of education (U.S. Census Bureau, 2008).

How is it that well-intentioned and concerted efforts continue to result in disparities? How can we make sense of these outcomes?

This chapter is designed to help you do just that. We'll begin by considering common assumptions made about people from traditionally marginalized groups. From there, we'll look at how two different perspectives (*critical* and *functionalist*) impact both assumptions that are made about students and subsequent school improvement efforts.

CRITICAL ANALYSIS: QUESTIONING ASSUMPTIONS

For many, critical analysis has been an extremely helpful tool in making sense of puzzling educational and social systems and outcomes. *Critical* here does not mean faultfinding but digging beneath the outward appearance, recognizing and analyzing assumptions about education and people with traditionally marginalized differences, asking why things are as they are (or why not a different way). Assumptions that impact our ability to provide equitable and excellent education include those concerning the following:

- Exceptionality
- Socioeconomic status
- Culture and race
- Parenting
- Religion
- Disproportionate labeling and segregated educational placements

Understanding the underlying assumptions helps with understanding how the privileged or marginalized identities of students connect with opportunities they have (or don't have) in our school system and in our society. Critical perspectives can be helpful in identifying power relationships and in recognizing oppressive systems—these are often masked by unexamined assumptions (e.g., segregated programs assumed to be maximizing opportunities to learn while they are in fact producing the unintended consequence of *limiting* opportunities to learn).

By their very nature, assumptions tend to go unrecognized and unexamined, making them especially problematic. Even just recognizing our underlying assumptions can be slippery and difficult—part of what makes them assumptions is that these are the things that we take for granted. Asking us to notice them is a bit like asking a fish to notice the water when what seems more important is the food, the predator, the potential mate. Yet the quality of the water makes an undeniable difference to fish, impacting their opportunities for food, for a mate, for survival. Similarly, the assumptions people make—individually, but especially collectively—make a significant difference in the opportunities and quality of life that our students have.

An Example: Assumptions About Parenting

As you might expect, assumptions affect how people are treated in educational systems. This applies to students and to parents, educators, and others involved in schools. As an example, consider the experience of Dixie Jordan, the parent of two children, as described in Hallahan and Kauffman (2000). Her oldest child is obedient and well-behaved. Her youngest has emotional/behavioral disabilities. She went from being a parent whom others considered exemplary to suddenly being assumed to lack basic parenting skills. She reflects:

When systems blame parents for causing their child's emotional or behavioral disorders, the focus is no longer on services to help the child learn better adaptive skills or appropriate behaviors, but on rationalizing why such services may not work. (quoted in Hallahan & Kauffman, 2000, p. 260)

Dixie's experience illustrates a commonly held assumption in our society: "Good" parents produce "good" children. Children who do not behave according to dominant norms are assumed to be the product of "bad" parenting.

This is reflected not only in personal reactions to children and parents (as illustrated above) but also in our educational and social policies. It might be logical to respond to students whose behavior challenges schools by making changes in the way that the students are approached *by schools*; however, in

> **Think About This:** What keeps us from examining the underlying structures of schooling? Why would professionals be more inclined to change students than change schools?

my experience, classes to improve *parenting* skills are much more likely to be recommended. This illustrates one of the central understandings from the school change literature: Reforms that are added onto the existing educational system (rather than requiring changes within it) are more easily incorporated into the "grammar of schooling" (Tyack & Cuban, 1995).

Assumptions About Other Groups

Next, consider other assumptions that have been commonly made about people based on their membership in particular groups in our society. In Figure 2.1, which assumptions are recognizable stereotypes? Why do you think some are recognizable as stereotypes, and some are not?

Where do stereotypes such as those in Figure 2.1 come from? Sometimes they are passed on through family and significant others. Such messages may be explicit (e.g., "those people expect everything to be handed to them") or implicit (e.g., "how about if you invite *[someone more like us]* instead?"). Sometimes they are embedded in media (e.g., people with disabilities depicted engaging in menial activities or Muslims represented as violent). They have also been embedded in school curricula (e.g., Native Americans represented as savages, White men as history's heroes). (To learn more about stereotypes, see Activity 2.A: Stereotypical Portrayals of Native and European Americans, Related Resources for Chapter 2, www.tcpress.com.)

Ironically, another means of transmission is by invisibility or omission. People from marginalized groups may be missing from high-status images (e.g., business owners rarely represented as women of color). Lack

Figure 2.1. Assumptions About Groups in Society

Category	Group	Some Traditional Assumptions (Not a Complete List)
Socioeconomic status (SES)	High SES	More motivated, cultured, able
	Low SES	Less motivated, cultured, able
Gender	Male	More intelligent and rational; strong physically and emotionally
	Female	Less intelligent and rational; physically and emotionally fragile
Culture/Race	Dominant group(s)	More capable, desirable, ambitious
	Marginalized group(s)	Less capable, desirable, ambitious
Perceived ability	Significantly above average	People who are needed by our society (e.g., to maintain national standing); as such, they are deserving of enriched opportunities and status
	Significantly below average	People who are in need of beneficence from our society; as such, they should be grateful for whatever is given/decided by those with greater perceived ability
Religious orientation	Protestant	Hard-working ("the Protestant work ethic")
	Jewish	Wealthy, but extract their wealth from the work of others (cf. Foxman, 2010)
	Fundamentalist	Ignorant
	Muslim	Violent

of personal knowledge and experience may also play a role. For example, if I didn't grow up knowing people who are fundamentalist, or Hispanic, or if I don't know that my friend is lesbian, I may be more likely to accept negative assumptions about people in these groups.

The list in Figure 2.1 is not, of course, all-encompassing; assumptions made about others vary depending on the situation and among individuals (Sleeter, 1995). For example, consider Figure 2.2 as a way to help think about different perspectives on the nature of "have-not" groups in U.S. society—those who have limited access to society's resources. (For the moment, please disregard the empty bottom row, Nature of "Haves.")

If you think about it, you can see the logic behind each perspective—even if you don't share it. If the society is assumed to be fair and open, that

Figure 2.2. Contrasting Perspectives on the Nature of Society and Societal Groups

	Dominant Position	**Marginalized Position**
Nature of Society	Our society is fair, open	Our society is unfair, rigged
Nature of "Have-Nots"	Lacking in ambition, effort, culture, language, etc.	Strong, resourceful
Nature of "Haves"		

Source: Multicultural Education, Critical Pedagogy, and the Politics of Difference, edited by C. E. Sleeter and P. L. McLaren, 1995, Albany: State University of New York Press. Copyright 1995 State University of New York Press. Adapted with permission. All rights reserved.

is, a meritocracy (the dominant position in the United States), then everyone has an equal chance to acquire society's resources (wealth, status, etc.). It follows, then, that when people have less, it must be their own fault. On the other hand, if the nature of society is unfair and rigged, it follows that people who have less must be strong and resourceful just to survive.

> **Think About This:** Looking at who gets into gifted programs helps us to see some of the ways privilege gets passed on in schools. Students from dominant groups (for example, White, middle-class, and able-bodied) are most likely to be served in those programs.

In summary, our assumptions have a major impact on how people are viewed by and treated in our society. Because we take assumptions for granted, it takes a conscious effort to realize we are making them. But making this effort to recognize how they operate in a particular situation is an important part of making sense of inequities we see in schools and society (a necessary but insufficient condition for reform).

LEARNING TO APPLY CRITICAL ANALYSIS

Over the course of many years in the field, I have been repeatedly confronted—and frustrated—by outcomes for students that fail to live up to

Activity 2.2: Analysis of "Haves"

Now return to the empty bottom row of the table in Figure 2.2; see if you can extend Sleeter's (1995) analysis to the nature of the "Haves" in our society (those who have greater access to society's resources).

educational policies, legal rhetoric, and my own values. As I discussed in the Introduction to this book, by learning to recognize and analyze the underlying assumptions of our work in schools, the broader societal context, and their impact on the lives of our students, I have gained greater understanding of—if not comfort with—our educational system. Part of this is greater understanding of how complicated and difficult is the task of equitable and excellent education. And although these understandings have come without a magic wand, they have made my efforts more politically savvy, more insightful, and more effective.

Here's an example of learning to recognize and question underlying assumptions from my own work in schools, in this case concerning students not keeping up with the rest of the class. Two assumptions underpinned efforts to teach these students:

1. We need to diagnose the student's underlying problem—what was wrong with the student, preventing him or her from keeping up with peers?
2. Having diagnosed the student's underlying problem, we need to provide a Special Program to fix it.

These two assumptions were applied to a variety of purported problems: differences in abilities, language, background knowledge and experiences, and so forth. Corresponding labels were assigned to programs and students representing the diagnosed problem: "handicapped," "linguistic disability," "cultural deprivation,"or "environmental deprivation." Experts on each problem were identified, and programs were set up to house and serve identified children.

Over time, advocacy groups have pointed out the pejorative connotations of these labels as well as the dangers of labeling as "deficient" students who speak different languages or come from non-European backgrounds. In some cases, terminology has changed. For example, students formerly labeled as having a linguistic disability are now referred to as English language learners; students formerly referred to as culturally or environmentally deprived may now be labeled "at risk" or simply poor. The underlying assumptions, however, remain the same: When students don't keep up with the rest of the class, the problem lies within the student (rather than within the educational system), and the solution is a Special Program, rather than making the general education program more responsive to all students.

A third assumption came into play in the development of Special Programs: Special Problems are best addressed in concentrated form. Thus, students with Similar Special Problems were placed together, making it more efficient for Special Problem Experts (e.g., ESL teachers, remedial education teachers, special education teachers, etc.) to "treat" them. (And yes, this medical language—"diagnosis," "treatment"—has been commonly used, reflecting the medical model on which special programs are often based.)

Over time, I came to question these assumptions as I saw the impact of our Special Programs on marginalized students. Despite our best efforts, being isolated in a special program was demoralizing for my students; they knew that they were there because of their failure in general education and had internalized an image of themselves as deficient. Those with multiple marginalized identities (e.g., poor or culturally diverse in addition to a disability label) in particular reacted with behavior considered inappropriate by their Special Problem Experts (like me).

These negative impacts are rationalized with the assumption that students should reach a point where the Special Problem label could be removed. However, this rarely occurs (at least during their school experience—many students have "six-hour" labels such as ELL or LD that may be largely irrelevant outside of the school walls, in their homes and communities).

Eventually, I took a position supporting students in inclusive classrooms. Working in that environment, it became clear to me that even though these students had more severe disabilities and their school experience was still imperfect, it was significantly better than a segregated program experience. For example, they frequently surprised us with how well and how much they learned. And although there was some teasing by students without disabilities, I saw much less than in the segregated program. (For a more formal analysis of research on outcomes of separate and inclusive programs, see Chapter 6.)

WE HAVE CHOICES AMONG PERSPECTIVES: HOW YOU SEE MAKES A DIFFERENCE IN WHAT YOU SEE

Depending on our perspective—how we look at things and how closely, through the lens of our backgrounds and expectations—we may see different things. For example, when confronted with the achievement gap between marginalized and privileged students, do we see marginalized students bogged down by their personal deficits? Or a society and educational system that systematically underserve the same groups over and over?

Perspectives differ in their attention to key issues such as power, decision making, and voice. Using traditional perspectives, we tend to take a relatively uncritical view, often without active consideration of issues such as who holds power in a particular situation (and who doesn't), how decisions are made, and which voices and evidence are given most

Activity 2.3: What Do You See in the Photograph?

Photo by Diana Lawrence-Brown

In looking at the image above, do you see the deer? You need to examine it closely; the deer is difficult to see. The deer is camouflaged by its surroundings, and the photograph was taken through a window screen. Similarly, with some students, we need to consciously peer past a screen or camouflage—for example, a screen of cultural perspective, a camouflage of language or other communication barrier—to be able to see more clearly. For a color version of this photograph, see the Related Resources for Chapter 2, www.tcpress.com.

weight. An identifying characteristic of critical perspectives is close attention to these issues. (See also Activity 2.B: Critical Perspectives, Related Resources for Chapter 2, www.tcpress.com.)

Note that those with marginal power are also those who tend to have marginal political, social, economic, and educational outcomes (Darder, Baltodano, & Torres, 2009). People with power, consciously or not, tend to act in ways that maintain their power, and that produce positive outcomes for those with whom they identify most closely. With a limited amount of power to go around in society and interests that are sometimes competing, those with marginal power tend to experience marginal outcomes. This is true even when they are the ones, according to official rhetoric, who are intended to benefit the most from various services and programs.

For example, *supported employment* is a vocational service intended for those with the most significant disabilities (Federal Register, 2001). It includes job development (developing a job that matches the strengths of the person rather than seeking an existing job) and job coaching (on-the-job training that is not time limited). However, instead of benefiting people with the *most* severe disabilities, this service is often provided to those with the *least* severe disabilities who aren't already working in the community. It's as if the assumption is that people with the least severe disabilities are somehow the most deserving of such jobs and services—despite the explicit language in the regulations.

FUNCTIONALISM AND CRITICAL PRAGMATISM: DIFFERENT WAYS OF LOOKING

One way to analyze educational systems is by comparing and contrasting critical and traditional perspectives toward individuals with marginalized differences, our schools, and our society. By examining assumptions, goals, and practices embedded within different paradigms, power relationships that impact outcomes for students can become more visible. Let's consider two (of many) possible perspectives: (1) *functionalism* and (2) *critical pragmatism* (Skrtic, 1995).

Assumptions of Functionalism

Functionalism is a dominant perspective used in our society, including in schools. The reason for the name functionalism is that from this perspective the system appears to be functional—that is, to be working pretty well for most people. While it may need some tweaking, it is not perceived as needing a major overhaul. Problems are viewed largely as existing within individuals who failed to benefit from a largely intact (functional) system. People in power assume that they know best, that their decisions affecting others are in the others' best interest. (To explore further the assumptions of functionalism, see Activity 2.C: Assumptions of Functionalism, Related Resources for Chapter 2, www.tcpress.com.)

Society is full of examples of the functionalist perspective at work—such as the Special Programs discussed in the previous section. Does it make sense to you that when a particular group is not well served by a system—such as students who don't experience intended outcomes from educational services—it is those students who should be expected to change? Why or why not? Under what circumstances?

Who do you think should determine the answer to that question? Does society benefit from efforts to improve outcomes for and participation of marginalized people? Do schools?

Outcomes of Functionalism

As you might imagine, a functionalist perspective often fits well with the mindset of people already in power—and others who are benefiting from the system as it is. Outcomes for those who are not may be discounted, and this may not be intentional. It is often thoughtlessness, not an active conspiracy against others. Most people with power are not evil masterminds, pulling strings to purposely disadvantage those from marginalized groups. But with functionalism at work under the surface, the system is viewed as working pretty well overall. As we've seen, efforts to improve outcomes for the rest are likely to take the form of fixing personal "deficits."

> **Think About This:** Critical analysts differ in their perspectives about the intentions of people in power. Some argue that people in power *are* intentionally working to disadvantage those from marginalized groups. Relate this discussion to the well-known quote from Audre Lorde: "The Master's tools will never dismantle the Master's house."

Freire elaborates on this aspect of a functionalist perspective toward marginalized groups: "The oppressed are regarded as the pathology of the healthy society . . . [these] 'incompetent and lazy' folk are then expected to re-create themselves in the image of dominant groups" (quoted in Darder, Baltodano, & Torres, 2009, p. 53). For example:

- Black people are expected to act White (e.g., in the way they talk or dress) to get ahead.
- Lesbian or gay people are expected to act heterosexual.
- Deaf people are expected to speak and to lip-read (even though most hearing people can't lip-read).
- Working-class people are expected to act middle-class.

Meanwhile, to dominant groups, their own behavior patterns are just normal—why *wouldn't* everyone else want to be that way? And shouldn't they, if they want to get ahead?

Assumptions of Critical Pragmatism

In this section, our comparison of traditional and critical perspectives continues, focusing now on a specific form of critical analysis known as *critical pragmatism* (Cornbleth & Waugh, 1995; Skrtic, 1995). As we've noted previously, applying critical perspectives means actively questioning appearances, common assumptions, and practices—looking deeper, looking below the surface—asking *why* things appear as they do. *Critical pragmatism*

Activity 2.4: Connections with Your Own Experiences

Was there a time when you were expected to change your feelings or behaviors to fit the dominant group, or you expected others to change to fit your expectations? How did you feel about these expectations? What are implications for educators and schools?

For example, if you attended a school in which you were not of the dominant religion, to what extent did the classroom/school accommodate and fully include you in activities and interactions? To what extent were you expected to assimilate, to accept the status quo?

Or if you went to a school where you *were* of the dominant religion, how much did you learn about people of other religions? What did you learn? That they were strange and exotic people who didn't do things right or normally?

Diversity presents many opportunities for cultural enrichment and critical thinking, but they can be easy to miss. Especially in a situation where our own background is mainstream, we will need to actively look for and develop such opportunities.

takes critical analysis a step further, posing pragmatic questions: "Who benefits?" "Who decides?" "What difference does it make?" So the *pragmatic* aspect of critical pragmatism means having a very practical bent—an explicit focus on outcomes, benefits, and consequences (cf. Durant, 1961).

Other important aspects of critical pragmatism are context and pluralism (Cornbleth & Waugh, 1995). *Pluralism* here means attending to multiple viewpoints—especially of those most affected by the decision. Rather than assuming that those in authority know best, it is purposefully dialogic, incorporating an ongoing give and take among stakeholders. This means consciously approaching conclusions with the assumption that they are provisional, open to further interpretation, and open to criticism. Critical pragmatism is also *contextualized.* Instead of assuming that what happens in one place would automatically work the same way in the next, we actively consider how the location, time, and school and host communities might shape what we think and what we do.

> **Think About This**: Mara remembers, "Growing up as a Jewish child in a largely Christian society, teachers sometimes said things like 'While all of us are celebrating *our* holiday, Mara and her family will be celebrating their special holiday.' It was clear that I was 'odd,' 'the other,' 'weird.' I didn't feel honored, I felt marginalized."

Consider the following illustration of context and pluralism from the perspective of critical pragmatism. Educators often view school reforms in other communities with skepticism, concluding, "That's great, but it won't work here." Reformers may view these skeptics as naysayers, lacking imagination, vision, and a willingness to change. But the pluralistic and contextual emphases of critical pragmatism mean that local issues, practicalities, beliefs, and details are sought out; to ignore or downplay them would undermine the reform effort from the start. Local stakeholders' concerns and ideas are taken seriously, especially those most affected by a decision to change (or to keep things as they are). They are integral to the dialogue from the very start, beginning with an analysis of the outcomes of the status quo. Where outcomes are disappointing, a strategy is crafted centering on the priorities, concerns, and local knowledge of students, educators, and community members who are most affected. For example, segregated programs are generally instituted with the assumption that outcomes will be better for the students served. If, however, outcomes are not found to be better, then students, educators, and community members need to come together to reform the service.

To summarize, critical pragmatism includes a practical focus on who benefits, pluralistic attention to multiple viewpoints, and careful consideration of local context and concerns. The goal of critical pragmatism is social justice—to change our practices to better fit our values (Skrtic, 1995).

For most educators, this means changing our schools to better serve *all* our students. In situations where stakeholders' values differ, specific professional development may need to be provided for effective collaboration and conflict resolution to take place. This can help the group to determine their shared values. Even if we don't agree on some important things, we can use our common ground to move toward a more just educational system; this is an essential aspect of lasting reform.

Outcomes of Critical Pragmatism

What difference does it make, if we adopt this more critical perspective? What I have seen in practice is that when we make a commitment to serve each student well and adopt an attitude of flexibility in our practice, the result can be instructional environments and experiences that benefit all students, improving outcomes for those in the middle and at the top as well as those who are struggling. (For more about specific strategies that support this multilevel instruction, see Chapters 7 and 8.) Because of the focus on dialogue, more voices are heard ("two heads are better than one"), and the proposed solution is more likely to be respectful of diverse groups. Then, because we actively take into account the particular context, there are fewer problems with overgeneralization from one situation to another. And finally (although there is no magic wand), there is greater potential for outcomes to improve because there is active and ongoing attention given to them.

Let's look again at the example of the achievement gap. An achievement gap is said to exist when certain groups of students systematically achieve at lower levels than other students; the greatest attention recently in the United States has been paid to achievement levels for students who are African American, Hispanic, and/or poor, in comparison to their Asian American, European American, and/or more wealthy counterparts.

In addressing an achievement gap from the perspective of critical pragmatism, several things happen. Diverse perspectives on the issue are sought, especially perspectives of those who are most affected (in this case, people who are African American, Hispanic, and/or poor). Close attention is given to examining the context, including location, time, and history of the school and host communities. There is a focus on practical consequences—not just *differences* in achievement levels, but the *impact* of those differences on those affected by the gap.

It's vital here not to neglect digging below the surface, asking why, identifying and questioning assumptions—the critical aspect of critical pragmatism. Without this part of the analysis, if the focus is on outcomes alone, the danger of "blaming the victim" increases. As a result, differences in achievement have, in the not-too-distant past, been pejoratively attributed to lack of ambition, cultural deprivation, and even genetic makeup of marginalized groups.

When both aspects of critical pragmatism are exercised, however, critical analysts come to very different conclusions about the nature of an achievement gap (DeShano da Silva, Huguley, Kakli, & Rao, 2007; Ladson-Billings, 2006; Lauter, 1966; Williams, 1969). Rather than lack of ambition, cultural deprivation, or genetic inferiority, they identify an *opportunity* gap attributable to factors such as low expectations and systematic exclusion, along with inequities in educational resources, in teacher qualifications and class size, in social connections and knowledge of social systems. The result is an entirely different approach to educational reform. Rather than putting oppressed people in the position of re-creating themselves in the image of dominant groups, the emphasis can become more practical and respectful, focused on equalizing educational factors through actions such as the following:

- Increasing the percentage of qualified educators
- Reducing class size
- Increasing social connections and knowledge of social systems
- Equalizing rewards of educational achievement

- Increasing expectations
- Eliminating systematic exclusion

Applying Critical Pragmatism: Questions to Ask

Now take a moment to apply what you've learned. Consider a social and educational situation from your experience, and then try to answer the questions in Figure 2.3. You may want to start by thinking of a student or students whose educational outcomes you find compelling. For example, do you know of a student who has done/is doing surprisingly well? Or maybe someone whose outcomes have been disappointing, perhaps due to being excluded, dropping out, and so on? You'll also find it helpful to consider the situation you are analyzing in terms of both highly specific, local aspects and larger societal and governmental aspects. (For more examples of using critical perspectives to understand real-world data and experiences, see Doyle & Reitzug, 1993, and Lawrence-Brown, 2000.)

Figure 2.3. Critical Pragmatism Applied to Inclusive Education

	Questions to Consider
Power & Decision Making	• Who decides what characteristics and abilities (e.g., languages, cultures, behaviors) are valued? What counts as a disability, and who has one? • Who decides which students are included in general education, and which are segregated in separate programs? • What alternatives to segregation are considered? What alternatives are missing or marginalized? • What is the rhetoric about how these decisions should be made? • In cases where practice does not match the rhetoric, how is power exercised to manage the situation?
Assumptions & Evidence	• What assumptions are made about people from marginalized groups? About educators, families? • What assumptions are made about schools? About separate programs (e.g., who is there, what happens, what does it lead to)? About inclusion? • What evidence is considered?
Benefits & Consequences	• Who benefits from separate programs? From inclusive classrooms? • What unintended consequences are there?

As you read the rest of this book, try to actively use the questions in Figure 2.3 to help you think about educational and social situations you encounter. Keep in mind the following as you apply this critical perspective to your own experiences and the other educational situations that you study:

- Recall the quote from Helder Camara at the very beginning of this chapter. Despite the greater insight that a critical perspective can facilitate, your enhanced understandings will not always be warmly received by others. Expect people with power to act in ways that maintain their own power and privileges (along with the privileges of those with whom they are closely connected). Even if it's not an active conspiracy against you, there may be negative consequences associated with disagreeing with powerful people and trying to change the status quo. In schools, untenured educators may be particularly at risk. For more discussion of successful school change, see Chapter 12.
- Despite the risks of rocking the boat, we must also consider the risks of habitually going with the flow. Outcomes of our current educational system are not equitable. Our personal and collective values and aspirations demand that we seek a society in which the gifts and talents of all students can be identified and developed. Experiences, perspectives, and contributions of particular groups must not be systematically marginalized, for this harms not only those who are marginalized but society in general.

GROUND TRUTH: THE PRACTITIONER'S VOICE

A Special Education Teacher

In my first year of teaching, I had a student with multiple disabilities stemming from Fetal Alcohol Syndrome. She was living in a homeless shelter in a very wealthy part of a major financial and cultural center. Her mom was working in a program cleaning city parks; she had not graduated from high school herself and therefore had difficulty helping Desiree with her school work. In addition, Desiree would often come to school hungry, and would talk about being locked in her apartment bathroom all night, as her mom was talking on the phone in a private conversation. Education was a cry distance away, as Desiree's social and emotional needs were very extensive.

I worked with Desiree day after day, initially just trying to meet her needs (according to Maslow's Hierarchy). Beyond school hours, I worked with Desiree's mother to create tools that she could use to support her daughter's academic growth while at home. For example, I recorded myself reading books on an MP3 player so that Desiree and her mother could read together at home or even on the subway.

Eventually, after I had earned their respect and trust, we started making significant progress academically. Desiree learned how to read, write, and solve basic math problems. Her mother saw the progress and became hooked on education as well. Unfortunately, Desiree did not perform at grade level on the state exams.

During the summer, my principal called me in for a meeting regarding Desiree's academic needs for the following year. I felt strongly that although she was not quite at grade level academically, the inclusion class was meeting her needs. However, the principal felt that Desiree would perform better in the self-contained 12:1 class. When Desiree's IEP (Individual Education Plan) meeting was scheduled in September, the principal did not invite me as the "special educator." Desiree's mother went into the meeting unprepared about the possible outcomes relating to Desiree's placement. She did not recognize *anyone*. By the end of the meeting, a decision was made to place Desiree in the 4th grade self-contained classroom. The principal had controlled the meeting to her advantage—Desiree would be placed in the self-contained class, offsetting the then-current male-dominated population and ensuring that students with behavioral disabilities would not be bussed to our school to fill that last spot. They had moved Desiree out of her LRE (Least Restrictive Environment).

As you have read, assumptions affect how people are treated in educational systems. In the case of Desiree, her mother's lack of education was noticed by my school principal. This weakness of hers was then used to move Desiree into a more restrictive environment. I believe that the principal lacked personal knowledge and experience in special education, and therefore did not see the positive effect that the inclusive placement had on the child. Quite possibly, the principal may have been concerned about her own position and fearful that the parents of the general education population would not want Desiree in their class.

REFERENCES

Brown v. Board of Education. (1954). 347 U.S. 483.

Cornbleth, C., & Waugh, D. (1995). *The great speckled bird: Multicultural politics and education policymaking.* New York: St. Martin's Press.

Crissey, S. (2009). *Educational attainment in the United States: 2007.* Washington, DC: U.S. Census Bureau.

Darder, A., Baltodano, M., & Torres, R. (2009). *The critical pedagogy reader, 2nd ed.* New York: Routledge.

DeShano da Silva, C., Huguley, J. P., Kakli, Z., & Rao, R. (2007). *The opportunity gap: Achievement and inequality in education*. Cambridge, MA: Harvard Education Press.

Doyle, L., & Reitzug, U. C. (1993, October). *A practitioner's narrative: Separatism and collaboration among special education teachers and other stakeholders*. Paper presented at the Convention of the University Council for Educational Administration, Houston, TX. ERIC No. ED392178

Durant, W. (1961). *The story of philosophy*. New York: Washington Square Press.

Education for All Handicapped Children Act of 1975, Pub. L. No. 94-142.

Federal Register. (2001). Part 361—State Vocational Rehabilitation Services Program. Retrieved from http://www2.ed.gov/legislation/FedRegister/finrule/2001-1/011701a.html

Foxman, A. (2010). Why I wrote "Jews & money." Retrieved from http://www.adl.org/ADL_Opinions/Anti_Semitism_Domestic/20101210-Oped+.htm

Hallahan, D. P., & Kauffman, J. M. (2000). *Exceptional learners: Introduction to special education* (8th ed). Boston: Allyn and Bacon.

Kelly, P. (2005). *As America becomes more diverse: The impact of state higher education inequality*. Boulder, CO: National Center for Higher Education Management Systems. Retrieved from http://www.higheredinfo.org/raceethnicity/InequalityPaperNov2005.pdf

Ladson-Billings, G. (2006). From the achievement gap to the education debt: Understanding achievement in U.S. schools. *Educational Researcher, 35*(7), 3–12.

Lauter, S. (1966). *Education and race*. New York: National Urban League. ED039296.

Lau v. Nichols (1974), 414 U.S. 563, 568

Lawrence-Brown, D. (2000). The segregation of Stephen. In Cornbleth, C. (Ed.), *Curriculum politics, policy, and practice* (pp. 103-138). Albany: State University of New York Press.

Schott Foundation for Public Education. (2009). *National Opportunity to Learn campaign: Federal recommendations*. Cambridge, MA: Schott Foundation for Public Education. Retrieved from http://www.otlcampaign.org/sites/default/files/resources/otl-federal-recommendations.pdf

Skrtic, T. M. (1995). *Disability and democracy*. New York: Teachers College Press.

Sleeter, C. (1995). Reflections on my use of multicultural and critical pedagogy when my students are White. In, Sleeter, C. & McLaren, P., Eds., *Multicultural education, critical pedagogy, and the politics of difference* (pp. 415–438). Albany: State University of New York Press.

Title IX, Education Amendments of 1972 (Title 20 U.S.C. Sections 1681–1688)

Tyack, D., & Cuban, L. (1995). *Tinkering toward Utopia: A century of public school reform*. Cambridge, MA: Harvard University Press.

United States Census Bureau. (2008). Disability data from the current population survey/annual social and economic (ASEC) supplement: Table 3. Mean earnings of persons 16 to 74. Washington, DC: United States Census Bureau. Retrieved from http://www.census.gov/hhes/www/disability/disabcps.html

Williams, H. (1969). To close the opportunity gap. *Junior College Journal, 40*, 1, 8–13.

CHAPTER 3

Multiple Identities, Shifting Landscapes

Janet Sauer

One of the core purposes of public education from its earliest days was to
transcend difference.

—Mark Fettes, "Imaginative Multicultural Education"

Key Principle 3: *Traditionally marginalized differences (including but not limited
to disabilities, cultural/linguistic/racial background, gender, sexual orientation,
and class) are best understood and responded to within a broader construct of
diversity. Each of us has multiple identities that can be represented or viewed in
different ways.*

All of us live within and travel through various sociocultural landscapes
in a global society. At times we might find ourselves in conflict between
the idea of American social/cultural diversity and the broader American
shared identity. Think about the increasingly diverse range of demographic groups represented in schools, including but not limited to characteristics, such as race, gender, socioeconomic status, or ability status. Within
each of these demographic characteristics there is also diversity. For instance, we can consider the heterogeneity among those referred to as African American and ask, what is the difference between African, African
American, and an African who is American (Scruggs, 2011)? Also, we do
not always fit into only one racial category. Further, people occupy more
than one location or characteristic of diversity, such as the transgendered
youth who might have a disability.

Students are phenomenally diverse (Nieto, 2000). Tension can emerge
between honoring this human diversity while also holding onto what one

might think of as a shared American identity that is often reflected in the media or in school curricula and practices. Examples might include saying the Pledge of Allegiance, eating fast food, or cheering for Team USA during the Olympics.

To assist in this interpersonal and intrapersonal journey, we create cultural models and "habits of conversation" (Gee, 2005). Gee explains how people engage in "habits of conversation" or daily discourse that can reveal their assumptions. In this case, we are asking you to pay close attention to the words or phrases used to describe characteristics. The focus of this chapter is to examine our human diversity and various shifting identities within the cultural context of schools. As pre-service and practicing educators we

> **Think About This:** How do ideas about America as a "melting pot" get in the way of honoring individual differences?

can reflect upon our personal experiences and how they might impact the students with whom we work. What are our habits of conversation and what beliefs and assumptions might they reveal about our understanding of the meaning of diversity? (See also Activity 3.A: Media or Literature Analysis, and Activity 3.B: Listening & Observing, Related Resources for Chapter 3, www.tcpress.com.)

School missions often include statements about "celebrating individual student strengths" or "honoring diversity." Are these statements lived out in the daily lives of educators and students? Is there an anti-bias or cultural diversity curriculum embedded across the course subjects? How does eating a cultural food once a year facilitate understanding of cultural values, or does it serve to reinforce cultural stereotypes? Educators, families, and invested community members seek a deeper understanding of what statements like "Celebrate Diversity" mean. What kinds of

Activity 3.1: School Mission Statements

Examine various school mission statements regarding what is written about diversity and how the school describes their efforts to address it. Is the word "diversity" used? If so, how is it defined? Ask teachers, administrators, students, parents and guardians, and staff if they are familiar with the mission statement and if they were involved in its development. Ask them for examples of ways in which the mission is lived out in the school curriculum and activities. Find out how the school determines if its mission statement reflects the school's priorities. Compare and contrast different school mission statements. Draft your own mission statement and after reading the chapter, revisit it and see if you might change it.

differences count in the diversity construct? Does it involve more than race, gender, and ethnic identities?

THE ART OF ACKNOWLEDGMENT

"I can't ignore my disability, why would you?"

—Karen, High School Student

Karen asked this question as part of a language arts curriculum called *Writing, Identity, and the Other* (Ware, 2001). She pointedly challenged her teachers, peers, and the community at large to acknowledge her identity as someone with a disability. Her question leads us to examine our assumptions about disability and our cultural norms regarding how to respond to and engage with people who experience disability. Despite decades of legislation and educational practices touting the values of human diversity, to ascribe the disability label to oneself or to another is to set the person apart from the majority, the typical, the norm group. The idea that educators should acknowledge disability disrupts traditional teaching taboos, which suggest that we should ignore a student's characteristics when those characteristics diverge from what is considered typical or expected for fear of stigmatizing that student.

> **Think About This:** It is troubling that color blindness regarding racial differences and making disabilities invisible are seen as desirable goals in education. What would happen if we noticed?

It is through interaction that underlying assumptions and prejudices surface. Labels typically stigmatize people, and school-age students are particularly vulnerable to bullying based on labels. Fifty percent of children are reported to be victims of bullying (Schoen & Schoen, 2010). Students with disabilities are two to three times more likely to be bullied than their peers (Van Cleave & Davis, 2006). While advocating for the Safe Schools Act, California state representative Linda Sanchez noted that LGBT youth are some of our nation's most vulnerable students, and some of the most frequent targets of bullying (U.S. Committee on Education and Labor, 2009, p. 72). Schools across the country have adopted anti-bullying curricula in an effort to keep students safe. However, researchers suggest such efforts are limited unless accompanied by schoolwide supports for

> **Think About This:** For many bullying instances, there are witnesses. They have to decide if they will remain a bystander or if they will intervene. What factors help them decide?

promoting healthy social interactions (Swearer, Espelage, Vaillancourt, & Hymel, 2010). (See also Activity 3.C: Making Schools Safe for All, Related Resources for Chapter 3, www.tcpress.com.)

In order to feel safe in schools, students need acknowledgment. They also need to develop an understanding of others who may look, sound, or behave differently from them. The creative writing activity about identity in which Karen and her classmates had participated was part of a humanities-based disability studies curriculum at an urban arts magnet high school. For Karen, a teenager who was perceived as disabled, the particular educational context, or social landscape, allowed her to be comfortable enough to identify with this marginalized group, to claim her membership in the disabled community. She felt she could not ignore her difference and wondered why others would try to. She challenged society in ways akin to the African American "Black is Beautiful" movement of the 1960s, the feminist movement that began in the late 1800s and reemerged during WWII and the 1970s, and the more recent lesbian, gay, bisexual, transgendered, queer, and intersex (LGBTQI) movements.

The tension Karen and her classmates expressed in their writing regarding differences of ability is similar to the phenomenon experienced by other marginalized groups defined by their race, class, culture, primary language, gender, or sexual orientation in stigmatizing ways. Steele (2010) highlights decades of research into social identities and how negative stereotypes are played out in the daily lives of college students based upon expected behaviors. For instance, in one study, women about to be tested in high-level math skills were broken up into two groups. Immediately before the test, the first group was reminded about successful women in math, whereas the second group was reminded about the cultural stereotype that women are not good at math. The impact of the statement on the second group was that their previous achievement in math was significantly depressed. Steele describes this phenomenon as "stereotype threat." In other words, assumptions based on stereotypes can directly influence student performance. (To learn more about stereotype threat, including who is affected and how, ways to reduce it, and criticisms of stereotype threat, visit www.reducingstereotypethreat.org.)

In our efforts to learn about what it might be like to "live in another's shoes," it is useful to be self-reflective. For example, a teacher researcher observed a 5th-grade girl named Taylour (Hairston, 2005). Taylour lived on a Hawaiian military base with her family. She was labeled legally blind and identified culturally as African American. She had albinism, which means an absence of pigment in her skin, hair, and eyes, and when the teacher asked her to describe herself, the child responded, "I'm colorless in a rainbow." Upon reflection, the teacher researcher wrote a poem asking, Who defines me? Who labels me? This is part of what she wrote:

I am defined by the color of my skin, the texture of my hair, the tone in my voice. I am defined by my femininity and grace, my sexual preference and the way I walk into a room or invade someone's space.

I am defined by my history and past. Stereotypes that were created based on hate and ignorance but linger and linger and linger—day after day—as the years pass.

I am defined by my financial status, the job I hold, my education and where I live, what type of car I drive, how I eat, who my husband is, his rank in the military, where my children go to school, the degrees I hold and my grade point average. (Hairston, 2005, p. 55)

This teacher began a reflective journey using poetry as a vehicle for examining stereotypes and identity.

THE RIGHT TO DEFINE ONESELF

When we enter new contexts, how do we introduce ourselves to others? Are there things we might avoid mentioning? What choices are involved regarding what (not) to disclose? Much is determined by our personal histories, by the larger society, and by our expectations of how those we are meeting will interpret our external identities.

What Is an Identity?

Identity is usually considered the defining characteristic(s) of a person. Philosophers, sociologists, psychologists, educators, and researchers have long studied the idea of identity, each field approaching the topic from a different vantage point and developing different theories. Identity theory involves self-efficacy whereby a person identifies with a set of characteristics and holds beliefs about his or her related performance (Stets & Burke, 2000). Jenkins (1994) suggests that it is through social interaction that personal identity is formed. *Internal* identities can be thought of as those attributes we acknowledge about ourselves. For example, we might think

Activity 3.2: Writing an Identity Poem

Consider how you might answer Hairston's questions. Then, write your own identity poem. What labels did you choose when describing yourself? What descriptors did you elect to leave out? Did the descriptors you edited out remind you of distressing events in your life?

of ourselves as smart because we attend college. We might identify with the teaching profession as one that is reputable, thus having a positive internal or personal identity. By contrast, our *external* identities are reflected by the clothes we wear, the color of our skin, or our spoken dialect. A student teacher shared how frustrated she felt when she spoke in her Southern dialect and others immediately judged her as unintelligent. Although she self-identified as an educated person, the North-

> **Think About This**: Not everyone in our society feels comfortable disclosing his or her multiple identities. What do you think stands in the way? How might we change that? How do your students choose to introduce themselves to you?

erners in her college classes did not seem to view her as such. Elementary and secondary students of mine who had speech or language differences expressed similar frustrations.

Some identities can be altered, and some cannot. By whistling classical music like Vivaldi within earshot of White strangers, a young African American male redefined himself as someone of the educated social class (Steele, 2010). He took action to define himself rather than letting any stereotype-based assumptions by others define who he was. Similarly, one of my pre-service teachers explained that she would purposefully use the Standard English dialect in school, but when at home with her family she typically spoke an African American vernacular. She identified with her African American culture in both contexts, but in different ways. While we form and reform our identities we may notice a change of status these identities offer in different contexts. For example, while my light skin, business-style clothing, and Standard English speech hold status in a parent-teacher conference, these same external attributes could be suspicious to youth of color in an urban high school. This awareness of how we are read by others and the related privileges associated with our identities are important to those who ascribe to social justice values and seek to enact inclusive classrooms. (To explore your own identity, see Activity 3.D: Creating a Self-Portrait, Related Resources for Chapter 3, www.tcpress.com.)

A Question of Labels

The relationship between identity construction and *labels* is not straightforward. The naming or labeling of a person "invokes meanings in the form of expectations with regard to others' and one's own behaviors" (Stets & Burke, 2000, p. 225). When a student is labeled as an English language learner, for instance, educators form specific expectations of the student's behaviors and academic performance. This becomes particularly troublesome for second-generation American immigrants who might be proficient in spoken English language but not literate. These students, often referred to as "Generation 1.5," are typically tracked into remedial low-track classes (Roberge, 2003); they struggle between their self-ascribed identity as typical Americans and the implications of being labeled an English language learner (ELL). This leads one to question who ascribes a label to whom, and what values are attributed to those labels. Wilkins's (2004) study of Puerto Rican youth illustrates the stigmatizing power of labels. The label in this case, a "Puerto Rican wannabe," was used by peers as an insult to describe "a particular kind of white girl . . . [who] rejects white middle class cultural style" (p. 104). The Puerto Ricans who viewed themselves as genuinely ethnically Puerto Rican ascribed the "wannabe" label to distinguish themselves from those they saw as perpetuating negative stereotypes. Self-ascribed labels, on the other hand, can reflect changes in identity in ways considered positive. For example, the change from "Indian" to "Native American" is described as an important step in developing a positive "collective identity" (Spencer, 1994).

It is difficult to know how a person might want to be referred to, so it is best to simply ask. As part of her work in culturally responsive teaching, Gay (2000) uses the prompt, "I am _____, but I am not _____," with students to assist in understanding how labels are often used as short-cuts to describe one another. A 7-year-old was quick to inform his teacher that although he had significant medical issues, he was "not a robot." Educators can discuss the importance of clarifying the difference between what characteristics students identify with and those they do not. The value ascribed to labels determines where they land in the social hierarchy. When the label is used to define a person, the definition of the label becomes the person's primary descriptor, and other attributes fall to secondary status or are forgotten. (See also Activity 3.E: Disable the Label, Related Resources for Chapter 3, www.tcpress.com.)

Words like "gay" and "retard" have returned to common parlance as general put-downs. A recent campaign titled "Spread the Word to End the Word" challenges the use of the word "retard." A public service announcement (PSA) for the campaign titled "Not Acceptable" (2012) begins with a Black man saying, "It's not acceptable to call me a nigger," and concludes with Lauren Potter, the actress with Down syndrome from the television series *Glee*, saying, "It's not acceptable to call me a retard." When writing about people with disabilities, the American Psychological Association (APA) suggests the use of person-first language. For example, write "a person with a disability" instead of "disabled person." Some people argue this is an infringement of their First Amendment rights to freedom of speech. In an online self-advocate journal, the editor wrote, "In principle, I support person-first language, as it arose from within our own community—unlike such euphemistic garbage as 'differently-abled' and 'special needs.' But in practice it's an impossible construction to maintain . . . too many syllables

. . . so we fall back on 'disabled'" (*New Mobility*, March 14, 2011). The issue, then, is perhaps less about the word itself, but rather the meaning *behind* the word and the negative assumptions and cultural stereotyping that accompany the use of the word in particular contexts.

Multiple Identities

We form and reform our identities. As explained earlier, we have internal and external identities. These identities are not easily separated, and they change over time depending upon the context and the values we attribute to certain descriptors or markers. We also can hold multiple identities at the same time, negotiating their value with others. At times our various identities might come into conflict with these values and the expected behaviors others assume of us based upon social norms. We may be discouraged (or inadvertently discourage others) from making personal identities public or claiming identities that the wider society deems to be unvalued and/or stigmatizing. Therefore, it is worthwhile to carefully consider how we choose to define our students and create the conditions that allow them to choose which identities they want to disclose.

SHIFTING LANDSCAPES AND IDENTITY VALUES

The values we attribute to certain identities are informed by our personal and cultural histories. They are reflected in our cultural models (Gee, 2005). One powerful example is the legacy of indigenous Americans

 Activity 3.3: Challenging "Naughty Words"

View the PSA "Not Acceptable" (www.youtube.com/watch?v=T549VoLca_Q) and the subsequent comments that illustrate the conflicting interpretations and defenses for using the word *retard,* and for likening it to other pejorative expressions. Also, read the online threaded discussion for *New Mobility* magazine titled "Crip, Gimp, and Other Naughty Words" (March 14, 2011, www.newmobility.com/browse_thread.cfm?id=144&blogID=10).

1. Restate the different perspectives.
2. Whose voice carries the most weight? Why do you think this is the case?
3. What is your perspective? Has it changed after watching the video and reading the discussion?
4. Choose two labels that you are comfortable using for yourself but wouldn't want others to use. Why?

Activity 3.4: Rubik's Identity Cube

Using the Rubik's Cube as a metaphor, draw an image that represents one of your identities on each side of a paper cube. For example, I might draw a book on one side to represent my teacher identity and draw a baby on another side to represent my identity as a mother. I can also make a small cube with related identities and combine it with other cubes to illustrate how some identities are hidden from certain views. New cubes made over time and hung together like a mobile offer an identity timeline.

University of Colorado Professor Leslie Grant described using this activity with "prospective teachers to reflect on their own multidimensional nature and consider their future students in the same way. They examined aspects of who they are, and how they are perceived and understood by others. We expanded the activity to consider what might go *inside the box*, aspects of their own make-up that—although not immediately visible—profoundly impact who they are."

See also Activity 3.F: Shifting Identities, Related Resources for Chapter 3, www.tcpress.com.

interpreted in modern culture. The APA (2005) acknowledged how Native American sports mascots have a particularly negative impact on the self-esteem of Indian children, but they also have negative effects on *all* students because they undermine indigenous American identity and perpetuate stereotypes.

Poet Janice Gould (2011) captured the conflicting feelings of her Native history, as recollected from growing up near the campus of the University of California, Berkeley, in the following excerpt:

Indian Mascot, 1959

Now begins the festival and rivalry of late fall,
the weird debauch and daring debacle
of frat-boy parties as students parade foggy streets in mock
processions, bearing on shoulders scrawny effigies of dead,
defeated Indians cut from trees, where,
in the twilight, they had earlier been hung.

"Just dummies," laughs our dad, "Red Indians hung
or burned—it's only in jest." Every fall
brings the Big Game against Stanford, where

young scholars let off steam before the debacle
they may face of failed exams. "You're dead
wrong," he says to Mom. "They don't mock

real, live Indians." Around UC campus, mock
lynchings go on. Beneath porches we see hung
the scarecrow Natives with fake long braids, dead
from the merrymaking. On Bancroft Way, one has fallen
indecorously to a lawn, a symbol of the debacle
that happened three generations ago in California's hills, where

Native peoples were strung up. (A way of having fun?)
Where did they go, those Indian ghosts? (pp. 1–2)

Gould's poem illustrates the impact of cultural histories on pres-
ent-day attitudes and identities. The painful legacy of Indian boarding
schools (see Chapter 6) is rarely discussed, but one can hear echoes of such
assimilation sentiments in calls for English-only curricula. Unsurprisingly, these students along with those referred to as Generation 1.5—whose
parents were immigrants but who grew up American—may experience
conflicting identities (Campbell, 2009).

Double-Minority Status

What about those of us who hold more than one marginalized identity? Consider the following comment from a Ball State University student
during a focus group meeting:

> My disability I can deal with. It makes the world I live in challenging yet
> "navigable," but to be black and disabled is most debilitating because it
> challenges mobility of the body and the mind. (quoted in Keys, Malone, &
> Russell, 1997, p. 1)

Issues involving people with *double-minority status* are being taken
up by national advocacy organizations. TASH (2010), the association for
people with significant disabilities, describes how their members who are
people of color have compounding negative experiences of racism and
discrimination based on perceived ability. The murder of Navajo teen
Fred C. Martinez Jr. illustrates the complexities involved at the intersections of marginalized identities. Sixteen-year-old Martinez was known to
his family and friends as being gay, an identity traditionally referred to
by Navajos as "two-spirited" bodies, a *nadleehi* (male-to-female *berdache*).
One of his teachers described him this way: "He had a woman's mind,

soul and heart in a man's body . . . If he had been a woman, he would have been the most popular girl in town" (Bartels, 2001). A reporter covering the crime wondered, "Did the attacker target Martinez because of his sexuality or his ethnicity?"

Blanchett (2010) addresses the complex relationship between hierarchies *within* disability categories. It is more acceptable to have a "learning disability" (LD) label than "mental retardation" (MR), which is the reason argued by Blanchett and others that White, middle-class boys are more likely to be labeled LD, whereas historically there has been a disproportionately high percentage of Black males labeled MR. Now, consider how students labeled with MR are usually taught in segregated classrooms (Smith, 2007) and students of color are often discouraged from taking advanced classes even when they show they can do the work, thus "racially stratifying" schools (O'Connor, Mueller, Lewis, Rivas-Drake, & Rosenberg, 2011).

To Claim or Not to Claim

Social hierarchies seem to play a role in whether or not people feel safe disclosing and claiming their marginalized identity. Some of us have privileges regarding what, how, and when to disclose certain identities. Which of our multiple identities do we claim? Do we have a choice and, when we do, might we consider "passing" instead? The idea of passing for someone other than ourselves is discussed in literature regarding sexual orientation (Kissen 1996) and race (Rottenberg, 2003). Similarly, migrant youth experience cultural dissonance as they "play White" in an effort for acceptance (Derrington, 2007).

The high school student Karen claimed her disabled identity, as a person with spina bifida (a physical impairment affecting the spinal tube) who likely requires mobility supports such as braces, crutches, or the use of a wheelchair. People with non-visible disabilities are also increasingly coming out, but it is noteworthy how some hold statuses that might mitigate their marginalized identity (e.g., Mooney, 2007, is a White male labeled as learning disabled, and Grandin, 2011, is a White professor who is also labeled autistic). As Sherry (2008) points out, "disability is always a sexed, gendered, racialized, ethnicized, and classed experience . . . [that] operates within a framework of multilayered and complex patterns of inequity and identities" (p. 75). (See also Activity 3.G: Learning from Autobiographies, and Activity 3.H: The UN Convention on the Rights of Persons with Disabilities, Related Resources for Chapter 3, www.tcpress.com.)

The multiple identities we all have and the shifting landscapes in which we experience social judgment should not be simplified by short-cut labels and stereotypes. We need to think deeply, critically, and reflectively about the ways in which school policies and practices influence students' (and our own) attitudes toward diversity, and whether or not it is worth the risk to claim one's marginalized identity.

CONCLUSION

"America was never, ethnically or racially, a homogeneous society," Campbell (2009, p. 198) wrote in the introduction to his work about North America's diversity. As educators, our job asks us to live in and respond to this diversity in our daily work. You might begin your response to this reading by using the critical reflective lens described in this book as you listen to yourself talking with colleagues, with your students, and with their parents. Educators who have taken this critical stance have found new ways of seeing their students and themselves. With greater understanding of themselves and their students, educators acknowledge ways in which our multiple identities contribute to a democratic society.

In their examination of inclusive educational dispositions, Theoharis and Causton-Theoharis (2008) discuss how educational leaders can create opportunities for students' emancipation from the educational system that has historically marginalized them. They suggest that informed and reflective educators take meaningful action to improve the opportunities for students who otherwise might feel marginalized. To not do so is to affirm the social inequalities described in this book. We need to listen to our students, like Karen, who have been traditionally marginalized, and not ignore them or their differences. If we agree with Fettes (2007), whom I quoted at the beginning of this chapter, that the purpose of education is to "transcend difference," we will be better equipped to respond to our students' multiple and changing identities when we respond within a broader construct of diversity.

GROUND TRUTH: A PARENT'S PERSPECTIVE

Punita Arora

I entered kindergarten in 1972 and loved the joy of school and my activities in Mrs. Wenzel's classroom. I was one among a group of others just like me. I learned about "Indians" and the story of the first Thanksgiving and was confused that my ancestors weren't "those Indians" (my parents emigrated from India). I remember the sometimes disturbing images of Native Americans in the news, demanding equal rights and respect, though my Indian family enjoyed equality. These images share a nebulous space in my memory of the Vietnam War, Black Pride, and the Women's Movement. As a 6-year-old, I became aware of my emerging identity as one and Other within the fabric of our society. Other-ness eventually fueled a passion for justice and a level playing field for all during an era of self-centeredness. My identity as Other would grow again, with the birth of my second baby, a beautiful boy with autism. He, too, strives to find his place and to create his own identity. My hope is that he focuses on what is possible. However, I fear that he will know the pain of being misunderstood, minimized, and marginalized as Other. Sadly, even now, my son lives in a world where many often miss the deeper truth that all those Others are other *people*, just like them.

GROUND TRUTH: A NATIVE AMERICAN PERSPECTIVE

Janice Gould
Professor of Women's and Ethnic Studies, University of Colorado

For convenience, American Indian people may use the term "Native American" or "American Indian" or "Indian" or their own tribal designation or something else (like "NDN"). It's complicated and an issue we've faced for a long time. For Indigenous people, there is so much that is *not* a part of the conversation on labeling. Beneath that governmental designation lies a history of paternalism and a denial of sovereignty, which is an issue both distinct and crucial for Native people.

REFERENCES

American Psychological Association. (2005). *APA resolution on recommending the immediate retirement of American Indian mascots, symbols, images, and personalities by schools, colleges, universities, athletic teams, and organizations*. Washington, DC: Author. Retrieved from http://www.apa.org/pi/oema/resources/policy/indian-mascots.pdf

Bartels, L. (July 7, 2001). Teen's death from hate? Cortez Navajo youth may have been slain for his sexual identity. *Rocky Mountain News* (Denver, CO).

Blanchett, W. J. (2010). Telling it like it is: The role of race, class, & culture in the perpetuation of learning disability as a privileged category for the White middle class. *Disability Studies Quarterly, 30*(2). Retrieved from http://dsq-sds.org/article/view/1233/1280

Campbell, G. (2009). Many Americas: The intersections of class, race, and ethnic identity. In A. Ferber, C. M. Jimenez, A. Herrera, & D. R. Samuels (Eds.), *The matrix reader: Examining the dynamics of oppression and privilege* (pp. 198–226). New York: McGraw-Hill.

Derrington, C. (2007). Fight, flight and playing White: An examination of coping strategies adopted by gypsy traveler adolescents in English secondary schools. *International Journal of Educational Research, 46*(6), 357–367.

Fettes, M. (2007). Imaginative multicultural education: Notes toward an inclusive theory. In K. Egan, M. Stout, & K. Takaya (Eds.), *Teaching and learning outside the box: Inspiring imagination across the curriculum* (pp. 126–138). New York: Teachers College Press.

Gay, G. (2000). *Culturally responsive teaching: Theory, research, and practice.* New York: Teachers College Press.

Gee, J. P. (2005). *An introduction to discourse analysis: Theory and method* (2nd ed.). New York: Routledge.

Gould, J. (2011). *Doubters and dreamers.* Tucson: The University of Arizona Press.

Grandin, T. (2011). *The way I see it: A personal look at autism and Asperger's* (2nd ed.). Arlington, TX: Future Horizons.

Hairston, K. R. (2005). "Colorless in a rainbow": An African American female with albinism in the Hawaii public school system. *The Review of Disability Studies, 1*(3), 53–66.

Jenkins, R. (1994). Rethinking ethnicity: Identity, categorization and power. *Ethnic and Racial Studies, 17*(197), 223.

Keys, L., Malone, J., & Russell, K. (1997). "Beyond inclusion": The reality of culture and disability executive summary. Indiana Governor's Planning Council for People with Disabilities. Retrieved from http://www.in.gov/gpcpd/2358.htm

Kissen, R. M. (1996). *The last closet: The real lives of lesbian and gay teachers.* Connecticut: Praeger Publishers.

Mooney, J. (2007). *The short bus: A journey beyond normal.* New York: H. Holt.

New Mobility. (2011, March 14). Crip, gimp, and other naughty words. Retrieved from http://www.newmobility.com/browse_thread.cfm?id=144&blogID=10

Nieto, S. (2000) *Affirming diversity: The sociopolitical context of multicultural education.* (3rd ed.). New York: Longman.

O'Connor, C., Mueller, J., Lewis, R.L., Rivas-Drake, D., & Rosenberg, S. (2011). "Being" Black and strategizing for excellence in a racially stratified academic hierarchy. *American Educational Research Journal, 48*(6), 1232–1257.

Roberge, M. (2003). Generation 1.5 immigrant students. Retrieved from http://www.sfsu.edu/~etc/?q=system/files/Roberge_article.pdf

Rottenberg, C. (2003). Passing: Race, identification, and desire. *Criticism, 45*(4), 435-452.

Schoen, S., & Schoen, A. (2010). Bullying and harassment in the United States. *The Clearing House, 83.* 68–72.

Scruggs, A. E. (2011). Color complex: When it comes to serving diverse students, colleges realize one size does not fit all, even within the same racial group. *Diverse Issues in Higher Education, 28*(2), 16–18.

Sherry, M. (2008). *Disability and diversity: A sociological perspective.* New York: Nova Science Publishers.

Smith, P. (2007). Have we made any progress? Including students with intellectual disabilities in regular education classrooms. *Intellectual and Developmental Disabilities, 45*(5), 297–309.

Spencer, M. E. (1994). Multiculturalism, "political correctness," and the politics of identity. *Sociological Forum, 9*(4), 547–567.

Spread the Word to End the Word. (2012, June 30). *Not acceptable* [video]. Retrieved from http://www.r-word.org/r-word-not-acceptable-psa.aspx

Steele, C. M. (2010). *Whistling Vivaldi and other clues to how stereotypes affect us.* New York: W. W. Norton and Company.

Stets, J. E., & Burke, P. J. (2000). Identity theory and social identity theory. *Social Psychology Quarterly, 63*(3), 224–237.

Swearer, S., Espelage, D.L., Vaillancourt, T., & Hymel, S. (2010). What can be done about school bullying? Linking research to educational practice. *Educational Researcher, 39*(1), 38–47.

TASH. (2010). Full inclusion of families of color in disability human rights organizations. Retrieved from http://tash.org/

Theoharis, G., & Causton-Theoharis, J. N. (2008). Oppressors or emancipators: Critical dispositions for preparing inclusive school leaders. *Equity & Excellence in Education, 41*(2), 230–246.

U.S. Committee on Education and Labor. (2009). *Strengthening school safety through prevention of bullying. Joint hearing before the Subcommittee on Healthy Families and Communities and the Subcommittee on Early Childhood, Elementary, and Secondary Education* (Serial No. 111-30). Washington, DC: U.S. Government Printing Office. Retrieved from http://www.gpo.gov/fdsys/pkg/CHRG-111hhrg50733/pdf/CHRG-111hhrg50733.pdf

Van Cleave, J., & Davis, M. M. (2006). Bullying and peer victimization among children with special health care needs. *Pediatrics, 118*, 1212–1219.

Ware, L. (2001). Writing, identity, and the other: Dare we do Disability Studies? *Journal of Teacher Education, 52*(2), 107–123.

Wilkins, A. C. (2004). Puerto Rican wannabes: Sexual spectacle and the marking of race, class, and gender boundaries. *Gender & Society, 18*(1), 103–121. doi: 10.1177/0891243203259505

CHAPTER 4

The Social Construction of Difference

Graciela Slesaransky-Poe
Ana Maria García

Key Principle 4: *Marginalized differences are socially constructed; how we respond to individual differences is impacted by factors such as history, culture/ geography, race, gender, and socioeconomic status.*

When I (Graciela) was invited to contribute to this book with a chapter on social constructions, I felt it was a great fit for me. I have been thinking about social constructions, differences, power, and privilege since 1990, when I arrived in Philadelphia from Argentina as a Fulbright fellow. Living in Argentina, as a middle-class young woman, I seldom felt different. Even though I am Jewish, my "Jewishness" was rarely a factor that set me or my family apart from the rest. I had never experienced being marginalized or excluded. I did not know what being "the other" meant until I arrived at the U.S. Embassy in Buenos Aires to get my visa to come to the United States. The visa application form had a box where I had to check my race. Without hesitation, I selected White; however, I was asked to change it. At that time, Latin American citizens were not supposed to select White. I was told instead to select "Other." Since my arrival in the United States, I have been "Other." Race, ethnicity, language, culture, religion, gender identity, and social status are concepts that my family and I deal with on a daily basis, not really fitting squarely into any box. My husband, who is Black; my biracial, Jewish children, one of whom does not match society's expectations of what it means to be a boy; and I, a Latina Jewish immigrant with a "heavy accent," grapple with these socially constructed categories and the effects that power, privilege, justice, equity, and opportunity grant or deny.

Similarly, I (Ana Maria) was challenged to deal with comparable issues given my own history. Born in Cuba, the granddaughter of Spanish immigrants, my family and I came to the United States as political refugees from communism and the Cuban Revolution. As foreigners in America, we were on the outside of the culture. We spoke no English, had no family here, and had to re-create a life with very few resources. Asking for aid at social agencies located my family as less, as not contributing, and as flawed somehow. We had to quickly learn how to change ourselves into Americans.

These lived experiences of being Other have shaped both of us in very particular ways and have brought us directly to do this work of social justice and social change. In this chapter, we use the lens of social construction theory to explore the social construction of categories such as race, disability, gender, and sexual orientation; how these constructions are enacted in schools; and the consequences they have for students and communities.

WHAT IS SOCIAL CONSTRUCTION THEORY?

Social construction theory is concerned with the ways we think about and use categories to structure our experience and analysis of the world. It rejects the longstanding view that some categories are natural, bearing no trace of human intervention and existing beyond the realm of human influence (Jackson & Penrose, 1993). More specifically, social construction theory argues that many of the categories that we have come to consider as natural, and hence unalterable and immutable, can be more accurately (and more usefully) viewed as the product of processes that are embedded in human actions and choices. According to Jackson and Penrose,

> [Social construction theory] *challenges our complacency in accepting the inequalities* which are permitted, if not encouraged, by specific kinds of categories and their application. Moreover, by enabling us to deconstruct categories which are previously viewed as indivisible and untouchable, the theory *offers new opportunities for redressing human divisiveness and inequities.* (Jackson & Penrose, 1993, p. 2, emphasis added)

Classifying Individuals and Groups

Social construction is a useful paradigm to understand all categories of social identity, including race and ethnicity, gender, sexual identity and orientation, class, disability, and religion. These culturally defined classifications are also significant in that they are structured as fundamentally different from one another. Thus, we expect people to be either White or Black, boy or girl, masculine or feminine, gay or straight, but never both or in between, reinforcing the notion that these categories are binaries or that they have mutually exclusive attributes. For example, when we see or meet a person who challenges our ability to quickly place him or her into a social category we are familiar with, we feel disconcerted and look for clues to help us figure out "what" that individual "is." This is the case when we meet biracial persons, transgender parents, or genderqueer students. (Genderqueer is a term used to refer to people who do not identify as or who do not express themselves as completely male or female.) We feel the need to know, "Are they White?" "Black?" "Is he/she a boy?" "A girl?" "A man or a woman?"

It is only when we come up with a response that makes sense to us, that we can move on and stop thinking about it. Interestingly, what people are and the ways they identify themselves can vary depending on the social circumstances and the cultural environment they are navigating, as beautifully illustrated in the following poem by Ryan Flores (2012).

Guess Who? (an exercise in lateral thinking)

to my mother I am *son*
to my father I am *hijo*
to racist hillbillies of the Midwest
I am *wetback*, *spic*, and *beaner*
to cholos at Armijo I am *gringo*
to officials at the State Department
I need "proof" of *citizenship*
to la gente de México I am *güero*
in the southwest I am *coyote*
at the University I am *Latino*,
Mexican-American, and *Chicano*
to the Census Bureau I am *Hispanic*
or *"more than one heritage"*
to mis abuelos I am *mezclado*
to those who hear me speak Spanish
I must be *Argentino* or *Español*,
because of light skin and green eyes
because of maternal Bohemian ancestry,
I muse and call myself *Chex-Mex* or *Czexican*
but I could be the *United States* of existence
I could be *America*
I could be your neighbor
your boss, your teacher, your student
I could mow your lawn,
cook your food
I could be you
So, who *am* I?

Activity 4.1: How Do You See Me?

After reading "Guess Who?," reflect on the many ways that society ascribes differing identities to the same person depending on region, experience, and history. Ask yourself how this affects an individual's sense of him- or herself and shapes how he or she experiences the social world.

The questions raised in Activity 4.1 are questions we generally do not discuss in schools because one common approach to dealing with difference is to deny or minimize its existence (see the "Color-Blind Racism" section later in this chapter, for example). However, the existence of categories of difference adds a great deal of richness to our lives. So, why is it that we do not talk about them? Because we learn to believe that by discussing differences such as race, disability, religion, or sexual orientation, we may be seen as divisive—as discriminating against people or groups of people. However, as Ore (2012) states, "it is not differences that are the causes of inequity in our culture. Rather, it is the meaning and values applied to these differences that make them harmful" (p. 2). For example, the problem is not that people of color are defined as different from Whites in the United States, or that people with disabilities are different from able-bodied people, or that gays and lesbians are different from straight people, or that Muslims are different from Christians. The problem is that Whites, men, able-bodied people, heterosexual people, and Christians "are viewed as superior and as the cultural standard against which all others are judged that transforms categories of '*differences*' into a system of racial '*inequality*'" (Ore, 2012, p. 2; emphasis in original).

Furthermore, how we define who is Black or White, who counts as Latina or multiracial, as disabled, as queer, is not an individual decision but rather a decision constructed by social policies and cultural ideologies. It is useful to take a social construction perspective to interrogate what has gone wrong when human rights are denied to some citizens. The right to marry, the right to education, health care, and adequate shelter and food—all are fundamental human rights but are distributed unequally among our U.S. population. They disfavor people of color, people of low socioeconomic status, single parents, individuals with disabilities, members of the lesbian, gay, bisexual, transgender, questioning/queer (LGBTQ) community, and some religious communities. It is important that we pause and ask ourselves why these categories and labels of *normal* or *deviant* are created in the first place, how they operate in everyday life, what their purpose is in the social structure, and how they play out in schools. Furthermore, the dominant categories are the ones that hold the hegemonic ideals—that is, the social, cultural, ideological, or economic influences exerted by a dominant group—which are taken so for granted as the way things should be that White is not ordinarily thought of as a race, middle class as a class, men as a gender (Lorber, 1994), or heterosexual as a sexual orientation.

The stratification by race, class, gender, disability, and sexual orientation constructs the gradations of a heterogeneous society's scheme. Thus, in the United States, White is A, and Black is Not-A; middle class is A, and working class is Not-A; straight is A, and LGBTQ is Not-A. As Jay (1981, cited in Lorber, 1994) explains, that which is defined, separated out, isolated from all else is A and pure. Not-A is impure, a random catchall, to which nothing is external except A and the principle of order that separates Not-A from society's point of view. In most socieites, man is A, woman is Not-A. Consider what a predominately White society would be like where woman was A and man Not-A. (Lorber, 1994). Or consider a society where Black is A and White is Not-A, or lesbian is A and straight is Not-A!

> **? Think About This:** How do these comments apply to religion in the United States (or elsewhere)? How have people's conceptions of what is A and Not-A changed over time?

Awarding Privileges

Social construction emphasizes the role of human interaction and culture in creating classifications and labels of difference and producing inequalities that become embedded in our social practices and ideas. Most important, understanding social construction of differences teaches us to pay attention to the power dynamics of race, disability, gender, and sexual orientation. Classification results in a differentiation of power, resources, and privilege.

In the late 1980s, McIntosh (1988) began to notice the *unearned privileges* her male colleagues had by virtue of their sex and gender. That is, these privileges were bestowed upon them not based on their merits, but solely because they were men. Upon further reflection, McIntosh realized that as a White, middle-class, college-educated woman, she, too, had privileges that her Black colleagues, both males and females, did not have. She created a checklist with 52 items that described the ways in which her privileges as a White woman gave her an advantage over other groups. Over the years, the original checklist was modified to reflect many of the other socially constructed categories. Today, one can easily find on the Internet McIntosh's original checklist, as well as many other privilege checklists that have been modified and adapted to socially constructed categories that are socially valued over others—to which society assigns power and prestige. These are the male, the Christian, the able-bodied, the middle- or upper social class, the heterosexual, the cisgender. (Note that *cisgender* and *cissexual* are

Activity 4.2: Identifying and Unpacking Our Own Privileges

Search online under the keywords: *Privilege Checklists*. Select the ones that reflect your identities. For example, if you are a White, middle-class, able-bodied, heterosexual, cisgender, female, Christian student, find the Privilege Checklists for race, class, disability, religion, gender, sexual orientation, cisgender, and so forth. While you read the checklists, consider carefully what experiences, thoughts, and feelings you identify with and are surprised by.

- What do these checklists indicate about who has power in U.S. society?
- How do you think that power and privilege could be experienced as a teacher? As a student? As a family? Imagine the experiences of a Muslim immigrant family in schools, or that of a student raised by her Black single mother who has three jobs but is still struggling to make ends meet.
- How is this power manifested?
- How are power and its codes transmitted across a culture?
- Who gets included, and who gets excluded?
- And finally, did this exercise help you realize the benefits of recognizing your own privileges, and how you could connect, perhaps, with students, families, and communities that may not enjoy the same privileges?

terms used to refer to gender identities where an individual's self-perception and presentation of his or her gender matches the behaviors and roles considered appropriate for one's sex. These terms are used in contrast to transgender or transsexual, where the affirmed gender identity and expression is incongruent with the birth anatomical sex and assigned gender.)

SOCIAL CONSTRUCTION OF IDENTITY CATEGORIES

In the following sections we will examine the social construction of race, disability, gender, and sexual orientation. As we do so, be mindful of Activity 4.2, and examine these constructs under the lenses of power and privilege.

Social Construction of Race

Although we think of race as biologically determined, according to the American Anthropological Association (1998), race in the United

States is a social mechanism invented during the 18th century to refer to those populations brought together in colonial America to provide slave labor. That is, race was used to draw lines between the owner and the slave, the master and the servant, those in power and the disempowered. Determining who is Black, White, or multiracial has continued to evolve over the years, as shown in the changes of the racial classifications on the U.S. Census over decades, which implies that race is not biologically grounded, but an ideological concept (Lee, 1993) with immense social implications. For example, let's look at the 1896 *Plessy v. Ferguson* case. Homer Plessy was a shoemaker in Louisiana whose skin was very light, who refused to ride the "Blacks only" section of the train. In the decision of the case, the U.S. Supreme Court ruled that any person with at least one Black ancestor was considered Black, and therefore Plessy was forbidden from riding the "Whites only" section of the train (Schutt, 2006). In 1920, the U.S. Census reflected a hardening of the absolute distinction between persons judged Black and White by dropping the categories involving mixed-raced ancestry, such as Mulatto. This change is often attributed to the historical and continuing importance of skin color, usually dichotomized in the United States into White and non-White, in defining race (Lee, 1993).

It is interesting how this dichotomization plays out in other countries. In the United States, for example, "if you are not quite White, then you are Black," but in Brazil, "If you are not quite Black, then you are White" (Fears, 2002, cited in Schutt, 2006, p. 103). Why is this important, you may ask? It is important because the way society and schools treat individuals, families, and communities of color affects the opportunities and the quality of life those communities will experience.

Many people of color in the United States have learned at an early age that society does not treat them fairly. They have learned not to trust authorities and social institutions which are biased against them. And this conclusion, though rarely spoken, has been studied and supported by evidence. Let's take for example, the findings of the Pennsylvania Supreme Court Committee on Racial and Gender Bias in the Justice System (2003). It was created to determine whether—and to what extent—racial and gender bias either exists or is perceived to exist in Pennsylvania's

> **? Think About This:** Those in the dominant or majority identity are often frustrated and sometimes angry when the labels they use for those in marginalized groups are inconsistent or shift over time. When three women of color shared their identity labels in class, one called herself "Black," another "African American" and another said, "I'm not Black or African American, I'm Jamaican." The White students were upset —they wanted to know the right thing to say, and this was too complex!

court system. After several years of investigation, the Pennsylvania Supreme Court Committee concluded that at least in some counties, race plays a major, if not overwhelming, role in the imposition of sentencing, including the death penalty, and that "there is a significant failure in the delivery of capital counsel services to indigent capital defendants in Pennsylvania, one that disproportionately impacts minority communities" (Committee on Racial and Gender Bias in the Justice System, 2003, p. 218).

Another case is a report from the American Civil Liberties Union (2007) about police bias in Rhode Island that states:

> Thoroughly documented results of a two-year study of traffic stops and searches in Rhode Island confirmed what many members of the minority community had long believed: minority drivers were far more likely than white drivers to be pulled over by police. In the same vein, the study conducted by Northeastern University, also found that blacks and Latinos, once pulled over, were searched at a much higher rate than Whites even though White drivers who were searched were more likely to be found carrying contraband. (p. 5)

The above practices are commonly referred to as racial profiling. Racial profiling is defined as any "practice in which a person is treated as a suspect because of his or her race [or] ethnicity . . . [This occurs when practices are enforced] against a person based on such characteristics instead of evidence of a person's criminal behavior" (American Civil Liberties Union, 2008, paragraph 2).

Race and Schools. Race plays a prominent role in today's social institutions, and schools are no exception. Students of color are routinely and systemically treated differently and given disparate opportunities than their White peers. Accounts of differential treatment can be found in everyday schools and classrooms across the United States and can range from the most complex to the most simple. Just as social institutions knowingly or unknowingly racially profile citizens, schools engage in the racial profiling of their students as well (Slesaransky-Poe, 2005a, 2005b). Evidence of racial profiling can be found in

- the over-representation of students of color referred to special education;
- the under-representation of students of color in gifted, honors, and other advanced placement settings;
- the disproportionate placement of students of color in the most restrictive learning environments, including self-contained, low-performing classes, programs, and tracks;

- the high number of students of color (relative to their White peers) being taught by teachers who are not certified in the subject they teach; and
- the high rate (relative to their White peers) at which students of color experience harsh discipline and punishment, with frequent out-of-school suspensions and expulsions and early and frequent referrals to the judicial and criminal systems.

A large number of students of color cross the border from normalcy to disability not because they are disabled but because schools are not able to support them in ways that allow them to succeed (Meyer & Patton, 2001). As a result, students of color experience inadequate services, low-quality curriculum and instruction, and unnecessary isolation from their nondisabled peers (Losen & Orfield, 2002). As stated in the 24th Annual Report to Congress on the Implementation of the Individuals with Disabilities Act (U.S. Department of Education, 2002), Black youth ages 6–21 account for 14.8% of the general school population. Yet they account for 19.8% of the special education population. In 10 of the 13 disability categories, the percentage of African American students equals or exceeds the general population percentage. The representation of African American students in the intellectual disabilities and developmental delay categories is more than twice their national population estimates.

This is very concerning. Students who do not need special education services but are referred to special education anyway may receive services that do not meet their needs; they may be misclassified or inappropriately labeled. In addition, placement in special education is attached to stigma and a culture of low expectations. High school graduation rates for students receiving special education services are significantly lower than for students in general education, and if, against all odds, students are able to complete their high school education, a diploma indicating that they were special education students holds a lesser value to pursue higher education or other related post-secondary opportunities. Not surprisingly, according to the National Center for Education Statistics (2011), the level of unemployment by race/ethnicity and selected levels of educational attainment for the year 2010 indicated that Blacks had the highest overall unemployment rate among young adults.

Color-Blind Racism. When our statuses are defined as having value within the social structure, we experience privilege—a set of (not necessarily) earned rights or assets belonging to a certain status (Ore, 2012). When our statuses are devalued, we experience discrimination and oppression. It is critical that we look at the above data and ask ourselves how it could be that in schools that serve a predominately White, middle- and upper-class student body, one can know which are the special education classrooms just by looking at the students' racial makeup, by noticing that students in the special education classrooms are disproportionally students of color? Why is it that the gifted classes have mostly White and Asian students? And most important, why is it that we are not doing anything about it?

Some educators say that they do not see the color of their students, that they are color-blind. They maintain that racial group membership should not be taken into account, or even noticed, despite research demonstrating that race is perceived automatically (Apfelbaum, Norton, & Sommers, 2012). According to Gordon (2005), color-blindness is a self-imposed blindness by White people, a refusal to see race and acknowledge White privilege. It is a complex ideology in which White people are taught to ignore race, a stance that ends by re-inscribing existing relations that privilege White people. Seeing race is considered to be "impolite"; it clashes with the U.S. mainstream "culture of niceness" (McIntyre, 1997, cited in Gordon, 2005). Color-blindness maintains that race does not exist as a meaningful category and posits that the benefits accrued to White people are earned by deserving individuals rather than systemically conferred. Noticing skin color becomes hazardous in that it endangers the status quo that benefits some (i.e., White people) and disadvantages others (i.e., people of color).

> **? Think About This:** This phenomenon—of not noticing difference—is a form of what is called "willful ignorance"—a systematic and adamant refusal to rethink our opinions and challenge our own assumptions even when presented with extensive information.

As you become a teacher, it is important for your own personal and professional development and for the impact that you will have on your students and their communities that you keep this issue front and center. Unfortunately, when presented with the racial inequalities just described, many pre-service and in-service educators fall in the trap of blaming the victim, that is, they consider these disparities to be the students' fault. They see these outcomes as an inevitable and natural consequence of the students' performance and discipline, parental lack of interest in education, quality of life, or even innate deficiencies by virtue of being Black, of lower socioeconomic status, or Other. These approaches are problematic because they deny the fact that these categories of difference are maintained as part of a larger system of oppression and privilege. These approaches excuse educators from examining their own prejudices and biases, which we all have. We are routinely bombarded by messages that reinforce prejudices. But it is our job as responsible educators to identify them and to be able to break the cycle of oppression so that we can collectively end institutionalized discrimination.

Social Construction of Disability

Historically, people with disabilities have been regarded as individuals to be pitied, feared, or ignored. They have been portrayed in the media as helpless victims, heroic individuals overcoming tragedy, and charity cases who must depend on others for their well-being and care. Even today, media coverage frequently focuses on heartwarming features and inspirational stories that reinforce stereotypes, patronize, and underestimate individuals' capabilities (Texas Council on Developmental Disabilities, 2012). Over the past decades, new laws and disability activism and advocacy have been slowly altering public awareness and knowledge, and these efforts are beginning to eliminate some of the negative stereotypes and misrepresentations.

About 54 million Americans—one out of every five individuals—have a disability. And those numbers are on the rise. Labeling of people as having disabilities in the United States has dramatically increased in the 20th century. During the same period, general education teachers came to see themselves as unqualified to teach the full range of students (Tyack & Cuban, 1995). Yet, the contributions of individuals with disabilities can enrich our classrooms, communities, and society at large as they learn, live, work, and share their lives with their peers and neighbors.

Most approaches to dealing with disability (formerly known as *handicapism* and sometimes referred to as *disableism)* are grounded on *ableist* beliefs and practices that justify systemic and individual bias, prejudice, and oppression against people with disabilities. Ableism holds the belief that disability in and of itself makes one in some way lesser—less deserving of respect, a good education, membership in the community, equal treatment, equality before the law, opportunities to prosper and live independently, and opportunities to have inclusive, self-fulfilling, and productive lives.

Ableist beliefs, systems, and structures are the real barrier to the integration and quality of life of people with disabilities. Examples of the negative effects of ableism for people with disabilities include social and physical isolation and unemployment, as well as a lack of accessible public buildings and restrooms, accessible and reliable public transportation, interpreters for the Deaf, and affordable and reliable at-home attendant care. In schools, ableism shapes the complaints by school district administrators and school board members about the financial burden of educating students with disabilities. Yet they may not question the cost of gifted education or the exorbitant prices of synthetic turf fields and other athletic facilities. Clearly, students who are very smart and those who are athletes are highly valued in most school communities.

Contrarily, anti-ableist approaches to disability are grounded on the social model of disability, one that removes the focus from the individual that needs to be fixed and locates it in society. An anti-ableist approach examines the social structures that prevent individuals from living independent, productive, included, and self-determined lives. In simple terms, it is not the inability to walk that prevents a person who uses a wheelchair from entering a building but the existence of stairs. The social model contends that if those barriers would disappear, people with disabilities would have the opportunity to live, learn, work, play, shop, travel, and worship as they choose.

The social model of disability is grounded on the disability rights movement and the disability studies academic discipline. As Linton (1998) states, disability studies offers a critical lens on the otherwise constricted, inadequate, and inaccurate conceptualizations of disability that have dominated academic inquiry, and our society. Disability studies is concerned not simply with the variations that exist in human behavior, appearance, functioning, sensory acuity, and cognitive processing but, more crucially, with the socially constructed meaning we attribute to those variations. The field explores the critical divisions our society makes in creating the normal versus the pathological, the insider versus the outsider, or the competent citizen versus the ward of the state (Linton, 1998), and this has immense implications in the ways we separate and provide instruction to students with disabilities. We have learned that separate is not equal, and yet the opportunities we provide, the curricula we use, and the environments we fabricate for students with disabilities are very different from those of their non-disabled peers.

Social Construction of Gender and Sexual Identities

How we define a woman, or a man, or a cisgender or transgender person is constructed on a very rigid baseline that separates the social from the physical and the social from the political. By this we mean that our gender identity and how we express our gender(s) are created in a particular time period and by particular societies, so they are neither universal nor ahistorical. Further, all gender expressions are both cultural and individual communications between oneself and another. For example, from the moment we are born we are gendered by those around us. Parents paint nurseries in pink or blue, blankets and clothing are similarly coded, and girls have barrettes and headbands put in their hair to identify them as girls (since as babies they are not physically gender-identifiable). This trend in differentiation and articulation of a gender marks our life course: the toys we are given, the sports we are enrolled in, and the emotions we are allowed to show vary by gender construction and constraint. There exists a false duality that separates the male from the female (biological sex) and the masculine from the feminine (gender) as if there were no in-between and within states of being. For example, the *sex binary* (either boy or girl) not only disregards the presence of the intersexual, but also of the many other variations of hormones, anatomical structures, and genitalia that comprise the human experience (García & Slesaransky-Poe, 2010; Slesaransky-Poe & García, 2009).

Furthermore, the ways in which the media reinforces socially constructed ways of being a boy or man, a girl or a woman, placing heterosexual marriage as the ultimate goal for every individual and the pursuit of "happily ever after" shapes society's understanding and expectations of gender and sexual identities and expressions. For example, the ways in which Disney movies and the most traditional fairy tales portray princesses and female characters as passive, helpless, and needing a male to rescue them, protect them, and bring them back to life or make them happy gives us one narrative upon which to build a feminine identity. This narrative relies heavily on the values of heteronormative courting, love, marriage, and family, and patrols the borders between and among the genders. (Heteronormativity can be defined as the pervasive and institutionalized ideological system that naturalizes and privileges heterosexuality as universal.) By reproducing itself through all of our social institutions and cultural practices, heteronormativity maintains power over non-conforming and resistant ways of gender identity construction. (See also Activity 4.A: Reflecting on Disney Princesses, Related Resources for Chapter 4, www.tcpress.com.)

In schools, we design activities that separate boys from girls, assign gender-stereotypical roles to them, and presume particular and distinct interests for boys and girls in activities and school functions. Students are offered gender-specific books featuring stereotypical heroes that affirm the normative roles of maternal nurturer for girls and physical provider for boys. Families raising gender-non-conforming children as well as educators are beginning to understand that there are many different ways to be a boy or a girl, all equally valuable and all OK ways of being. They are learning together how to support students who challenge society's assumptions of what it means to be a boy or girl; to defy the narrowly defined socially constructed gender binary that constrains children and ourselves; and to provide opportunities for children to feel comfortable, well adjusted, and confident just the way they are, finding their fluid places along the gender continuum (Slesaransky-Poe, 2013). Thinking about gender as a social construction could help educators understand that gender non-conformity may be unusual but it is not unnatural; that challenging the very binary categories that we use to think about gender not only frees those who do not fit tightly into any box, but also frees those students who feel the need to police their peers' gender conformity, with name-calling, harassment, and even the extreme of physical assault.

Social Construction of Sexuality and Sexual Orientation

Until recently, it was believed that humans were born with a sexual nature and that the natural order created two sexual types: heterosexuals and homosexuals. Scientists thought that a science of sexuality would reveal the nature of the sexual instinct and its normal and abnormal expressions (Seidman, 2010). Now sexuality and feminist scholarship, as well as the lived experiences of diverse individuals, have revealed that the existence of only two sexual types is not the case—that sexuality is fundamentally social. That is, how we act, the meaning we give to certain behaviors, and how we present our desires and our bodies are shaped by the social world around us. Also, the classification of sex acts into good and bad or acceptable and illicit is a product of social powers; the dominant sexual norms express the beliefs of the dominant social groups (Seidman, 2010).

Unknowingly, from a very early age, we begin to mold children and to push them to adhere to the heteronormative society we live in. Even as young as preschool age, we tend to ask girls if they have a boyfriend, or boys if they have a girlfriend; we celebrate and reinforce their "house play" in the dramatic play area, and we become very uncomfortable and confused when they break the heteronormative rules and expectations we have come not only to accept but to deem normal and natural. This takes many forms in our classrooms. We show images that reflect the standard referent of boys, girls, and gendered normativity. We ask children to tell us about their mothers and fathers, thereby erasing the same-sex parents that many of our children have.

There is so much educators can do to combat this taken-for-granted mindset, such as using teaching materials, visual aids, books, and narratives that positively represent a variety of family configurations. This provides healthy opportunities for students who have two moms or two dads, or a single dad, or who are being raised by grandparents, to see themselves represented and affirmed in their classrooms and schools. In addition, by providing those positive examples, we not only help students who may be questioning their own gender identities or sexuality and who could greatly benefit from positive examples of what is natural and possible, but we could also help those students and adults who feel justified to tease, harass, or bully those who are different from their own gender and sexual identities and expectations.

According to the latest School Climate Report by the Gay, Lesbian, and Straight Education Network (GLSEN, 2011), eight out of 10 LGBT students feel unsafe and afraid in school. The majority of LGBT youth have heard homophobic remarks not only by their peers but by their teachers and other students' parents as well. Most of these students have also reported high levels of verbal and physical harassment and aggression in schools; many skip school at least once a week because they fear harass-ment. We know that educators can make a difference in the school expe-riences of LGBT students and students who are raised in LGBT families. According to GLSEN (2011), the following are indicators of support for LGBT students:

- presence of a safe school policy that includes explicit protection based on sexual orientation and/or gender identity and expression
- curricula that are inclusive of the lives of LGBT people
- presence of supportive teachers or school personnel
- presence of student clubs that address LGBT issues (such as Gay-Straight Alliances or diversity clubs)

When these supports are in place, students report a decrease in negative school experiences; there is an increase in staff intervention in name-calling and bullying as well as an increase in positive educational out-comes (e.g., lower absenteeism, students more likely to want to go to college, higher GPAs). It is every teacher's responsibility to keep students safe, and to be mindful that when students are kept on the margins of a group because they are different from the norm they are less able to learn. Instead, their energy is depleted and diverted from learning and growing to coping and surviving.

THE INTERSECTIONALITY OF IDENTITY

While we have discussed the social construction of race, disability, gen-der, and sexual orientation as separate phenomena, in reality they occur simultaneously and interrelatedly. It is critical that we underscore the im-portance and reality that we all embrace a multiplicity of identities and that they are dynamic and fluid. Additionally, it is important to see people as whole beings—for example, as a White woman with disabilities, as a multiracial lesbian of low socioeconomic status, as a Black highly edu-cated immigrant. Further, becoming aware of the social constraints of a particular identity or category does not necessarily mean possessing an awareness of how the privileges of other identities may be creating op-pression on other individuals. For example, my (Ana Maria) white skin and blue eyes privilege me at the same time that my queerness does not. As May-Machunda (2005) reflects:

> As an African American woman, I have regularly encountered and learned to address stigma and disadvantages resulting from racism and sexism.

However, being denied privilege in some systems of oppression has not pre-cluded holding privilege in another. Furthermore, having insight into the ways one or two other systems of oppression work does not guarantee auto-matic sensitivity to oppression in a different system. Similarly to people ben-efiting from White or male privilege, I have lived much of my life oblivious to those privileges upon which I, as an able-bodied person, unconsciously cashed in on daily. (p. 78)

The notion here is that identity is mitigated by the interactions among the varying social statuses that we hold. For example, one's experience of race is shaped by one's gender or sexual orientation and the value that is socially attributed to that particular orientation. As another example, the word or category *woman* is inadequate in defining the rich and critically different statuses of women depending on race, ability, and sexual orien-tation. Being a White heterosexual woman is not a shared experience with the Latina lesbian, or with the White woman with a disability. Our iden-tity—or more correctly our *identities*—are negotiated in the particulars of time, space, and the social and lived experiences of each of us. (For further discussion of the concept of intersectionality, see Chapters 3 and 5.)

CONCLUSION

We have explored the processes that construct and reinforce categories of difference so that we will better understand how they impact our and our students' lives. We have discussed how systems of inequality are socially created and how, by challenging an essentialist view of social categories, we hope to break the cycle by which these ideas have been used to legiti-mize human actions that grant advantages to some categories over (or at the expense of) others (Jackson & Penrose, 1993). We also explored how we can gain a greater understanding of how to transform such systems into ones characterized by equality for individual students' educational and social experiences in their communities.

Our personal and professional experiences as well as our responsi-bilities as educators ignite our commitment to expose the ways in which members of marginalized categories are treated in schools, and how our educational system continues to create and maintain power imbalances, to oppress communities, to stigmatize, and to foster social isolation and exclusion. We are passionate about addressing these topics because we are convinced that each of us can and should make a difference in work-ing toward social justice.

We need to continue to look critically at the decisions we make and the effects they have on our students and their communities. And that takes practice. It is not achieved by reading this chapter or this book, or by taking a class. Unlearning privilege and unlearning biases require intentional and purposeful action, as there are many things in our daily lives that lead us toward developing prejudice, toward acting unkindly to others, without having any intent to do so (Smooth, 2011).

We hope that you will be able to challenge the deep-rooted assumptions so present in today's schools that stigmatize and profile certain students, and that you are able to create safe environments for you and your students where differences are acknowledged and affirmed, not muted or hidden. May you find the strength you will need to challenge and dismantle the matrix of domination that privileges a few and continues to oppress, exclude, silence, ostracize, and Otherize many. May you find the way to be a leader in your school by treating your students and their families with the highest respect, kindness, compassion, understanding, and humanity.

GROUND TRUTH: THE VOICE OF A PARENT/EDUCATOR

Ellen Skilton-Sylvester
Professor, School of Education, Arcadia University

As an educational anthropologist and the mother of adopted biracial twins who have learning disabilities, and as someone who has always felt that my own identities have most often been invisible and misunderstood, this chapter feels like a welcome breath of fresh air. Like Slesaransky-Poe and García, I have often felt like the boxes that people want to put me and my family in don't feel comfortable or accurate.

As I read this chapter, I was reminded of several key anthropological ideas that have been central to my teaching and the work I do with pre-service teachers. First, context matters. We are not the same person at home as we are at school or the same person when we are with our friends or with strangers. How we do on activities and assessments in one context may not say much about what we are able to do in other contexts. As a mentor and educational anthropologist, Fred Erickson used to say, "People are always making sense." They may not be making sense to us, but they are making choices that make sense to themselves. Second, generalizations about particular groups of people are usually wrong and sometimes dangerous; the particular matters. Finally, as noted literacy scholar Brian Street has said, "Culture is a verb." We often treat culture as a noun, as if it doesn't move and change. We act as if it is a thing that exists outside of us rather than a process through which we shape experience as it shapes us. Nothing could be farther from the truth.

Much of my own scholarship has focused on the experiences of Cambodian women and girls in U.S. classrooms, where the "model minority" myth about the academic and economic success of Asian Americans has had powerful and disastrous implications for their schools and communities, making the needs of this community invisible. In one painful example, assumptions about Asian kids being "good at math" led to an informal policy decision at the elementary school of three sisters I worked with. Over several years the Cambodian children were pulled out from math to attend English classes because "math would come easily for them" (Skilton-Sylvester & Chea, 2010). When each of the three sisters struggled with algebra, educators were surprised but should not have been. If teachers and administrators had been more familiar with social construction theory, they might have realized that what it means to be Asian American and a student is not set in stone but connected to the particular experiences of families and individuals.

And when I look at my experiences as a mother, I am constantly and personally reminded of the impossibility of discrete categorization. My daughters are biracial twins, but to the outside world, one looks Black and the other looks White. Their academic trajectories are also impossible to categorize simply. I like to say that they are intellectuals who struggle with spelling and math. Are they smart? Amazingly so. Do they struggle with some parts of school? Absolutely. In my personal and professional life, I continually live and work at the intersection of "yes/and" rather than "either/or." Graciela and Ana Maria are inviting us, I think, to embrace this space in our classrooms and communities. In my mind, nothing could be more important.

REFERENCES

American Civil Liberties Union. (2008). *Racial profiling: Definition.* Retrieved from http://www.aclu.org/racial-justice/about-campaign-against-racial-profiling

American Civil Liberties Union. (2007). *The persistence of racial profiling in Rhode Island: A call for action.* Rhode Island Affiliate, ACLU. Retrieved from http://www.aclu.org/pdfs/racialjustice/riracialprofilingreport.pdf

American Anthropological Association. (1998). *American Anthropological Association statement on "race."* Retrieved from http://understandingrace.org/about/statement.html.

Apfelbaum, E. P., Norton, M. I., & Sommers, S. R. (2012). Racial color blindness: Emergence, practice, and implications. *Current Directions in Psychological Science, 21*(3), 205–209.

Committee on Racial and Gender Bias in the Justice System. (2003). *Final report of the Pennsylvania Supreme Court Committee on racial and gender bias in the justice system.* Retrieved from http://friendsfw.org/PA_Courts/Race_Gender_Report.pdf

Flores, R. (2012). "Guess Who?" In A. L. Ferber, K. Holcomb, & T. Wentling (Eds.), *Sex, gender, and sexuality: The new basics* (2nd ed.) (p. 108). New York, NY: Oxford University Press.

GLSEN. (2011). *National school climate survey: LGBT youth face pervasive, but decreasing levels of harassment.* Retrieved from http://www.glsen.org/binary-data/GLSEN_ATTACHMENTS/file/000/002/2105-1.pdf

García, A. M., & Slesaransky-Poe, G. (2010). The heteronormative classroom: Questioning and liberating practices. *The Teacher Educator, 45*(4), 244–256

Gordon, J. (2005). White on White: Researcher reflexivity and the logics of privilege in White schools undertaking reform. *The Urban Review, 37*(4), 279–302.

Jackson, P., & Penrose, J. (1993). Introduction: Placing "race" and nation. In P. Jackson & J. Penrose (Eds.), *Constructions of race, place, and nation* (pp. 2–26). Minneapolis: University of Minnesota Press.

Lee, S. M. (1993). Racial classifications in the US census: 1890-1990. *Ethnic and Racial Studies, 16*(1), 75–94.

Linton, S. (1998). *Claiming disability: Knowledge and identity.* New York: New York University Press.

Lorber, J. (1994). *Paradoxes of gender.* New Haven, CT: Yale University Press.

Losen, D. J., & Orfield, G. (2002). *Racial inequity in special education.* Cambridge, MA: Harvard Education Press.

May-Machunda, P. M. (2005). *Exploring the invisible knapsack of able-bodied privilege.* Unpublished Paper. American Multicultural Studies, Minnesota State University Moorhead. Retrieved from http://www.library.wisc.edu/edvrc/docs/public/pdfs/LIReadings/ExploringInvisibleKnapsack.pdf

McIntosh, P. (1988). White privilege and male privilege: A personal account of coming to see correspondences through work in Women Studies. Working Paper #189, Wellseley College Center for Research on Women, Wellesley, MA.

Meyer, G., & Patton, J. M. (2001). On point… On the nexus of race, disability, and overrepresentation: What do we know? Where do we go? National Institute for Urban School Improvement. Retrieved from http://www.urbanschools.org/pdf/race.pdf.

National Center for Education Statistics. (2011). *The condition of education 2011.* Retrieved from http://nces.ed.gov/pubs2011/2011033_3.pdf.

Ore, T. E. (2012). *The social construction of difference and inequality: Race, class, gender, and sexuality* (5th ed.). New York: McGraw-Hill.

Schutt, R. K. (2006) *Investigating the social world: The process and practice of research* (5th ed.). Thousand Oaks, CA: Pine Forge Press.

Seidman, S. (2010). *The social construction of sexuality* (2nd ed.). New York: W.W. Norton & Co.

Skilton-Sylvester, E., & Chea, K. (2010). The other Asians in the other Philadelphia: Understanding Cambodian experiences in neighborhoods, classrooms and workplaces. In M. Osirim & A. Takenaka (Eds.), *Global Philadelphia: Immigrant communities, old and new* (pp. 270–191). Philadelphia: Temple University Press.

Slesaransky-Poe, G. (2005a, November) Meeting the needs of English language learners with disabilities: From least restrictive to most inclusive environment. Keynote Address. PennTESOL East Conference. Immaculata University, Pennsylvania.

Slesaransky-Poe, G. (2005b, April). Racial profiling in education: A new dimension to the unfulfilled promise of *Brown v. Board of Education*. Showcase Presentation. Presented at Council for Exceptional Children Convention and Expo 2005, Baltimore, MD.

Slesaransky-Poe, G. (February, 2013). Adults set the tone for welcoming all students. *Phi Delta Kappan*, 94 (5):40–44.

Slesaransky-Poe, G., & García, A. (2009). Boys with gender variant behaviors and interests: From theory to practice. *Sex Education, 9*(2), 77–86.

Smooth, J. (2011). How I learned to stop worrying and love discussing race. Retrieved from http://www.youtube.com/watch?v=MbdxeFcQtaU

Texas Council on Developmental Disabilities. (2012). *People first language*. Retrieved from http://www.txddc.state.tx.us/resources/publications/pfanguage.asp

Tyack, D., & Cuban, L. (1995). *Tinkering toward Utopia*. Cambridge, MA: Harvard University Press.

U.S. Department of Education. (2002). *Twenty-fourth annual report to Congress on the implementation of the Individuals with Disability Education Act*. Retrieved from http://www2.ed.gov/about/reports/annual/osep/2002/index.html

CHAPTER 5

Same Struggle, Different Difference:[1] Linking Liberation Movements

Mara Sapon-Shevin

Key Principle 5: There are many parallels between different civil rights movements, including those movements representing groups that have been discriminated against on the basis of characteristics such as disability, gender, sexual orientation, national origin, race, and language.

Although disability is a form of diversity, diversity should not be considered a disability. In the introduction to a special issue of the *Journal of Teacher Education* entitled "Unsettling Conversations: Diversity and Disability in Teacher Education," Pugach, Blanton, and Florian (2012) note that, "given the longstanding rhetoric of preparing teachers for diversity, there has been comparatively little discussion about the role of special education within the larger discourse of diversity of race, class, culture" (p. 235). Indeed, the discourses around more general multicultural education and special education have remained oddly and significantly disconnected.

For both areas, there is a history of semi-inclusion or marginalization within preservice education programs. Disability issues tend to get presented (if at all) to general educators in a course called "Introduction to Exceptionality" or "Survey Course on Special Education." This course often entails learning a laundry list of disabilities, how to identify them, and how to refer them to the right "elsewhere." Rarely is it a political analysis of special education, and seldom is it integrated into other course work.

Multicultural education is often similarly relegated to a separate course on "Multicultural Education" or "Teaching in a Diverse Society," which is often disconnected from the rest of the teacher preparation program. In many cases, this course consists of a list of different racial and ethnic groups and their contributions to society, with some attention paid to how to teach correctly to/about each group. Rarely is it a political analysis that considers how all aspects of education might be framed in sociopolitical ways (Sapon-Shevin & Zollers, 1999).

This chapter situates struggles for full inclusion for people with disabilities within the context of other liberation movements for people who have been marginalized and oppressed. By understanding the commonalities—and differences—among groups that have experienced oppression, we can better work for a shared vision of liberation and effective advocacy strategies that cross labels and forms of difference.

EXAMINING THE RELATIONSHIP
BETWEEN DIVERSITY AND DISABILITY ISSUES

Although a re-examination of how special education and multicultural education are addressed is important, this must be done critically, or we risk false comparisons and distinctions or conflation of the two areas. What is the relationship between broader diversity issues and disability? What would we learn by looking at the intersections of different identity issues and how they are addressed in schools (Meyer, Harry, & Sapon-Shevin, 1996)? Pugach, Blanton, and Florian (2012) ask:

> How can we work together to advance a more complete vision of diversity, one that does not merely attach "disability" to a long list of social markers of identity, but rather works from the assumption—and indeed the fact—that the children and youth for whom we prepare educators do not have just one diversity identity, but rather multiple diversity identities that interact with and nest within one another in different and often complex ways? (p. 235)

Critiquing Deficit/Medical Models of Difference

Other chapters have discussed the problems and dangers of conceptualizing difference as something that needs to be fixed. Although it is certainly true that there exists extensive prejudice and discrimination against people who are read as different, assuming that the solution to this negative response is to change the object of that discrimination leads to troubling practices and fails to address underlying cultural norms about difference.

When a young man was harassed and bullied in his high school for being "gay" (although he had never, in fact, embraced that label

Activity 5.1: What Do the Books Say?

Examine textbooks on diversity or multicultural education, and look at whether/how disability is included. Note what topics are covered and to what extent.

Talk to a classmate who has read a different textbook and compare the ways in which a social/political lens is or is not invoked throughout your respective texts; consider the implications of this for school policies, practices, curriculum, and pedagogy. If the information in the textbook you examined were the only information on disability you received in a teacher education course, what kinds of attitudes and beliefs about students with disabilities and their inclusion in general education do you think you would have?

himself), he was told that if he would only "straighten up" and not be so engaged in the arts, not be so gentle and "soft," then the problem would be solved. The principal was unwilling to examine the underlying homophobia in the school culture or to discipline the students who had tied the young man up in a volleyball net and thrown him in a garbage can. The onus of change was placed on the student who was experiencing harassment. The existence of programs

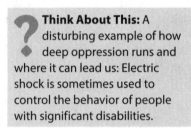 **Think About This:** A disturbing example of how deep oppression runs and where it can lead us: Electric shock is sometimes used to control the behavior of people with significant disabilities.

(known as "conversion therapy" or "reparative therapy," which may include electric shock) designed to "re-program" or "cure" (defined as embracing heterosexuality) people who identify as gay/lesbian/transgendered is clear evidence of how deep the oppression runs and where it can lead us.

Some parents have chosen to have their children with Down syndrome undergo surgery in order to change their facial appearance. They argue that since society discriminates against people with this syndrome, they can increase their child's future opportunities by decreasing the chances that their child will be read as having Down syndrome. While changing attitudes is far slower work, and one must assume that parents making this choice have their child's best interests at heart, it is troubling that we want to "fix" the object of ill treatment rather than address our own and others' limited, dangerous, and damaging responses to perceived differences and putative disabilities.

Activity 5.2: Looking at Our Own Experiences with Prejudice

Think about a time you have seen someone mistreated because of his or her gender, race, ethnicity, religion, dis/ability, or other physical or behavioral characteristic.

Generate two sets of solutions to correct the situation you observed: one that requires the target of oppression to change and another that addresses why people engage in prejudicial or discriminatory ways.

Now evaluate each solution:

1. How possible is it—for example, can a Black person become White if he or she tries harder?
2. What assumptions about difference and normality underlie each solution?
3. Who benefits or loses from this solution?
4. How does each solution affect our functioning and success as a multicultural, diverse society?

Why Conflating Diversity and Disability Is Problematic

Deficit perspectives form the foundation of traditional special education (as well as other segregated systems). But by locating disability within a critical perspective on marginalized differences more generally, the implication is *not* that other marginalized differences should be viewed as impairments—quite the contrary. Adopting this perspective means *rejecting* traditional deficit-oriented perspectives that position differences (including disability) as inferior, incompetent, or less than normal.

The conflation of race with disability, for example, is extremely problematic. As pointed out previously, the extensive evidence that students of color are routinely over-referred to special education should force us to look at racial prejudice, poverty, and other societal issues rather than to make assumptions about racial inferiority or causality (Ferri & Connor, 2006). It is a very real concern that *traditional* conceptions of disability are conflated with race in a social and economic system built on assumptions of inferiority of non-Whites (and people with disabilities) and in an educational system that routinely misidentifies students of color as having disabilities (Ball & Harry, 1993). It is vitally important for special educators to confront the intersection of special education with race, class, and culture, including how misinterpretation of non-dominant cultural values and practices contributes to oppression of non-dominant groups, even if inadvertently (Pugach & Seidl, 1998).

In a book chapter entitled "A Dialogue We've Yet to Have: Race and Disability Studies," Ferri (2010) discusses the challenges and potential gains of increasing the intersection between research on disability oppression and research on racism. Similarly, Erevelles, Kanga, and Middleton (2006) write that scholars in "critical race theory and disability studies have rarely explored the critical connections between these two historically disenfranchised groups within educational contexts" (p. 77).

This is, however, far more than a call for "cultural sensitivity in disability issues." A study by Ford (1992) surveyed administrators in Ohio and found that most of the special education administrators perceived that special education teachers who work with African American students should participate in multicultural education in-service training that focuses directly on issues relevant to African American youth. But nowhere was there mentioned the over-referral of students of color to special education, class issues, and so forth. Instead, the focus was defined as issues of cultural awareness, understanding of differences, appreciating diversity, valuing diversity, and a commitment to the maintenance of diversity.

Similarly, Garcia and Malkin (1993) expressed a need for special education services to be culturally and linguistically appropriate. They focused on (1) the language characteristics of learners with disabilities who are bilingual that will assist in the development of a language plan; (2) knowledge about cultural factors that influence educational planning and services; (3) characteristics of instructional strategies and materials that are culturally and linguistically appropriate; and (4) characteristics of a learning environment that promotes success for all students. But again, this was still very much a special education framework—how to do special education better—rather than any radical reconstruction of what special education is or means or how it relates to issues of race or class.

RECOGNIZING CONNECTIONS AMONG OPPRESSED AND MARGINALIZED GROUPS

Marginalized groups have not all been oppressed by the same methods, at the same times, and to the same degree. But each has been treated unjustly and can connect in mutually beneficial ways around civil rights and social justice concerns. When examining the history of oppression and discrimination against various groups of people throughout time, marginalized groups are connected not by physiological similarities (be they disability, race, gender, etc.) but by sociological similarities (the way they've been treated by dominant groups). That is, there are some similarities in what discrimination looks like.

- *Stereotypes:* Generalizations are made about a group and assumptions are made about individuals based on that belief (Black men are dangerous; Chinese people are good at math; women aren't mechanical; people with significant disabilities aren't sexual beings).
- *Stigmatizing/limiting labels:* People in marginalized and oppressed groups often experience labels (single words) that are generally negative and prejudicial ("faggot," "fatty," "retard," "slut," "wetback").
- *Limited representation and/or misrepresentation:* People in various categories are often either invisible (in the media, for example) or are represented in extremely limited or prejudicial ways. For example, commercials for products rarely include people who are not thin and "attractive"; children's books rarely include non-Christians in stories.
- *Segregation:* Based on some characteristic or putative characteristic, people in marginalized groups are often forced or encouraged to participate in separate schooling, employment, recreation, and so on.
- *Unequal opportunities/loss of rights:* People may be denied opportunities based on their identities—for example, gay parents who lose custody of their children upon the death of their partners; women who are not allowed to participate in certain sports; or people with disabilities who are denied access to higher education.

Despite the commonalities among various oppressions—racism, sexism, homophobia, ableism, classism—there are salient differences as well. Identities and characteristics that are sources of oppression vary in their visibility, contexts, permanence, and histories. Learning to become good

 Activity 5.3: What Do We Learn from TV?

Watch three hours of mainstream television programming and note the stereotypical and prejudicial labels and language that are used. How do characters talk to one another: Do you note teasing? Mean comments? Negative comments about differences? Racial and ethnic epithets?

Share with a partner what you found, and discuss how you would go about addressing these negative exemplars with your students in order to make them more sensitive to the power of language.

allies to those experiencing oppression requires understanding distinctions and recognizing that support and activism to redress discrimination may be different; that is, we cannot assume that how one advocates for a person with a physical disability provides a model for how to advocate for someone in a religious minority.

But various marginalized groups may share a vision for a strength-based educational system rooted in a view of human difference as essentially valuable, not deficient. Ball and Harry (1993) describe the following goal of multicultural and social reconstructionist education:

> to reform the school program so that all students experience success, social equity, and cultural pluralism . . . [and are prepared] to use political analysis of inequities inside and outside of school and to use collective social action to redress inequality. (p. 432)

Acknowledging Differences in Past Struggles

Unfortunately, liberation and civil rights movements directed at challenging oppression and discrimination against a particular group have not always been inclusive of all people, nor have they recognized the ways in which various oppressions are linked. The civil rights movement of the 1960s struggled with the homophobia of the time; Martin Luther King Jr., who fought for the rights of African Americans, nonetheless distanced himself from Bayard Rustin (a Black gay man) who had been active as his organizer and speechwriter. Rustin's sexuality was seen as too problematic and an obstacle to racial equality. (See Murray and Menkart, 2004, for excellent resources for teaching about the civil rights movement.) The women's movement did not embrace lesbians, fearing that it would damage their image and power. The disability organization ADAPT at first did not want to include people with cognitive disabilities. The LGBT movement, although it includes a "T" for transgendered, has often not included and sometimes actively rejected people who are transgendered.

Unfortunately, it is not true that someone who has been oppressed him- or herself will automatically be thoughtful, sensitive, and active about combatting other oppressions.

There are settings in which people engage in "competitive oppressions" discussions—"You think it's hard being a Jewish lesbian with a disability? Try being an African American gay single parent!" Such discussions are generally unproductive and interfere with finding common ground and addressing underlying hegemonic privileges and discourses that reinforce multiple oppressions.

Activity 5.4: How Do Struggles for Social Justice Connect?

Examine resources (there are many available online) that tell the histories of the civil rights movement, the women's movement, the disability movement, and the LGBT liberation movement.

   Make note of which struggles included which constituencies and which were omitted. What does this tell you about coalition-building, prejudice within liberation movements, and the potential for embracing shared agendas?

Ferri (2010) warns, however, that assuming that coalition work will be straightforward fails to acknowledge the differences in the struggles and the ways in which success might be constituted differently. She explains:

> We must also acknowledge and account for differences in political and economic power between ourselves and any potential ally. Finally, we must determine a mutually beneficial goal that we both stand to benefit from the alliance. It is from this position of shared self-interest that fuels a sustainable coalition. (pp. 147–148)

Becoming Effective Allies Against Oppressors

How do we get better as allies? What gets in our way? How do structural constraints keep us separate, and who benefits from that separation? Robin Smith and I have led a workshop activity for many years that begins by asking participants to describe a time that they engaged in one of the following actions:

- interrupted oppression of some kind (or attempted to)
- failed to interrupt oppressive behavior or language

After the participants share with a partner, we construct a chart that asks the following questions:

- If you tried to interrupt the oppressive behavior, what made that possible for you?
- If you didn't try to interrupt the behavior, what got in your way?

Figure 5.1 presents a typical set of responses.

Figure 5.1. Challenging Oppression

What Made It Possible	What Got in the Way
Had strong feelings	Had strong feelings
Was in a position of power	Didn't have any power in situation
Had a relationship with the oppressor	Had a relationship with the oppressor
Knew what to say	Didn't know what to say
Had the "facts" that helped me	Knew it was wrong, but didn't have enough information
Had practiced doing this	Tired/gave up
It hit me at a personal level	It hit me at a personal level
It was my role as teacher/adult	Fear of retribution, loss of job, safety

Discussions after the activity often center on the ways in which our ability to be good allies is impacted by our lack of knowledge (times when we are so unaware of how prejudice is being enacted that we don't even see it) and our lack of strategies for challenging oppression. It is always interesting that sometimes having a personal relationship with the oppressor makes it easier to challenge the op-

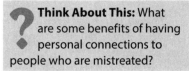

Think About This: What are some benefits of having personal connections to people who are mistreated?

pression ("I couldn't hear that kind of language from my best friend"), and sometimes makes it harder ("He's my uncle, so I didn't want to say anything"). Similarly, being a member of the oppressed group sometimes allows us to speak up strongly since we have more information and more vested interest, but sometimes membership in the targeted group immobilizes us and renders us less effective.

In addition to the need for more courage in becoming *upstanders* rather than bystanders (see the organization at www.glsen.org), we may lack a knowledge base. For example, if we don't realize that a large number of African Americans are lactose intolerant, we might invite African Americans to a dessert reception at which we serve only different types of cheesecake. If we are ourselves heterosexual, then a party invitation that says "For you and your husband/wife" may not strike us as problematic. Our ability to challenge behaviors and policies hinges on our knowledge about diverse populations. Lifetimes of segregation and interaction with only a small range of people impede our ability to be thoughtful, informed, and powerful allies. This is another strong argument for the importance of inclusive education—so that we can be smarter about diversity issues and increase the likelihood that we will have personal connections to those who are mistreated and they can have more knowledge about us and our struggles as well.

Activity 5.5: Taking It to the Streets

All liberation movements have chants and slogans that are designed to get a broader group of individuals interested in the cause. Imagine yourself at a rally—Who is there? What do you want? What would it look like? How would you know when you had achieved it? Experiment with some chants or slogans that would make your issues of liberation from oppression more understandable to others.

What do we want?

Liberation
Autonomy
Dignity
Inclusion
Recognition
Respect
Justice/fairness

When do we want it?

NOW!

UNDERSTANDING THE CONCEPT OF INTERSECTIONALITY

One key to developing strategies for addressing multiple oppressions and becoming a better ally for all students is understanding the concept of *intersectionality*—the systematic study of the intersections of race, ethnicity, class, gender, sexuality, and the other dimensions of difference mentioned previously. The multiple identities our students bring to the classroom can include race; color; ethnicity; Deafhood; geographic origin; immigration status; language; caste; socioeconomic class background; employment status; sex; gender; gender identity and expression; family configuration; sexual orientation; physical, developmental, or psychological ability; veteran's status; age or generation; religious, spiritual, faith-based, or secular belief; physical appearance; environmental concern; and political affiliation. Although two individuals may both identify as people of color and homosexual, other identities (such as class, gender, size, and religion) may substantially affect the ways in which those individuals are viewed, treated, and challenged (Clark, 2002).

Erevelles and Minear (2010) highlight the complexities of intersectionality:

Activity 5.6: How Have *We* Challenged Oppression?

Engage with classmates in the workshop activity described above in Figure 5.1, and identify areas in which you feel you need to learn more in order to be a better ally.

Talk about times in which you missed that something oppressive had even happened because you lacked critical knowledge or sensitivity.

Formulate a plan to increase your knowledge, your courage, and your skills in challenging oppressive behavior.

> If one is poor, black, elderly, disabled, and lesbian, must these differences be organized into a hierarchy such that some differences gain prominence over others? What if some differences coalesce to create a more abject form of oppression (e.g., being poor, black, and disabled) or if some differences support both privilege/invisibility within the same oppressed community (e.g. being black, wealthy, and gay)? (p. 129)

In teacher education, discussion of these dimensions has typically evoked debates about discrimination, equity, affirmative action, diversity, and inclusion. But teacher educators have also seen that they must expand their conceptions of multicultural education and diversity education by recognizing students' multiple identities. Clark, Brimhall-Vargas, and Fasching-Varner (2012) note that, increasingly, young people are moving away from singular identities (i.e., based only on race or ethnicity or nationality or gender or religion, among other dimensions of difference) that many of the adults who work with them—especially as educators—still hold to with steadfast allegiance. As a result, a generational

Activity 5.7: What's It Like Being *Me*?

Which of your identities do you think people attend to most? Which of your identities are less visible to others but still critical to you?

What kinds of oppression have you experienced relative to any of your identities, and what would you want from an ally?

Respond to the following two statements:

1. "To be my ally you have to know me and something about my oppression—that my oppression happened."
2. "To be a full ally to me, you have to take into account all my identities."

gap, rooted in outmoded understandings and experiences of multicultur-alism, exists that can challenge the development of the crucial student/teacher relationship-building that is foundational to student success.

A more sophisticated understanding of issues of intersectionality and multiple identities can help educators and students to become better allies toward those experiencing marginalization, exclusion, and bullying.

CONCLUSION

Expanded advocacy for all students who have been denied equitable ac-cess to educational opportunity is a critical step in transforming a racist, heterosexist, classist, and ableist system. There are some common needs in achieving fully inclusive education across many forms of difference. Recognition of these similarities can help us move toward collaborative advocacy in creating a world that is just. Figure 5.2 details the advocacy and actions we must take in order to address social injustice across cate-gories; recognizing and enacting the shared solutions can make our work all the more powerful.

Achieving a just, equitable society is not just about schools, but schools can be important sites of struggle and reform. Only when we recognize our common humanity can we begin to create real and lasting change.

GROUND TRUTH: THE VOICE OF A SPECIAL EDUCATION PROFESSOR

Kagendo Mutua, Ph.D., University of Alabama

I was born, raised, and educated in Kenya and came to the United States in the 1990s as a graduate student. For the past twelve years or so, I have been living in the South where I teach special education in a large research university. My reflection centers on an incident that happened to me last year. This incident happened during a lunch where, as a member of a search committee, I along with other committee members was accompa-nying a candidate to lunch. The venue was a large, (read: grand) Greek revival architecture, plantation-style, members-only club where well-to-do locals meet for buffet-style lunch and fraternize with members of the university community. Needless to say, the largest proportion of daily diners is White.

The rest of my group had gone to the buffet. I was standing poised to hang my handbag over my chair when my attention was caught by the snapping of fingers by an elderly White woman who was sitting at the table directly in front of me with two others. I recall standing there, quietly looking at her, taking in tiny details of her appearance: a bony hand that may have been dainty in her heyday, perfectly manicured red lacquered nails, coiffured grey hair piled in a beehive hairstyle at the top of her head. I recall thinking how she looked like an air-brushed image with not a strand of hair out of place . . . lifeless, yet emitting currents in pent-up waves of extreme irritation/hostility.

She looked severe. Her lips were pursed and haughty.

Before it sunk in that it was me that she was summoning with snaps of her long bony fingers that glinted menacingly in the measured light of the period dining room, she realized her mistake and turned her gaze to scan the room for the interchangeable server. I turned back to look behind me at who it was that she was calling with haughty impatience. I did not see anyone behind me but tables of other diners who were heartily enjoying their meals and engaged in conversations. Quizzically, I turned to her, squinting as the fog slowly cleared from my brain. In that interminable moment of realization, with the confused haze clearing from my brain, I experienced a belated dawning of the realization that carried in it a poignant history of who she saw when she looked at me. That I was professionally dressed in my favorite (and stylish, I might add) Ann Taylor suit (and therefore could not have been visually confused for a uniformed waitress) was irrelevant.

This incident forced upon me the recognition and acknowledgment of the acute messiness of intersectionality and the ways that even the most astute discussions of intersectionality often miss its psychological dimension. Merely acknowledging and recognizing oneself (or others) as the site for multiple identities of oppressions fails to contend with the psychological issues that those oppressions bring to bear. My utter consternation and failure to instantaneously grasp what the woman was doing resulted not from a failure to intellectually know myself as a site for multiple oppressed identities, but rather as a result of a not psychologically seeing myself the way she did. I did not instantly see the history that was always already present in me as a bearer (read: brandisher) of the historical physical marker of subjugation—a Black woman in the South. I did not see myself as her server/servant, so her snap of the fingers did not transport me to a historical moment that bestowed upon her the position of mistress and I her maid/servant thereby naturalizing her behavior. Akin to Ralph Ellison's *Invisible Man*, she rendered mute my other identities by "simply refusing to see me." Living in the interstices of intersectionality is a constant (and tiring) negotiation between Ellison's invisibility and Dubois' double-consciousness.

That day, the Almond Ball—the famed dessert of the establishment— left a distinctly bland taste in my mouth. The woman's microaggression had made sure of it.

Figure 5.2: Working for Social Justice Across Oppressions

Problem	What Would Help?
Categories and identities seen as real, immutable, and permanent	Understanding the social construction of differences; re-examination of idea of "normative" or "normal" in describing people
Seeing differences as deficits, problems, or characteristics that need to be changed	Engaging in thoughtful and critical analysis of various kinds of differences—those that should be celebrated, those that should be embraced, and those that might (with the expressed desire of the person in question) be changed or remediated
Strong reliance on stereotypes, generalizations, and assumptions about the Other	Seeing people as individuals, avoiding over-generalization across groups, stereotypes, and assumptions
Difference as justification for removal for special services and differential treatment	Differences occasion thoughtful analysis and responsiveness within a broader context
Fairness seen as getting the right people into the right groups or categories; belief that certain children do deserve or need a different education	Critical examination of access to educational opportunities and the ways these intersect with identities, power, privilege, and prevailing social and cultural norms and expectations
Belief in the fairness of testing procedures, and the ability to justify segregation, tracking, differentiation based on labels	Critiques of the politics of evaluation and rejection of high-stakes, standardized tests to determine future access to instruction and learning opportunities
Justification of segregated practices based on the differential needs of individuals	Ability to distinguish forced exclusion from voluntary segregation (choosing to be with others like you in some way)
Reliance on the voice, experience, and expertise of professionals outside the group that is subject to discrimination	Understanding the importance of voice and autobiography, hearing people's stories, knowing that the people with the label are in the best place to talk about their own lives and futures; serious attention to issues of agency and choice, control and power
Defining success as assimilation, elimination of differences, and common expectations and experiences	Focus on advocacy and self-advocacy, not cure. Acknowledgment of need to empower others to take control over their own lives, communities, destinies

Source: Sapon-Shevin and Zollers, 1999

NOTE

1. The expression "Same Struggle, Different Difference" was coined by Dan Wilkins, whose incredible artwork can be found at www.thenthdegree.com.

REFERENCES

Ball, E. W., & Harry, B. (1993). Multicultural education and special education: Intersections and divergencies. *Educational Forum, 57*(4), 430–437.

Clark, C., Brimhall-Vargas, M., & Fasching-Varner. (2012). Occupying academia: Re-affirming diversity. In C. Clark, K. Fasching-Varner, & M. Brimhall-Vargas (Eds.), *Occupying the Academy: Just how important is diversity work in higher education?* (pp. 1–20). Lanham, MD: Rowman & Littlefield.

Clark, C.(2002). Effective multicultural curriculum transformation across disciplines. *Multicultural Perspectives, 4*(3), 37–46.

Erevelles, N., Kanga, A., & Middleton, R. (2006). How does it feel to be a problem? Race, disability, and exclusion in educational policy. In E. Brantlinger (Ed.), *Who benefits from special education? Remediating [fixing] other people's children* (pp. 77–99). Mahwah, NJ: Lawrence Erlbaum.

Erevelles, N., & Minear, A. (2010). Unspeakable offenses: Untangling race and disability in discourses of intersectionality. *Journal of Literary & Cultural Disability Studies, 4*(2), 127–146

Ferri, B. A.(2010). A dialogue we've yet to have: Race and disability studies. In C. Dudley-Marling & A. Gurn, *The Myth of the Normal Curve* (Chapter 10). New York: Peter Lang.

Ferri, B. A., & Connor, D. J. (2006). Reading resistance: Discourses of exclusion in desegregation and inclusion debates. New York: Peter Lang.

Ford, B. A. (1992). Multicultural education training for special educators working with African-American youth. *Exceptional Children,* October/November 1992, 107–114.

Garcia, S. B., & Malkin, D. H. (1993). Toward defining programs and services for culturally and linguistically diverse learners in special education. *Teaching Exceptional Children, 26* (1), 52–58

Meyer, L., Harry, B., & Sapon-Shevin, M. (1996). Issues in research on school inclusion and multiculturalism in special education. In J. A. Banks & C. A. McGee Banks (Eds.), *Multicultural education: Issues and perspectives* (3rd ed.) (pp. 334–360). Boston: Allyn & Bacon.

Murray, A., & Menkart, D. (2004). *Putting the movement back into civil rights teaching.* Washington, DC: Teaching for Change.

Pugach, M. C., Blanton, L. P., & Florian, L. (2012). Unsettling conversations: Diversity and disability in teacher education. *Journal of Teacher Education, 63*(4), 235–236.

Pugach, M. C., & Seidl, B. L. (1998). Responsible linkages between diversity and disability: A challenge for special education. *Teacher Education and Special Education, 21,* 319–333.

Sapon-Shevin, M., & Zollers, N. (1999). Multicultural and disability agendas in teacher education: Preparing teachers for diversity. *International Journal of Leadership in Education Theory and Practice, 2*(3), 165–190.

CHAPTER 6

Evaluating Assumptions; Examining Evidence

Diana Lawrence-Brown

Whatever affects one directly, affects all indirectly. I can never be what I ought to be until you are what you ought to be. This is the interrelated structure of reality.

—Martin Luther King Jr., 1965

Key Principle 6: Educational services in the United States were developed and continue to be based on largely unexamined assumptions about what is beneficial for certain students (e.g., that effective education for diverse students requires a separate program) that are unsupported by outcomes research (e.g., direct comparison of outcomes from inclusive and separate programs).

Separate educational programs have been commonplace in the educational history of the United States. Although segregation on the basis of race is most notorious, students have frequently been segregated on the basis of dis/ability, gender, religion, cultural/linguistic background, and class. As you begin reading this chapter, what are your thoughts about separate educational placements for various groups? How do you connect the Martin Luther King Jr. quote at the beginning of the chapter and the two photographs in Figures 6.1 and 6.2?

In some cases segregated schooling has been voluntary; for example, families may choose a religious education either at home or at a school organized by their faith community. More problematically, it has been imposed, as in the instance of Whites-only schools. In the southern United States, of course, it was African American students who were excluded. In the West, Native Americans and students of Mexican or

Figure 6.1. Segregated School, West Memphis, Arkansas, 1949

Source: Ed Clark/Getty Images

Figure 6.2. Willowbrook State School, Staten Island, New York, c. 1976

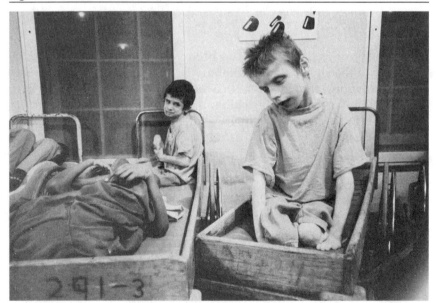

Source: William Bronston, MD, "Public Hostage, Public Ransom." Bronston's photo essay can be viewed at http://www.mncdd.org/extra/wbrook/willowbrook.html

Activity 6.1: "Among Their Own Kind"

Compare and contrast the following examples of segregation on the basis of the belief that it is best for people to be among their own kind:

1. *A Raisin in the Sun* (Hansberry, 1957) character Karl Lindner, bearing the message that residents of the White neighborhood where the Younger family is about to move agree that people are happier when they live among their own kind. He offers to buy the house back at a small profit to the family.
2. *The Reichsfolk Declaration* (a description of National Socialism, by its supporters), http://cosmicreich.wordpress.com/the-reichsfolk-declaration/
3. *The Rise of Professionals and Institutions* (a description of the historical rationale for institutionalization of people with disabilities), http://www.npr.org/programs/disability/ba_shows.dir/pos_chld.dir/highlights/exptcare.html

Asian descent were similarly segregated. Involuntary segregation is often justified by those exhorting it as best for people to be "among their own kind."

In some cases, it is less clear whether segregation is voluntary or imposed. For example, schools in the United States are often segregated by social class. At times this is caused by social stratification in neighborhoods (i.e., wealthy families live in certain neighborhoods; poor families live in others, each with their own neighborhood schools). Is this separation voluntary, or imposed?

It also results from private school tuitions that are out of reach for most families. Again, is this voluntary, or imposed? Try to think about this from the perspective of higher and lower socioeconomic status (SES) groups. Does your answer vary depending on the SES of the group you are considering?

> **Think About This:** It's really hard to talk about segregation being voluntary unless people feel that they have a real choice. When educators say, "The parents wanted the child in a segregated setting," we have to ask what the other options were and how they were depicted (i.e., "We'll put your son in a regular class, but he'll have no friends and they won't teach to his needs").

In the sections that follow, we look at outcomes of various forms of segregated education.

OUTCOMES OF SEGREGATED SCHOOLING

What are the outcomes, then, of segregated or inclusive education for various groups? We begin by looking at education segregated by social class, followed by racial/cultural background and dis/ability.

Education Segregated by Social Class

Anyon's (1981, 1992) work is notable among the many researchers who have documented the outcomes of education stratified by social class. Many people are not surprised to learn of disparities in resources such as educational materials and equipment, in number and preparation of staff. However, Anyon demonstrated that not only these resources but access to particular forms of knowledge varied according to social class, even in public elementary schools under the same state curriculum requirements and in some cases using the same textbooks. In the elite school (representing the top 1% in income), what and how students learned reflected preparation for executive roles in society. These children, for example, were taught to reason out rules or steps on their own, to connect curriculum content to current events and social issues, to take the lead in classroom discussions and activities, and to present themselves precisely and authoritatively in person and in writing. In contrast, in working-class schools, what and how students learned prepared them more for roles as laborers. For example, schoolwork involved mainly rote learning of isolated facts, rules, or steps to follow, with little attention paid to context, choice, or decision making. (For more about Anyon's work and how it is being used in today's schools, see tcla.gseis.ucla.edu/reportcard/tools/pdf/anyon.pdf.)

It is not surprising, therefore, that students with significantly lower socioeconomic status have significantly lower educational achievement. However, even modest efforts to increase resources available to poor families can significantly improve school success for their children (Greene & Anyon, 2010).

Problematic outcomes have also frequently been documented in connection with *tracking*, where general education classes within the school are grouped by educational focus and perceived aptitude. For example, there may be a college preparation track for high achievers, a middle track for students considered average, and a basic track for students who are struggling or seem unmotivated by schoolwork. It is also important to recognize the connection between tracking and social class. Each track is associated not only with disparate educational offerings but with disproportionate social class membership. For example, students in the basic track at the secondary level are likely to be offered vocational rather than college-preparatory coursework, and to be mainly students of lower socio-economic status. In contrast, students in the upper track are often offered not only college-preparatory coursework necessary for choice college and career options, but even the opportunity to begin earning college credit before graduating from high school. And yes, they are disproportionately of higher socioeconomic status.

Think About This: For a powerful rebuttal to the idea that it's bad teachers (and not lack of resources) that are responsible for low-achieving poor kids, watch the film *The Inconvenient Truth Behind "Waiting for Superman"* (http://gemnyc.org/2012/05/20/the-inconvenient-truth-behind-waiting-for-superman-now-online/).

Teaching methods used in separate tracks also vary. For example, though it might be argued that students in the basic track (often viewed as unmotivated low achievers) are most in need of *engaging* learning opportunities, they are often taught using rote drill-and-practice methods. In contrast, students in the advanced track are more likely to be taught using enriched educational opportunities involving creativity, problem solving, and hands-on exploration of topics connected with their interests (Sapon-Shevin, 1994/1995). Similarly, it might be argued that low achievers are most in need of opportunities to learn critical thinking (due to their subjugated status in society); again, however, it is students in the advanced tracks who are most likely to be offered such an education.

Segregation on the Basis of Race

Perhaps most widely known in the United States are negative outcomes for segregated African American students. In *Brown v. Board of Education* (1954), litigants famously demonstrated that "separate is not equal," leading to the outlawing of segregation by race in the United States. In an important precedent to the *Brown v. Board of Education* case, a California court had proclaimed "separate is never equal" (*Mendez v. Westminster,* 1946), overturning segregated schools in California. (For a short video about the *Mendez v. Westminster* case, visit http://www.teachers-domain.org/asset/osi04_vid_mendez/.) It must be noted, however, that problems with segregation by race and associated inequitable outcomes persist today. Long-fought-for gains made to integrate schools have been significantly undone—and separate is still not equal. As in the past, highly segregated schools today tend also to be very poor schools; students in these schools have distressingly low graduation rates (Lockett, 2010).

Extreme Segregation: Residential Facilities

Institutionalization of People with Disabilities. An extreme form of seg-regated education is placement in residential facilities; parents are per-suaded to institutionalize their children with disabilities so that they can receive the specialized care they need. The photograph in Figure 6.2 earli-er in the chapter was taken at Willowbrook, a state-run residential school located in New York City and the subject of an exposé contributing to the closure of many institutions. It is important to understand that the shameful conditions of institutionalization—educational, emotional, and physical neglect; physical and sexual abuse—are not anomalies but com-mon characteristics of institutional life. Consider the following comments from Seymour Sarason's foreword to *Christmas in Purgatory* (Blatt & Kap-lan, 1974), a photo essay documenting conditions in a variety of public institutions in different states:

> As the years went on, it became increasingly clear to me that the conditions I saw... were not due to evil, incompetent or cruel people but rather to a concept of human potential and an attitude toward innovation which when applied to the mentally defective [sic], result in a self-fulfilling prophecy. That is, if one thinks that defective children are almost beyond help, one acts toward them in ways which then confirm one's assumptions. . . . Dr. Blatt . . . has been under great pressure from many quarters to reveal the names of the institutions visited, but . . . [he] would not go back on promises made to those persons who permitted him to make this study. He wished, also, in not naming names, to *avoid creating the impression that this problem is a local rather than a national one.* (p. ii, emphasis added)

Native American Boarding Schools. Also institutionalized have been Na-tive American children, involuntarily transferred to far-off boarding schools where they were subjected to physical and emotional neglect and abuse. Although they apparently received more instruction than people institu-tionalized for having disabilities, they were humiliated as "savages" whose culture and families were deemed inferior and whose "salvation" was to come through Americanization and the elimination of Native culture. The following is a notorious quote from Richard Pratt (1973), the superintendent of the U.S. Training and Industrial School in Carlisle, Pennsylvania, in 1892:

> A great general has said that the only good Indian is a dead one, and that high sanction of his destruction has been an enormous factor in promoting Indian massacres. In a sense, I agree with the sentiment, but only in this: that all the Indian there is in the race should be dead. Kill the Indian in him, and save the man.

Activity 6.2: Compare and Contrast Institutionalization Experiences of Two Different Groups

Compare and contrast these two videos:

1. *Assassination of a Culture (Indian Boarding Schools)*, available at http://www.youtube.com/watch?feature=endscreen&NR=1&v=LtrIF6xbkwM (approximately 15 minutes)
2. *Institutions to Independence*, documenting the experiences of people with disabilities in institutions and in the community, available at http://www.mncdd.org/institutions-to-independence/independence.html (30 minutes)

Questions for Reflection and Discussion:

1. In what ways were the goals of institutionalization of these two groups similar or different?
2. How do their experiences seem similar or different?
3. What educational, social, and cultural outcomes do you see?

Segregation on the Basis of Disability Labels

Despite widespread disregard for such forms of institutionalization, and for programs that segregate students by characteristics such as race or national origin, people often believe nonetheless that segregated school programs are best for students with disabilities. There is a certain logic to this—when students with disabilities don't achieve at expected levels in general education classrooms, it has been assumed that a separate program could be designed to better meet their needs.

What evidence do we have to support the claim that students with disabilities actually learn

Think About This: Canadian Justice Murray Sinclair concluded that Native American boarding schools are an example of genocide. Do you agree? According to the United Nations Treaty on Genocide (1948), genocide is: any act committed with the idea of destroying in whole or in part a national, ethnic, racial, or religious group. This includes acts such as the following:

- Killing members of the group
- Causing serious bodily or mental harm to members of the group
- Deliberately inflicting conditions calculated to physically destroy the group (the whole group or even part of the group)
- Forcefully transferring children of the group to another group

Activity 6.3: Analyzing Outcomes

Conduct your own analysis of the outcomes research outlined in Activities 6.A and 6.B in the Related Resources for Chapter 6, www.tcpress.com. Each study directly compares outcomes for students with disabilities served in separate special education programs to outcomes for similar students with disabilities who are included in general education classrooms. Answer the following question: Do students with disabilities learn more in self-contained classrooms?

more in separate programs? Surprisingly little. In study after study, separate programs fail to outperform general education classrooms with inclusive supports (cf. Bunch & Valeo, 1997; Freeman & Alkin, 2000; Hunt, Farron-Davis, Beckstead, Curtis, & Goetz, 1994).

In light of the outcomes research, consider the following statement:

> Special education functions to legitimize and maintain a system of tracking and segregation that "amounts to a denial of access to knowledge" (Seidl, 2001, p. 400) as well as a self-devised explanation for the failure of schools to serve all students well. (Pugach & Seidl, 1998)

Do you agree? Why or why not?

IMPACT OF A CRITICAL PERSPECTIVE

Educational rhetoric describes the purpose of separate services as beneficial to students; however, the lived experience of students and educators within these systems often renders the rhetoric threadbare (e.g., Lawrence-Brown, 2000). In response, people (like me) who originally accepted the rhetoric at face value may begin to reject the arguments supporting the system and begin to work for change (Freire, 2009), to bring our practices closer to our values (e.g., see Think About This—A "Light Bulb" Moment, this chapter).

CONCLUSION

The research outcomes presented here are consistent with my own experience. Segregation of people with marginalized differences rarely has the result of enhancing their status, reducing their stigma, or helping them to gain access to valued roles in society. Although the students I taught in segregated

? **Think About This—A "Light Bulb" Moment:** I (Diana) was having a conversation with a central-office type who had very limited background and experience with people with significant disabilities. We were in the process of greatly expanding our community-based instruction so that each student would receive instruction in real-life settings in the local community at least once a week. She really didn't understand why it was important for *every* student, wondering if some were "too disabled to get anything out of it." She was also concerned about whether or not the local people were "really ready" to interact with our students.

As I struggled with how to explain (why the possibility that some anonymous group of people might be discomfited should not take precedence over another's access to the community), the light bulb came on—this was not just a pedagogical issue—*it was a civil rights issue.* (Really, it felt more like a gong than a light bulb.)

Understanding that access to the community was more than a pedagogical issue had an enormous impact on me. I became even more committed in advocating that no one should be excluded, and gradually more articulate in being able to explain why. My colleagues and I were ultimately successful in establishing a zero-reject policy; this experience was part of an ongoing process of understanding more and more about disability rights and oppression.

Now I routinely explain inclusion as a civil rights issue, often drawing connections with civil rights movements and issues of other groups.

programs did learn, they did not learn at the level of those I taught in inclusive programs—they could not, without full access to the general education curriculum. In addition to interfering with their learning, being segregated also interfered with their self-concept, their social skills, and friendships. Small wonder that some developed behavioral concerns as time went on.

Of course, our concern is not limited to groups traditionally marginalized in our society. Segregation also damages dominant groups. In my experience in inclusive classrooms, students from dominant groups benefited from push-in supports provided in the general education classroom. With separate programs, of course, they cannot. Separation also engenders fear; it prevents those from dominant groups from appreciating the potential of the Other, and hinders society from benefiting from their contributions. It is extremely difficult to recognize the strengths, gifts, and vitality of people you never have the opportunity to get to know.

At this point in my educational career, I can no longer justify segregated educational placements, particularly those that are involuntary. Even when students and families segregate themselves voluntarily, it is incumbent upon responsible educators to ask why. For example, reminiscent of

historical approaches to educating other marginalized groups, a number of
school districts have developed separate, "gay-friendly" schools as a haven
for LGBTQ students whose educational, emotional, and physical well-being
are threatened in their neighborhood
schools (Kilman, 2010). But is another
form of segregated schooling the appropriate response to this very serious
problem? Is that our best solution, given
what we know about the effects of (even

Think About This: What
are the powerful stories
that we can share with one
another that will help someone
understand? The story must be
told without anger or rancor
and be one that teaches and
raises consciousness through the
narrative rather than seeking to
punish the listener for his/her
ignorance.

well-intentioned) segregation on both dominant and marginalized groups?

Physical integration must be backed up by accommodations and
other supportive conditions that make it possible for the full range of
students to meaningfully participate, setting the stage for recognition
and development of their potential, their distinctive gifts, and their contributions (Lawrence-Brown, 2004). Specifically what this looks like and
how it can be accomplished are the subject of the chapters in Part II of
this volume.

As we shall see in the upcoming chapters, everyone benefits from
multicultural, universally designed instruction in well-supported, inclusive classroom communities where all are viewed as valuable members
with differing voices, strengths, abilities, and contributions. These responsive pedagogies benefit all students, not just those considered "diverse"
(Zirkel, 2008).

What is the cost of well-supported, inclusive general education classrooms? Certainly they are more expensive than unsupported general education classrooms—but the significant cost of segregated services that
function in the shadow of traditional general education classrooms must
also be entered into the calculation. For example, typical school districts
spent 31%–63% more per pupil for special education in 2005 (computed
from data provided in Alonso & Rothstein, 2010). Although more and
more students are being included, 39% are still placed in separate special education classrooms for 20%–100% of their school day (U.S. Office
of Special Education Programs, 2011). And as we have seen, this is despite a dearth of evidence suggesting that students learn more in separate
classrooms. I am not suggesting that we decrease spending on our most
vulnerable students—far from it. Rather, I'm suggesting that these funds
follow the child to the general education classroom, as suggested by both
the research evidence and the legal presumption under federal law favor-
ing placement of students with disabilities in general education. Support
services such as those for English language learners, gifted students, and

Activity 6.4: Now You Know—Now What?

As we close the chapter, consider the poem below. If you like, also revisit the quotation at the beginning of the chapter and the photographs in Figures 6.1 and 6.2. What connections can you make between the excerpts from Robert Frost's poem, "Mending Wall," and segregated education? Other forms of segregation?

Mending Wall

Before I built a wall I'd ask to know
What I was walling in or walling out,
And to whom I was like to give offence.
Something there is that doesn't love a wall,
That wants it down.

. . . .I see him there
Bringing a stone grasped firmly by the top
In each hand, like an old-stone savage armed.
He moves in darkness as it seems to me,
Not of woods only and the shade of trees.
He will not go behind his father's saying,
And he likes having thought of it so well
He says again, "Good fences make good neighbours."

those at risk academically or behaviorally can also follow the student back to the general education classroom. In this way, all students can benefit from high expectations, and high levels of support.

This chapter has reviewed outcomes related to various enactments of segregated schooling—some perhaps familiar, others not. On your own or with a small group, reflect on actions that you might take as an educator given the nature of this evidence.

GROUND TRUTH: AN EXPERIENCED TEACHER'S PERSPECTIVE

Rosemary Rotuno-Johnson
Veteran Special Educator

Rosemary is a 12-year-veteran special educator with experience teaching adolescents identified as having disabilities who has taught in both inclusive and pull-out settings. She comments on the impact on general education environments when students with disabilities are effectively included:

General education environments are made richer by the addition of students with disabilities. In the most ideal classrooms, educators are differentiating instruction and assessments on account of the students with the most obvious learning differences. As a result, many students benefit from the broader variety of activities, projects, and student collaborations found in these classrooms.

REFERENCES

Alonso, J. D., & Rothstein, R. (2010). *Where has the money been going?* Washington, DC: Economic Policy Institute. Retrieved from http://www.epi.org/page/-/pdf/bp281.pdf

Anyon, J. (1981). Social class and school knowledge. *Curriculum Inquiry, 11,* 3–42.

Anyon, J. (1992). Social class and the hidden curriculum. In G. Colombo, R. Cullen, & B. Lisle (Eds.), *Rereading America: Cultural contexts for critical thinking and writing* (pp. 524–540). Boston: Bedford Books.

Blatt, B., & Kaplan, F. (1974). *Christmas in purgatory.* Syracuse, NY: Human Policy Press.

Brown v. Board of Education. (1954). 347 U.S. 483.

Bunch, G ., & Valeo, A. (1997). *Inclusion: Recent research.* Toronto: Inclusion Press.

Freeman, S., & Alkin, M. (2000). Academic and social attainments of children with mental retardation in general education and special education settings. *Remedial and Special Education, 21*(1), 3–18.

Freire, P. (2009). From *Pedagogy of the oppressed.* In A. Darder, M. Baltodano, & R. Torres (Eds.), *The critical pedagogy reader, 2nd ed.* (pp. 52–60). New York: Routledge.

Frost, R. (n.d.). "Mending Wall." Retrieved from http://www.publicdomainpoems.com/mendingwall.html

Greene, K., & Anyon, J. (2010). Urban school reform, family support, and student achievement. *Reading & Writing Quarterly, 26*(3), 223–236.

Hansberry, L. (1957). *A Raisin in the Sun.* New York: Random House.

Hunt, P., Farron-Davis, S., Beckstead, D., Curtis, D., & Goetz, L. (1994). Evaluating the effects of placement of students with severe disabilities in general education vs. special classes. *Journal of the Association for Persons with Severe Handicaps, 17*(4), 247–253.

Kilman, C. (2010, Spring). "Homo high." *Teaching Tolerance, 37.* Retrieved from http://www.tolerance.org/magazine/number-37-spring-2010/homo-high

Lawrence-Brown, D. (2000). The segregation of Stephen. In Cornbleth, C. (Ed.), *Curriculum Politics, Policy, and Practice.* Albany: State University of New York Press.

Lawrence-Brown, D. (2004). Differentiated instruction: Inclusive strategies for standards-based learning that benefit the whole class. *American Secondary Education, 32*(3), 34–62.

Lockett, T. (2010, Spring). Unmaking *Brown. Teaching Tolerance, 37.* Retrieved from http://www.tolerance.org/magazine/number-37-spring-2010/unmaking-brown

Mendez v. Westminster School District. (1946). 64 F. Supp. 544 (S.D. Cal. 1946).

Pratt, R. (1973). "The advantages of mingling Indians with Whites." In F. P. Prucha (Ed.), *Americanizing the American Indians: Writings by the "Friends of the Indian" 1880–1900* (pp. 260-271). Cambridge, MA: Harvard University Press. Retrieved from http://historymatters.gmu.edu/d/4929/

Pugach, M. C., & Seidl, B. L. (1998). Responsible linkages between diversity and disability: A challenge for special education. *Teacher Education and Special Education, 21* (4), 319–333.

Sapon-Shevin, M. (1994/1995). Why gifted students belong in inclusive schools. *Educational Leadership*, December 1994/January 1995, 64–70.

Sarason, S. (1974). Foreword. In B. Blatt & F. Kaplan (Eds.), *Christmas in Purgatory* (p. ii). Syracuse, NY: Human Policy Press. Retrieved from http://www.mnddc.org/parallels2/pdf/undated/Xmas-Purgatory.pdf

Seidl, B. (2001). Review of the book *Advances in special education: Multicultural education for learners with exceptionalities. Early Childhood Research Quarterly, 16*(3), 395–402.

United Nations. (n.d.). *Convention on the prevention and punishment of the crime of genocide, New York, 1948*. Retrieved from http://www.cyberschoolbus.un.org/treaties/genocide.asp

U.S. Office of Special Education Programs. (2011). IDEA Part B: Educational Environment. Table B3-2: Number and percentage of students ages 6 through 21 served under IDEA, Part B, by educational environment and state: Fall 2011. Retrieved from https://www.ideadata.org/arc_toc13.asp#partbLRE

Zirkel, S. (2008). The influence of multicultural educational practices on student outcomes and intergroup relations. *Teachers College Record, 110*(6), 1147–1181.

PART II

ENACTING INCLUSIVE EDUCATION

CHAPTER 7

Building Inclusive Communities

Stacey N. Skoning
Kathryn Henn-Reinke

Key Principle 7: *All children are valuable members of classroom and school communities, with differing voices, strengths, abilities, and contributions. Inclusive communities embrace and expand children's sociocultural repertoires while also dealing with controversy and conflict in creative and constructive ways.*

Children and youth are complex and often have multiple identities. While this can make teaching diverse classrooms challenging, it also makes the environment rich, exciting, and dynamic. This chapter addresses how children with a range of talents and needs can learn and work together in a democratic and ever-changing community.

RECOGNIZING STRENGTHS

When I (Stacey) first met Rolland, he was in kindergarten. He was labeled as having autism and as non-verbal, but he watched everything going on around him. As he prepared to begin 4th grade, I was excited to learn that I would be his special education teacher.

Educators' Mindsets

I met with his 3rd-grade teacher to begin learning about his skills and abilities. Unfortunately, his 3rd-grade teacher followed a deficit-driven model of instruction and told me only what he could not do. It was a long list. Rolland was not toilet trained, he did not have any speech, and none of the communication systems they tried with him had worked. He was described as tactilely defensive; had a limited diet; "stimmed on" door hinges, coins, and other small objects (he rolled them in his fingers continuously if allowed); and was physically aggressive. "In short," I was told, he was "functioning at the level of a two-year-old" and would "always function at the level of a two-year-old."

The philosophy of Rolland's teacher—that she needed to fix what was wrong with her students—had devalued Rolland, his skills, and his abilities. He was viewed as having no skills and deemed unable to participate in both the general education curriculum and the regular education classroom. This view alienated him from his peers. He was rarely in the general education classroom, did not join his peers without disabilities even for lunch, and had limited interactions with children and other adults in the building. Most of his day was spent in a special education room, where he worked one-on-one with an adult assigned to him.

Think About This: The concept of mental age (e.g., "functioning at the level of a two-year old") is an example of unintended consequences of well-intended efforts. Originally developed to assist the layperson in interpreting IQ scores, it unfortunately has also led to low expectations, reduced opportunities to learn, and stigmatization of many students with significant disabilities.

How can we include students like Rolland in our regular education classrooms? First, we need to change our own mindsets as educators. We need to recognize that all children are valuable members of their classrooms and school communities, with differing voices, strengths, abilities, and contributions. To do this, we need to stop focusing our time and energy on determining how smart our children are, and instead identify how they are smart. Knowing children's skills and abilities will help us determine better ways to teach them. One way to reframe the discussion is through the lens of Howard Gardner's (1983, 1999, 2008) Theory of Multiple Intelligences. This theory is addressed in more detail in Chapter 8.

Identifying the strengths of our students is an important first step in recognizing and challenging the status quo that otherwise suppresses the voices of these children and youth. It was the first step in providing access for Rolland to both the general education curriculum and regular education classroom settings. Knowing their strengths allows us to determine more appropriate ways to teach our students. (For a description of the application of Gardner's Theory of Multiple Intelligences to the identification of Rolland's strengths, please refer to Activity 7.A: Applying Gardner's Theory of Multiple Intelligences, Related Resources for Chapter 7, www.tcpress.com.)

Group Work in an Inclusive Setting

How did this approach help Rolland? Near the end of the 4th-grade school year, he was working in a small group in his regular education social studies class. He was part of a group of four children—two boys (Rolland and Juan) and two girls (Haley and Nadia). Juan was an English learner (EL) and had an emotional/behavioral disability (EBD) label. Haley was labeled gifted and was a strong reader and writer. Nadia was a typical learner with no other educational labels. The group was preparing to put on a play about coming to America and entering through Ellis Island.

After the group finalized their scripts (under Haley's expert guidance), the group decided to split their remaining work. Haley and Nadia began making the props that the group would need for their performance. While they worked on props, Rolland and Juan began their work on the backdrop they needed. Juan drew a large desk in the center of their paper. Then he turned to Rolland.

> *Juan*: "What should be here? I don't know what else to draw."
> *Rolland*: (with assistance from his paraprofessional, typed the following on his communication board) "F-L-A-G"
> *Juan*: "Oh yeah! If they're coming into this country for the first time, there'd have to be a big U.S. flag there welcoming them to our country!" (He quickly added a flag on a stand next to the desk.)
> *Juan*: "What else should we put on here?"
> *Rolland*: "C-L-O-K"
> *Juan*: "Yeah! We need a clock on the desk to know what time they come in to put it on all the paperwork."

The boys continued this process with Rolland offering Juan suggestions and Juan drawing those ideas for about 20 minutes as they completed the design of the backdrop for their play. Eventually, the group of four came back together to color all of the pictures on their backdrop. In this way, all of the children's skills were used as they worked together to achieve a common goal.

In addition to their group goal, each student had individual goals. Juan had social skills goals in his IEP related to working well with others in small groups. Roland had communication goals in his IEP related to interacting with peers, communicating using his devices, and maintaining appropriate classroom behavior. Haley had a plan with the gifted and talented program to work on expressive writing skills well above her grade level. All four children also were working to achieve their district benchmarks in social studies. This activity provided all of the students with opportunities to practice skills that fell outside of

? Think About This: Cooperative learning with individualized roles can also be used to differentiate instruction in more traditional classroom activities.

Activity 7.1: Can Do Profile

In the examples in the text, how were strengths used and valued? How were weaknesses compensated for or accommodated?

Think about someone you know well who struggled in school. Record what that person was able to do in a variety of settings. Use this knowledge to create a "Can Do Profile" for that person. (Directions for completion of a "Can Do Profile" can be found in Activity 7.B: Can Do Profile, Related Resources for Chapter 7, www.tcpress.com.)

Be prepared to share the insights you gained about how to approach teaching, learning, and assessment with this individual.

the general education curriculum, within the general education lesson, and met general education curricular goals.

EMBRACING AND EXPANDING CHILDREN'S SOCIOCULTURAL REPERTOIRES

In addition to their strengths and abilities, children's sociocultural backgrounds have implications for how students learn about their world and how educators successfully or unsuccessfully incorporate these student repertoires into the teaching/learning/assessment process in the classroom. While cultural groups can include disability culture, those living in poverty, and religious and other groups, a focus on English learners (ELs) in this section will serve to highlight many of the circumstances common across these groups. Misunderstandings on the part of educators regarding issues of language learning and cultural differences have frequently resulted in over- or under-representation of ELs in special and gifted education programs.

Psychological and Social Issues

In bilingual and multilingual education we often see the term *psychosociolinguistic development*. A great deal of information can be gleaned from this term that has a bearing on the education of ELs. The psychological impact of being uprooted, sometimes violently, from one's homeland may certainly have an effect on a child's academic learning and interactions with educators and other students at school. Several years ago I (Kathy) had two children in my class from war-torn El Salvador. When the fire alarm went off unexpectedly one day, they instinctively dove under their

Activity 7.2: Benefits of Diversity

Create a drawing or other form of artwork that expresses the benefits of diversity. Why is having a diverse classroom important? (An example of a young child's artwork demonstrating the benefits of diversity can be found in Figure 7.A, Related Resources for Chapter 7, www.tcpress.com.)

desks. It made me realize how high their level of anxiety was about their personal safety. Academically, they were very successful, so it was only through experiences like this one that I gained clues into their perceptions of their surroundings and could take steps to assure them of their safety.

Socially, students also may experience many transitions. Obviously ELs are surrounded by a new culture and a new language, but in addition there may be other changes that have an impact on the social well-being of the children. For example, they may be moving from remote rural settings to large urban centers and must adjust to city life. Living conditions in their host country may be very crowded, at least initially, as several family members may share a single apartment that they can afford only by living together. Families may be separated for long periods of time, and children may suffer from loneliness and homesickness. Older siblings often are put in a situation called "accelerated role-taking" and must serve as child-care providers or translators for their families, taking on major responsibilities at an early age. Within the community or school setting, students may recognize that they are not well accepted in their schools and experience discrimination. Education may have a very different status in the new culture, and it may be challenging for families to deal with different expectations in attendance, interactions between educators and students, level and type of schoolwork, and so forth. Very often immigrant children struggle as much with these issues as they do with new academic and linguistic expectations. Having an understanding of these factors helps educators respond more fully in meeting the social/emotional needs of students, especially ELs.

Attention to these issues by educators can have a very strong impact on student learning. It is critical that we focus on acculturating students into the new culture, while assisting them in maintaining connections to their home culture. Conversely, when students are expected to reject their home culture and assimilate into the new culture, it leaves them feeling that somehow their home culture was inferior or unworthy in comparison to the new culture. As a result, they may feel less compelled to put much effort into their work at school. Attention must be paid to the ways that ethnicity, socioeconomic class, and other cultural contexts impact the strengths and needs of students if we are to educate diverse groups of children successfully. We need to be aware that ignoring these differences can lead to their being viewed as deficits. Instead, community strengths can be developed from these individual differences (Cummins, 2002).

Linguistic Issues

Linguistically, there also are many issues to consider when teaching English learners. Most language learners progress through predictable stages of language acquisition. These stages are similar across the first and subsequent languages that are acquired. Most states have testing requirements for measuring the progress of ELs in learning English and the results of these tests are placed in students' files. Educators benefit from examining these data and from understanding that the development of social language takes approximately 2–3 years, but the development of academic language needed for success in school takes much longer, often 5–10 years. For example, a teacher is puzzled because one of her students appears to communicate very well with everyone in English (social language level), but does not do well in school subjects (academic language level). A review of the child's language testing scores indicates that she is at a level 3 in English. Since level 7 reflects native-like fluency in English, the teacher now knows that the child needs much more support in developing receptive and expressive understanding of academic language in the content areas and can make appropriate adaptations in the curriculum for this student.

In serving as consultants, we were often confronted with general classroom teachers who confused language learning with reading disability. In one instance, a teacher planned to recommend one of the children with whom we were working for special education testing because he was reading below grade level and had demonstrated little growth over the past several months. The ESL/bilingual coordinator pointed out that the child was at a level 2 in English language acquisition, which is still a very beginning level. She also highlighted the tremendous progress the child had made in learning English since arriving from Mexico at the beginning of the school year. This child was in fact progressing at a reasonable rate and simply needed more time to acquire English language skills while bringing additional strengths and skills to the classroom community.

Indeed, sometimes it can be difficult to differentiate among developmental language learning, social/cultural adjustment issues, and disability. In cases where children are placed in bilingual educational settings, this task is often easier in the sense that educators can determine if progress is being made in L1 (the first language) but not L2, which would indicate that the issue is one of language acquisition in L2. If the child is not progressing in either language, this may be an indicator of a more serious problem. But sometimes this is more challenging and complex than it appears on the surface. For example, ELs occasionally take on selective mutism, because they are traumatized due to the emigration/immigration process, or they find the educational setting so overwhelming that they are not able to speak or respond in school, though they may continue to speak in their L1 in home or play settings. One student did not speak for several months, though she would complete some of the independent writing assignments. A few months later, she whispered her responses to one of the other students, who would relay them to the teacher. This teacher did not force the student in any way, but continually searched for opportunities and invitations for the student to communicate in ways that were comfortable for her.

Often language learning across the two languages of the student will be very uneven, and educators might be tempted to characterize students as alingual or not having any language. This notion is being strongly rebuked as researchers explore the language learning patterns of bilingual children who come to school after having spent several years in the United States (Escamilla, 2006; Hamayan, 2010). These children are able to respond to many concepts in L1 and many others in L2. Rather than declaring a lack of proficiency in one or both of the languages, these researchers are advising us to look at the level of linguistic and conceptual understanding the children have when their learning is considered as a whole. By providing supports to expand learning in both languages and to allow children to use what they know in both languages simultaneously, we encourage them to draw on all of their previous learning.

> **?** **Think About This**: People view language learners in different ways. Multilingualism is a valued characteristic in many parts of the world. However, Americans often view those whose native language is not English with scorn, and assume that everyone should speak English—even as visitors to other countries.

Culture in the Classroom

A secondary bilingual teacher travels to Spanish-speaking countries frequently. On every trip she searches for artifacts to bring back, because she understands the importance of representing the cultures of her students in the classroom. The students react with surprising enthusiasm when they enter the room and notice *papel picado* (intricate cut paper squares) hung from the ceiling or that there are copies of the latest magazines in Spanish on the counter. She buys sets of novels on these trips that are written by Spanish authors, because she knows that culture and Spanish literary style will be authentically represented in these texts. She arranges integrated discussion groups with students from various Latino cultures, because she knows that differences in values, traditions, and expectations will be expressed in the books. The discussions provide opportunities for students to learn about and understand cultural differences they may have among their classmates, even though they are all Latinos/as. While monolingual educators do not have the luxury of reading with their students in their L1, it is still important to have books that represent the cultures of the students in the classroom and to use quality children's/young adult literature as one avenue to learn more about the cultures of the students in the classroom.

The bilingual teacher also recognizes that many of the students are expected to work to help support their families and that by the age of 15 or 16 they would no longer be attending school in their country of origin. She has many discussions with students and their parents about the necessity of education to succeed in the United States. This district is very proactive in supporting the needs of their EL population. They have multiple avenues for determining their linguistic, social/emotional, and academic needs and implementing effective programs to address these needs. Nearly 100% of the ELs who remain in the district graduate, which is a strong testament to the efforts of the teachers and administrators.

Often, general classroom teachers assume that there is little parent involvement in schools in other countries because it is difficult to get parents to participate in school activities in the United States. Nothing could be further from reality. I (Kathy) have visited schools in Spanish-speaking countries where parent groups put on lavish meals and presentations for their visitors. Parents crowd school events and honor the teachers of their children in special ways. Schools in the United States that have strong participation from their immigrant parents have school personnel who speak the language(s) of the families, personally invite parents to various functions, and provide services that are useful to families. They are also the schools that are inclusive in these invitations and recognize that the extended family unit in many immigrant homes is very broad and many family members besides the parents or caregivers may wish to participate in school functions, attend parent/teacher conferences, or support their relatives in meetings with teachers and administrators.

? Think About This: It is so common to hear that parents "don't care" about their children because they don't come to school functions, completely ignoring all the ways their circumstances may differ from other parents: jobs that don't allow time off, lack of transportation, the right clothes, language barriers, no childcare, and so forth.

SIOP Model

The Sheltered Instruction Observation Protocol (SIOP) Model (Echevarría, Vogt, & Short, 2008, 2010) is an instructional approach that many EL teachers have found to be very successful, and it can be used by general classroom teachers as well. It is very versatile for educators working in inclusive classrooms that have one or more English learners. The key elements of SIOP include language and content objectives, building background, comprehensible input, scaffolding, interaction, active learning, and review and assessment. (For examples of SIOP in K–12 lesson plans, visit www.cal.org/siop/resources/lessonplans.html.)

Educators' use of culturally responsive pedagogy, multiple intelligences, and universal design principles, along with SIOP, supports learning for ELs who have or do not have special educational needs. All English learners benefit from rich, receptive, and expressive language and educational experiences that enable the students to progress both linguistically and academically. Attention to specific linguistic skills and strategies further supports second-language development. Providing choices in learning experiences and linking prior knowledge to new learning are simple, yet effective and authentic ways to integrate students' cultures into the learning process and enrich the classroom experience for all students. A good example of SIOP would be a science lesson that surveys student understanding of concepts, is hands-on, provides lots of TPR (Total Physical Response) or movement activities to assist students in remembering and understanding key vocabulary and concepts, and includes many opportunities for development of listening and speaking skills.

GROUND TRUTH: THE PRACTITIONER'S VOICE

Jill Williams
High School Special Education Teacher

Candy rarely comes to school on time, and when she does she is disheveled and not focused, carrying an odor of cat urine on her body and backpack. Students scurry to find new seating as Candy places her backpack in her seat of choice and the offensive odor fills the room. Candy's regular education teacher approaches me as to how he should deal with the situation.

Students who come from a low socioeconomic background may experience situations all too similar to Candy's—situations that cause them increased anxiety and decreased school performance. All her life, she has experienced a low-educational-level home plagued by unemployment, abuse, neglect, and exposure to inadequate or inappropriate experiences. In addition, she takes care of her younger siblings after school, assisting them with homework as well as trying to complete her own in between fights, cooking, cleaning, and friends.

Candy's experiences at home often carry over into the school day as she snaps at not only students but her teachers. Why? No one gets it. Candy is expected to be a student at school while acting as caretaker and guardian to her younger siblings at home. Additionally, she must suppress her anxieties when bill collectors are calling and knocking on the door. Candy is left home to deal with adult situations while only having the life skills of a teen. She waits for phone calls from police that her mom is in jail due to drunk driving and now has the burden of getting her siblings ready for school, walking them there, and getting back to the high school for her own day to start. There is no food in the house, she keeps the secret of mom's arrest from her younger siblings, and she wonders the rest of the day what mood her mom will be in when she and her siblings come home after school.

Educators are infuriated with Candy as she shows up late with incomplete homework and the odor of cat urine; she already has the threat of truancy fines hanging over her head due to all the days of school she has missed. Her teachers' conversations follow a certain pattern when the subject of Candy's school performance comes up: "She needs to suck it up and get the work done." "I'm not just giving her a grade because she has it a little rough." "Why should Candy be treated any differently than the rest of the students—we all have problems in our lives." "We have students that have jobs, are in sports taking high-level classes, and are on the honor roll; Candy should just get it together and get her work done." The conversation is the same for each child in a family crisis similar to Candy's. Can educators really be that insensitive to their situation or do they just not get it?

We talk about differentiating assignments for ELs and students with other labels recognized by the government, yet there is little guidance for educators on how best to differentiate learning for those with a less-than-stellar home life. Candy's situation is not unique to my school or to her alone; there are many students in a similar position. It is time to recognize these situations and plan differentiated lessons so all students can grow in their learning. It is time for educators to get to know their students. Educators must find their strengths and create unique and appropriate assignments for those students to show their understanding of the content.

Activity 7.3: Culture in Your Educational Experiences

In small groups, ask each other about the types of school experiences that were or were not helpful to you, who your favorite teachers were and why, and how the culture of the students was represented in the classroom. Develop suggestions for schools and educators about what could have made your educational experiences better.

 Activity 7.4: Representation of Culture in the School

Think about schools you have visited. How was culture represented throughout the school and the curriculum? Analyze the way culture was represented in this school, and determine if you think it was a superficial or meaningful representation of the culture of the students.

DEALING CONSTRUCTIVELY WITH CONTROVERSIAL ISSUES

Like any community, an inclusive classroom plays host to controversy and conflict, both of which are an integral part of life. As educators , we should approach these common issues as teaching opportunities for us and learning opportunities for our students. Effective facilitation of a controversial issue or a conflict that arises is crucial to enhancing students' growth as members of a classroom and—by extension—of a wider democratic community.

It is our view that at least part of the purpose of education is to think about how we view others, encourage diverse groups of children to work together, and support issues of social justice. Inclusive education is complex and important in the creation of a democratic society (Sapon-Shevin, 2007). Conflict often is a necessary part of social change and is an important part of teaching democratic principles (Apple, 1988, 1993). To prepare our students to function as intelligent and contributing members of our democratic society, we must give them increased responsibility for themselves and their behaviors while supporting their growth (Curwin, Mendler, & Mendler, 2008). In a shared classroom community, where educators and students work together to establish a positive democratic environment, students learn and practice conflict-resolution skills and hear the perspectives of others. Solving authentic problems together builds that sense of shared community needed in an inclusive classroom (Kohn, 1996).

Many of the pre-service educators with whom we work express concern about including controversial issues or mediating the conflicts that occur naturally in a group of people. We encourage them not to avoid these opportunities but rather to plan for their inevitable appearance. Taking time to examine a unit or lesson for potential moments of disagreement or diverging opinions results in a teacher who is better prepared to mediate them. Therefore, we need to use such moments as teaching/learning opportunities and not hide, run from, or focus too narrowly on them. Below, we discuss two instances where in-service and pre-service teachers worked through controversial issues in ways that resulted in positive growth experiences for all concerned.

Our first example is from a charter school that serves highly advanced students, many of whom are twice-exceptional; that is, students identified as having gifts and talents as well as learning disabilities. A 5th-grade teacher determined that her students were becoming far too clique oriented and tended to exclude classmates. After she noticed that students who were twice-exceptional were the majority of those excluded, she opened up the issue to a whole class discussion, without mentioning names or specific instances. Acting as a facilitator, she elicited ideas for ways to include all students in activities, both in class and during recess. Students voted to enact two ideas they felt were most workable: personal goal-setting to find out at least one new fact each week about someone in the class, which they would share at a Friday sharing time; and identifying students they did not know well and writing a weekly affirmation about one of those people.

Think About This: The fear of "Will I get in trouble for this?" often interferes with more complex conversations about context, gathering support, age-appropriate resources, etc.

After two months of these activities, the teacher reported that students were more apt to choose to move out of their usual cliques during group activities, and she observed positive changes in supportive communications between previously disconnected groups within the class. Moreover, the Friday sessions became a much-anticipated way of noting positive interactions between peers, and the students even asked the 6th-grade teacher if she would continue them next year. She agreed enthusiastically, because her colleague mentioned how much better she had come to know students because of what she heard shared about them each week.

In another school, a student teacher confronted controversy while working with 7th-graders, who used the term *gay* to describe anything boring, stupid, or unusual. Rather than merely telling students not to use the word, he engaged students in discussion about why they used it, what it meant to them, and who might be affected by it. He also asked students in groups to make posters that suggested better words to use than *gay*. This activity extended to the school hallways when students asked if they could make several signs and hang them around the school. With the principal's permission, this plan was approved, resulting in an example of how a classroom activity can have a broader impact on developing a more inclusive school community. After the discussion and poster project, the student teacher noted that he was much more careful about the language he used daily, particularly after one student said, "You said the movie was 'lame.' Isn't that kind of like saying it's 'gay'?" (See the amazing resources at www.welcomingschools.org for specific information on addressing diverse families and the epithet "That's so gay" with students.)

As alluded to earlier, heterogeneous groups will result in increased opportunity for instances like those presented above to arise. Many shy away from inclusion because they have to answer hard questions and respond to difficult interactions during collaborative activities. It is for this reason that communication is key. In the above examples, educators and students came together to talk about issues. Teachers acted as facilitators rather than judges or lecturers. The discussions shed light on concerns and led to opportunities for students to think critically about potential solutions and outcomes, which they were able to implement effectively with the assistance of the teachers. Second, that modeling of useful communication was possible because the educators involved were open to the idea of shared governance and community responsibility. They recognized that because the learning community was affected, the community needed a voice in how the situations might be resolved. This is important modeling for young people who will continue to deal with conflict in and out of school. Third, although these educators put the responsibility for change on the students themselves, they also reflected on the roles they played and their own shortcomings. Sometimes it is the teacher who needs to adapt and grow, not the student, and the key is developing the self-critical, reflective mindset that can result in those important leaps forward as a professional educator. Analyzing the classroom in this way also reinforces the idea that we all have different strengths and weaknesses, that we all are valuable members of the community, and that we can work together for the betterment of the group. Educators in inclusive classrooms will always encounter controversial issues, but as demonstrated above, these moments can be both educative and rewarding for students and professionals alike.

GROUND TRUTH: THE PRACTITIONER'S VOICE

Ann Mickelson
Early Childhood Teacher Educator

I want to describe two examples of contrasting approaches to including children with autism in early childhood settings. In the first example, a 4-year-old labeled as autistic was observed to get up and wander the classroom during circle time. The teachers in his classroom resorted to restraining him to physically prevent him from leaving the group. This not only upset the student but certainly affected the other students as well. Learning was sacrificed for physical placement with the group.

In sharp contrast, the teachers in the second example took a different approach with 2-year-old twins with autism who participated in a parent-child group that also included a circle time. They resisted sitting with the group during the songs, and the teachers decided to give them some space and time, rather than force them to sit. The teachers quickly noticed subtle observation and even some participation such as subtle imitation of hand movements from the twins as they moved about the periphery of the classroom. This was pointed out and celebrated with all staff as well as the parents and a plan was made for an adult to shadow each twin to model the songs and movements and encourage one-on-one interaction and participation. Over time, the subtle observation and participation was replaced with full engagement from the back of the room. Gradually the twins moved closer and closer with planned support from adults until they were fully engaged in participation and sitting with the group.

The child in the first example did not come to enjoy circle time and undoubtedly experienced numerous missed learning opportunities. The twins, on the other hand, eventually came to learn valuable skills across developmental domains that enhanced their participation in the parent-child group and in their educational careers and social lives.

 Activity 7.5: Classroom Controversy

Work in a group of four pre-service educators. Each member of the group should meet with a teacher (or students) and learn about areas of controversy found in an actual classroom and how these issues are addressed. The group should compile and analyze the responses for all of the interviews. They may wish to focus on which interventions are student centered and which are teacher centered, and which ones guide students to deal most effectively with these issues. Analyze ways to deal with different types of controversy in the classroom.

Activity 7.6: Shared Governance

Shared governance is an effective way to create a classroom where all students feel represented, safe, and empowered. Explore ways to develop shared governance in your class. Brainstorm goals for shared governance, and determine how to develop and assess these goals throughout the semester. Reflect on the impact these goals have had on your learning and on your participation as a class member.

CONCLUSION

As all of the examples in this chapter demonstrate, there are a few guidelines for educators that, when implemented well, help our children and youth to feel valued, to be contributing members of their classroom communities, to expand their sociocultural repertoires, and to handle controversy constructively. We must celebrate the unique gifts of each student in our classrooms and build on each of his or her strengths. We must support our students' individual learning goals and styles. We must recognize their unique backgrounds and cultural experiences and use these to enhance the learning of the entire group. Finally, we must build a supportive community of learners who enjoy learning and helping one another learn new skills and understand new concepts.

GROUND TRUTH: A PARENT'S PERSPECTIVE

Ann Freid
Parent

This chapter reminded me about something within myself that I realized after my daughter was born with Down syndrome. I never thought of myself as a racist until after she started school. I realized that if I wanted everyone else (her classmates, teachers, neighbors, entire society) to accept and appreciate my daughter for who she is (a child with Down syndrome), then I, myself, had better start accepting and appreciating *everyone else who is different from me*. I now am much more understanding and accepting of *all* people, whether their difference from me be color, ability, socioeconomics, body size, sexual orientation, or anything else. If I want everyone to accept *my* daughter, then I can't be a hypocrite and judge or alienate others.

REFERENCES

Apple, M. W. (1988). *Teachers & texts: A political economy of class & gender relations in education*. New York: Routledge.

Apple, M. W. (1993). *Official knowledge: Democratic education in a conservative age*. New York: Routledge.

Cummins, J. (2002). Beyond instructional techniques and standardized assessments: Implementing classroom interactions that foster power, identity, imagination and intellect among culturally diverse students. *Contact, 28*(2), 21–31.

Curwin, R. L., Mendler, A. N., & Mendler, B. D. (2008). *Discipline with dignity: New challenges, new solutions* (3rd ed.). Alexandria, VA: ASCD.

Echevarría, J., Vogt, M., & Short, D. (2008). *Making content comprehensible for elementary English learners: The SIOP Model*. Boston: Allyn & Bacon.

Echevarría, J., Vogt, M., & Short, D. (2010). *Making content comprehensible for secondary English learners: The SIOP Model* (2nd ed.). Boston: Allyn & Bacon.

Escamilla, K. (2006). Semilingualism applied to the literacy behavior of Spanish speaking emerging bilinguals: Emerging biliteracy or biiliteracy? *Teachers College Record 108*(11), 2329–2353.

Gardner, H. (1983). *Frames of mind: The theory of multiple intelligences*. New York: Basic Books.

Gardner, H. (1999). *Intelligence reframed: Multiple intelligences for the 21st century*. New York: Basic Books.

Gardner, H. (2008). *The 25th anniversary of the publication of Howard Gardner's Frames of mind: The theory of multiple intelligences*. Retrieved from http://www.howardgardner.com/papers/papers.html

Hamayan, E. (2010). Separado o together? Reflecting on the separation of languages of instruction. Retrieved from http://www.languagemagazine.com/?page_id=2704

Kohn, A. (1996). *Beyond discipline: From compliance to community*. Alexandria, VA: ASCD.

Sapon-Shevin, M. (2007). *Widening the circle: The power of inclusive classrooms*. Boston, MA: Beacon Press.

CHAPTER 8

The Art of Inclusive Teaching: Developing a Palette to Reach All Learners

David J. Connor
Subini A. Annamma

It is not our differences that divide us. It is our inability to recognize, accept, and celebrate those differences.

—Audre Lorde

The boldness of asking deep questions may require unforeseen flexibility if we are to accept the answers.

—Brian Greene

Key Principle 8: Students learn in many different ways. In order for students to be successful, educators must be flexible in their approaches, drawing from a repertoire of methodologies that value differentiation and support individualization.

Let us begin by introducing three diverse students. Please keep these snapshots in your mind's eye as you read through this chapter.

- Carmen is a 10th-grade student whose parents immigrated here from the Dominican Republic before she was born. She is fluent in both English and Spanish, and while she enjoys talking about many topics (from contemporary clothing to historical fiction) in either language, she also struggles in the act of writing in either

language. Carmen's essays are short and disorganized. She likes
to avoid writing at any cost.

- Darrell is a 7th-grade African American student who is highly
  popular with peers, great at basketball, a math whiz, and loves
  to use technology for interactive games. He was identified as
  having Attention Deficit Hyperactivity Disorder (ADHD) in 3rd
  grade, and he struggles to remain focused on tasks at hand in the
  classroom.
- Pei is a 5th-grade Chinese American student who likes to learn
  about animals from around the world. She has cerebral palsy, uses
  a wheelchair, and is currently about 2 years behind standardized
  expectations in math. Pei also has been assigned a full-time
  paraprofessional to assist with all person-to-person interactions
  via a communication board.

These are three random children that could be in any 5th-, 7th-, or
10th-grade class. What were your first reactions to reading about Carmen,
Darrell, and Pei? Why do you think that you reacted in these ways?

TOWARD NORMALIZING DIVERSITY: RESPONDING TO
NATURAL VARIATION WITHIN THE CLASSROOM

As educators, we are interested in contemplating what might work for
these three students in their classrooms. We raise the issue of what works
because teaching and learning are far more complex endeavors than how
they're traditionally presented in college classes, textbooks, internships,
scripted lessons, and claims of "scientifically proven" programs. There is
not a step-by-step, easy-to-read manual that serves as a recipe book for
fail-safe instruction. Teaching is and always should be viewed as a work
in progress, one that is contingent upon the dynamic interactions between
educators and students. We believe that an educator has the ability to enable or disable a student's learning. By that we mean that every decision
made has the power to connect or disconnect a student.

The challenge posed by this chapter is for current and potential educators to recognize how students in their classrooms learn in different ways
and to create an environment in which diversity is the norm. Effective
educators honor their students' diverse learning styles, and their beliefs
impact all aspects of teaching, including developing curriculum, planning
lessons, creating engaging activities, providing opportunities to process
and apply information, and assessment. A major point that we wish to
make clear is that educators who have not unpacked harmful and mis-
leading notions of the norm (including controversial taken-for-granted

practices such as developmental milestones, grade-level expectations, and literacy progress) tend to see children who do not fit the norm as being deficient rather than simply manifesting difference. In brief, shifting the focus of teaching from traditional notions of "normalizing," "fixing," "correcting," and "remediating" children to one of constantly refining and improving instruction helps educators see what is possible within their locus of control. It is imperative that students who have been historically segregated, deemed too different, or generally marginalized are fully integrated in all aspects of instruction along with typical students. Being part of a diverse classroom benefits children considered typical and high achieving as well as those identified as disabled. Of equal importance is that educators benefit from greater interactions with student diversity that accurately reflects the citizens within our democracy.

> **? Think About This**: The current focus on high-stakes testing and standardized curriculum negatively affects educators' abilities to be responsive to student diversity. How might you resist this focus in order to meet students' needs?

CREATING A TEACHING PALETTE FOR ALL LEARNERS

We begin this section by articulating certain assumptions. Most educators want their students to successfully grow academically, socially, and emotionally—to be motivated and engaged and to provide evidence of their growth. Given the nature of how students learn differently and the fact that many represent a variety of groups that have oftentimes been excluded from or marginalized within the curriculum, reaching every student can initially appear as a daunting task. However, there are many ways to recognize, understand, and plan for student differences. In the following subsections we describe six elements that can be combined to create a framework for learning. In some respects, it is useful to conceive each element as a color on an artist's palette. Note that each color can be used by itself to create a desired impact, as each element is a powerful approach in its own right. Sometimes, two or three colors can be used in combination to create new shades, different hues, and interesting juxtapositions. Combining all six colors, through matching or mixing, has the potential to maximize options within the art of teaching. Used together in thoughtful ways, the colors provide an effective framework that can guide all aspects of teaching and learning.

A. Acquire a Strength-Based View of Students

It is imperative to *always* begin by recognizing what students can do before identifying their areas of need. If this is not done, then educators are (often unconsciously) using a deficit-based lens that can have a profound negative effect on students. For many educators who have been enculturated into a traditional special education mindset, this means becoming conscious of this type of practice and developing different approaches to considering human differences (see Chapters 3, 7, and 10). Activity 8.1 provides ways to learn about students' interests in order to acquire a strength-based view of students.

B. Plan Using Universal Design

Universal design is a simple-but-revolutionary concept that is within the reach of all educators (Burghstahler & Cory, 2008). The original use of the concept hails from architecture and arose during the 1960s with the requirement to create new buildings accessible to citizens with different mobility needs. Ron Mace, the leader of the universal design (UD) movement, discovered that rethinking how buildings were traditionally configured actually benefited *all* users (Mace, Hardy, & Place, 1991). So while UD was originally intended to recognize the needs of people with disabilities, the flexibility it provides has benefited the entire population. For example, corner curb cuts for wheelchair users benefit people who wheel strollers, roll luggage cases, or are delivering large or heavy items that need to be wheeled.

In connecting the principles of universal design to classroom practice, the concept of *universal design for learning* (UDL) arose. Simply put, a teacher who plans with UDL in mind creates a hospitable classroom for *all* students by providing access to the curriculum for everyone. This approach eliminates or significantly reduces the need to "retrofit" accommodations. The Council for Exceptional Children (1999) described universal design as

> design of instructional materials and activities that makes the learning goals achievable by individuals with wide differences in their abilities to see, hear, speak, move, read, write, understand English, attend, organize, engage, and remember. Universal design for learning is achieved by means of flexible

Activity 8.1: Learn About Student Interests

Think about the descriptions of Carmen, Darrell, and Pei at the beginning of the chapter.

- What are their interests?
- What might be other areas of interest?
- How can you find out?

curricular materials and activities that provide alternatives for students with differing abilities. These alternatives are built into the instructional design and operating systems of educational materials—they are not added on after the fact.

The nine principles of UDL (Burgstahler & Cory, 2008) are listed below. Accompanying each is a question that serves as a checklist to educators.

1. *Equitable Use.* Is the design of the learning environment and lesson (hereafter referred to as "the design") useful to all people?
2. *Flexibility of Use.* Does the design accommodate a broad array of individual abilities and preferences?
3. *Simple and Intuitive.* Is the design straightforward and easy to understand, regardless of a user's knowledge, experience, language skills, or current concentration level?
4. *Perceptible Information.* Does the design communicate necessary information to the user, regardless of ambient conditions or the user's sensory abilities?
5. *Tolerance for Error.* Does the design minimize hazards and the adverse consequences of accidental or unintended actions?
6. *Low Physical Effort.* Can the design be used efficiently and comfortably, and with a minimum of fatigue?
7. *Size and Space for Approach and Use.* Does the design consider appropriate size and space in providing for approach, reach, manipulation, and use regardless of all students' size, posture, or mobility?
8. *A Community of Learners.* Does the instructional environment promote interaction and communication among students and between students and faculty?
9. *Instructional Climate.* Is the instruction designed to be welcoming and inclusive, where high expectations are espoused for all students?

The principles of UDL guide educators to meeting the needs of a variety of all learners—regardless of ability, language, sexual orientation, and so on (Rose & Meyer, 2008). As practitioners, we both strive to incorporate these principles into our own teaching.

An Example in Motion: A World History Class. In my high school world history class where we studied the history of U.S. involvement in Iraq, I (Subini) taught students with varying levels of ability, including LaDonika, who was considered gifted and getting ready for college; Collin, who had a 3rd-grade reading level and got frustrated when he had to write more than a few sentences; and Donovan, who had serious emotional difficulties and needed to move around to counter feeling trapped. In order to create access to the same content for all my students, I built on their strengths and gave them practice in areas where they needed to improve. To reach all students in the class, I did the following:

- I used the jigsaw method for featured readings in which the class is split into a number of groups, each with a particular text to focus upon and then share with the whole class. This approach reduced the individual reading load of all students while still allowing each person to have access to the same amount of information. In addition, the teacher has the option of providing texts of different lengths and complexity.
- I created PowerPoints of lectures that had visuals, media clips, and interactive dialogue to engage and support comprehension of concepts.
- I varied activities that accompanied all lectures so that students were actively engaged in having oral debates, creating maps, filling out graphic organizers, and participating in group discussions.
- I incorporated physical activity into every one of our lessons each day. It could be as small as students moving into different groups to taking part in gallery walks where they circulated to analyze quotes and record their opinions, to something more involved, such as role-playing important historical scenarios.

> **Think About This:** Asking students to sit still for long periods of time, coupled with the elimination of recess in many schools, has a serious impact on student behavior and learning and often leads to referrals to special education for hyperactivity, particularly for boys—an alarming trend.

- I rotated student jobs every week. These jobs were often tailored for certain students to increase movement or provide a chance to practice social skills.
- I differentiated note-taking. Some students took their own notes while others had notes already printed out with a word or phrase missing, which reduced the amount of writing required.
- I solicited students' expertise and knowledge whenever possible. We connected background knowledge by sharing stories of experiences with conflict, experiences with war in general, and experiences with the Iraq War. Many students had relatives serving in the Armed Forces, which helped them make personalized connections to the content being studied.

- I individualized final projects in a variety of ways. With initial approval and ongoing discussions with me, final products included skits, drawings, comic strips with explanations, models, and so forth.
- I allowed students to use their first language when discussing a concept. They then had to explain it to me in English so I could check for understanding.

While we have shared a high school–level example, it is important to recognize that the principles of UDL can be used in classrooms of any level (Rose & Meyer, 2008). For example, in elementary school, each student can learn about one U.S. state and present to the class, and this presentation can look different for each student; in middle school, students can write the biography of a selected family member; in high school, students can be given a choice of how they wish to share their knowledge—orally or in writing. Activity 8.2 provides an opportunity to begin to build these supports for students by starting small.

C. Differentiate Instruction

Another movement within education that has gained ground since the late 1990s is the concept of differentiated instruction. Carol Ann Tomlinson (1999, 2001), a groundbreaking educator focusing on instruction for all types of learners, has been instrumental in providing clear examples of how educators can practice many aspects of teaching in a flexible manner. By looking at these different aspects of teaching—such as selecting lesson content, deciding upon a process for engaging student learning, and determining what constitutes satisfactory evidence of student work— educators can decide upon ways to structure their lessons and provide opportunities for all students to be engaged and learn.

 Activity 8.2: Start Small!

Keeping in mind either Carmen, Darrell, or Pei, study a 5th-, 7th-, or 10th-grade lesson featured in one of your textbooks or on the Internet.

1. Locate an instance in which the student will be able to participate.
2. Identify a part of the lesson in which the student is not able to fully participate.
3. State what you'd change about this lesson to provide increased access to curriculum and materials or increased engagement for the student.

An important part of differentiating instruction for students with widely different ability levels (e.g., see Activity 8.3) is providing different roles for different students within the same activity. In Pei's case, it doesn't matter that there is no existing group that matches her ability level. Her individualized goals can be addressed in any group (not necessarily the lowest one). These goals may include lower-level academics (as above) or goals that are often not considered to be part of the general curriculum at all (e.g., communication, motor, and social skills).

Some goals, however, are best addressed outside of the classroom, in the natural environment for each particular skill. Dressing goals might be taught in the locker room; learning to cross the street safely requires community-based instruction.

And, of course, all of this will require people supports such as special education teachers, paraprofessionals, and/or therapists.

Tomlinson also encourages teachers to consider three other areas pertaining to the student. These are each learner's readiness, interest, and learning profile, considered in relation to the tasks at hand within a given lesson. Each of these areas provides a possible window into the learner that can, in turn, open a door that gives them access into the learning experience.

We realize that these ideas can sound a little abstract at first, so let's consider how they can appear in action. The main idea to remember is that each choice is purposeful, selected to ensure that children are connected to learning in ways that support them. Let us consider differentiation methods, for example, in a 5th-grade math class on solving word problems involving fractions.

- *Differentiating Content.* All students will receive a mini-lesson on ways to approach problem solving. Students can then be divided into four groups based upon word problems featuring specific mathematical methods of operation. All groups can contribute during a whole-class share-out.
- *Differentiating Process.* Students can be assigned (or given the choice) to work alone, in pairs, or in groups of four.
- *Differentiating Product.* The common goal is to have students solving word problems involving fractions, and this can be done in several ways. Students can orally explain how they solved the problem, demonstrate their approach by writing on the blackboard or smart board, or demonstrate to the class while using manipulatives.

As you can see, these approaches require preparation that is, by and large, manageable. Yet let's consider reasons *why* a teacher may have planned her class this way.

Activity 8.3: Spotlight on Pei

Some possibilities in contemplating differentiating instruction for Pei include having her

- work on understanding fractions with the dominators of 2, 3, 4, 6, 8 (content);
- work with a peer tutor to discuss customized word problems and involve Pei in solving them via her communication board (process); and
- demonstrate solving three examples of subtracting fractions with the same denominator, using a laptop and appropriate software—overseen by her paraprofessional (product).

Questions:

1. What might be some other examples?
2. How could this assignment be more connected to Pei's interests?

- *Differentiating by Student Readiness.* In creating groups to use fractions within one of the four basic mathematical operations, the teacher places students who have not yet fully mastered multiplication or division into groups of addition and subtraction. Also, should student groups complete the problems, the teacher can provide a more complex question in the same operation or perhaps a multiplication question for a group that had previously addressed subtraction. It is also worth pointing out that less skilled students should not always be placed together, as this reinforces notions of set hierarchies among students.

  Being able to customize teacher support for students is crucial at these junctures, which are often unpredictable and in the moment. Customizing teacher support may include a variety of options such as a special education teacher co-teaching, push-in support from other professionals (e.g., speech pathologists, occupational therapists, literacy coaches), or other options. What is essential here is that in order to support the classroom teacher to meet the students' individual needs, there must be frequent collaborative planning time for the instructional team. In other words, one teacher is not responsible for designing and implementing all supports; it is the responsibility of the instructional team.

- *Differentiating by Student Interest.* The word problems themselves are based upon the interests of the students, involving sports, shopping, eating, and television. Students are allowed to tackle the three problems within each group in any order.
- *Differentiating by Student Learning Profile.* Allowing students to share how they problem-solved in different ways permits them to play to their strengths (e.g. orally, writing it out for the class, demonstrating with manipulatives, choosing a group representative or two).

In sum, these ways to differentiate instruction maximize student access to the curriculum, providing ways for all students to become, and stay, connected to content knowledge and academic skills. Activity 8.4 provides questions educators can ask themselves when planning for differentiation possibilities.

Think About This: It's important to keep "differentiation" from becoming a more sophisticated form of tracking—with some students getting enriched, exciting curriculum and others being judged to be unable to participate.

D. Use Multiple Intelligences

During the 20th century, intelligence was largely assumed to be innate, fixed, and measurable by tests that produced a quantifiable score. By asserting the existence of *multiple intelligences* (MI), Howard Gardner (1983) helped change this perception. In brief, Gardner claimed that our society had been overusing a highly prescriptive and therefore limited understanding of intelligence that hinged on academic performance in literacy and numeracy. As a result, other forms of knowing and doing had traditionally been minimized, dismissed, or overlooked. While this trend of privileging literacy and numeracy has continued within education systems to this day, educators have found Gardner's ideas extremely useful in facilitating learning. Let us take, for example, the math class example described above involving problem solving with fractions. In teaching students as a whole class, in small groups, or as individuals, the teacher could use MI through the following techniques:

- recognizing key words and their meanings (language: "word smart")
- once the problem is understood, deciding the procedures (logical-mathematical intelligence: "number/reasoning smart")
- encouraging some students to create clear visual representations of the problem (spatial intelligence: "picture smart")

Activity 8.4: Differentiation Possibilities

Select a content area/unit with which you are very familiar, such as letter-sound correspondence (phonemic awareness), rhyming words, adding decimals, ancient Egypt, Arthur Miller's *The Crucible* (1952), the colonization of Africa, or Darwin's Theory of Evolution.

What are some of your ideas for differentiation possibilities according to:

Content? *What* is being taught, that is, the same concept in different ways.
Process? *How* students are engaging with the information, for example, research, solving, discussing, etc.
Product? *What* students do/create that provides evidence of their knowledge, for example, a list, a letter, an essay, a demonstration, etc.

- giving student groups the option of using their bodies to convey the problem such as by standing next to one another, taking steps, and so forth (bodily-kinesthetic intelligence: "body smart")
- creating a rhyme to remember the steps in a mathematical operation involving fractions (musical intelligence: "music smart")
- forming groups in which students can talk amongst themselves (interpersonal intelligence: "people smart")
- providing time for all students to think individually before sharing in pairs how they would begin to attack the problem (intrapersonal intelligence: "self smart")
- connecting problems to what is being studied in science, such as the migration of birds or the population growth of rodents in urban areas (naturalist intelligence: "nature smart")

While it is impractical to think of every lesson in terms of using all MI, at least two or three can be incorporated into lessons based on the ways students in your class learn, with a conscious attempt to infuse all of them multiple times over the course of the semester (Kagan & Kagan, 1998). Activity 8.5 provides a chance to consider ways to access multiple intelligences and build strength-based responses for Pei, Darrell, and Carmen.

Think About This: We need to make sure that *all* students get opportunities to develop all of their intelligences—rather than always having students work in their area of strength or preferred learning mode. For example, what happens if Marcus is always the one who draws the pictures and Magda always uses her extensive linguistic skills?

Activity 8.5: Strength-Based Approach

Using the information that you have about Pei, Darrell, and Carmen, what might be each student's strongest intelligences that could be built upon? What are their less developed areas, and how does this impact their learning process?

E. Embrace Multiculturalism

The use of a multicultural curriculum is essential for an inclusive classroom, as it provides opportunities for all groups within society to be recognized (Gay, 2003). At its heart, multiculturalism embraces pluralism, namely the belief that many cultural groups exist within, and contribute to, society. It challenges the dominance of the traditional educational canon of White, European, middle-class values and knowledge, and instead seeks a more diverse curriculum. Given that the majority of teachers and other educational decision makers are of social backgrounds that mirror the traditional educational canon, and the nation's classrooms contain 40% children of color (100% in many urban areas), there exist potential problems of cultural dissonance—meaning educators and their students do not understand each other's actions, reactions, interactions, learning habits, and expectations. In becoming culturally responsive teachers, all educators can build on the diversity of race, ethnicity, abilities, and sexual orientation of the

> **Think About This:** Unfortunately, rather than really learning about different cultures, schools often reduce multiculturalism to the "food, holidays, and music" of other countries. What stands in the way of more sociopolitical ways of thinking about diversity?

students in their classes (Florence, 2010). Being a culturally responsive teacher can be done through understanding and leveraging the cultures of students in classrooms. A culturally responsive teacher recognizes what funds of knowledge students have access to in their home communities and notes how that culture can influence students' repertoires of practice—which, in turn, should influence a teacher's teaching style (Gutierrez & Rogoff, 2003; Moll, Amanti, Neff, & Gonzalez, 1992). Consider the following possible factors:

- Emergent bilingual students may come from cultures where group conversation, similar to that in classrooms, is a rare practice. Moderating the type of interactions, scaffolding the class

Activity 8.6: Parents as Funds of Knowledge

- In what ways might the educational experiences of Carmen's parents be different than that of their daughter?
- What are some ways in which educators can promote strong relationships with families whose first language is not English?
- How might you respond to a mother who complains that her "normal" son shouldn't have to be in a class alongside Pei, who is not really learning the same thing and looks to to the mother like a distraction to others?

discussions, and assigning roles within groups serve to show understanding and respect for students' culture while helping them learn to appreciate other cultural ways of knowing and doing.

- Many cultures value verbal practices and conversation more than lecture-based learning. Teachers can structure lessons to balance key information for everyone via lecture, with topics for students to analyze in partners or groups.
- Some cultures emphasize group achievement over individual distinction. Creating opportunities for groups to present and share, rather than individuals performing, is another option.
- Parenting practices vary; in some cultures parents expect all learning to occur in school, while other parents seek to monitor and assist their children in doing homework.

Activity 8.6 provides ways to address parental interactions.

F. Employ Flexible Grouping

Learning why, when, where, and how to group students throughout a lesson is a key ingredient of inclusive classrooms (Valle & Connor, 2010). Once educators know their students, they gain a sense of how to best balance lessons between

1. teaching the whole class vital information for all students;
2. using various forms of student groups for specified content or skills; and
3. conferencing with individual children or youth for customized feedback.

In using these possibilities, teachers provide multiple ways in which all students can learn and share their knowledge. Several examples of various uses of flexible grouping include the following.

Whole Class

- Brainstorming about a particular topic (gender roles, emotions, why we have laws, equality, etc.)
- Checking in for meaning at any time during the lesson ("Let's review some of the main ideas so far about . . .")
- Summarizing at the end of class

Small Groups

- Cooperative learning among heterogeneous groups (such as studying a body organ in order to later present to the class)
- "Jigsaw," which involves several small groups working on different aspects of the same topic before coming together to share (e.g., aspects of a particular culture)
- Acting scenarios that allow students to dramatize the content area such as modeling types of triangles, creating equations using students, imagining phenomena in history from various perspectives (such as Columbus's arrival in the "New World" or the Underground Railroad)

Dyads

- Buddy reading that involves taking turns in reading and answering questions
- Think-Pair-Share, where students must first spend time originating thoughts, ideas, or responses before sharing with a partner
- Teaming students to problem-solve and double-check their answers to assigned questions (e.g., five math problems)

Individuals

- Quickwrites, which require all students to write their immediate thoughts in narrative or bulleted form (e.g., "What comes to mind when I mention the phrase 'Global Warming'"?)
- Double-entry journals, with one column for questions and quotes and the other for comments, promoting personalized interaction with the text

Activity 8.7: Benefits of Flexible Grouping

Explore the following questions:

- Why might Darrell benefit from being in a small group for part of the class?
- Why might Pei gain from whole-class instruction?
- Why might Carmen sometimes need to work alone?

- Graphic organizers, such as the timeline of an individual's autobiography

Each of these permutations requires a set of management skills that are acquired over time, partly through informed decision making, a willingness to take calculated risks, and trial and error. With time, teachers learn to move among these formats within most lessons, thereby providing a variety of ways in which students come to interact with one another while learning the knowledge and skills of the curriculum. Flexible grouping avoids the practices of permanent labeling, which can reify perceptions of ability and create stigma for those associated with the low group (see Activity 8.7 for flexible grouping considerations). The most important thing to remember with flexible grouping is that the grouping shifts and students should not be relegated to a group based on ability for long periods of time.

Summary

While we offer a simple analogy between teaching and painting (see Figure 8.1), we recognize that it can take a while to master each color; some educators are familiar with all colors, while others know a few; it takes a degree of informed experimentation when mixing colors; and some educators believe teaching is more akin to science than art. That said, we believe each one of the elements described in this section provides an opportunity to create a fluid, living, inclusive classroom, one that changes from day to day. In the next section, we sample a few activities to show how selected elements look in motion (see Activities 8.8 & 8.9).

IDEAS IN ACTION:
PRACTICAL APPLICATIONS WITHIN INCLUSIVE CLASSROOMS

Now that you've thought about the ideas laid out in this chapter, here are some ways to incorporate them into a lesson plan. Our case-study

Figure 8.1. Teaching Palette for All Learners

composite addressed some of the six elements of a framework for learning in an inclusive high school classroom attended by Carmen. In the following lesson on Practicing Perspective, keep in mind the strengths of students (*Element A*). Note that we used a literacy focus, but this lesson plan could be used in several content areas, as we believe that these methods, strategies, and resources can be included in all content area classrooms.

In sum, we wish to reiterate that this chapter (and this section in particular) illustrates ways in which teacher choices are vitally important in terms of how children/youth feel acknowledged, included, represented, and respected. In addition, educators come to feel empowered through the choices they make regarding their teaching.

Scenario

This high school class is made up of 30 students and two teachers, one a special education teacher and one a content area teacher. The students

 Activity 8.8: Discussion Questions

Many educators (and non-educators) believe that teaching can be viewed as a technical endeavor that simply requires executing a task, step by step.

- What are the implications of viewing teaching as a science or an art?
- Do you believe that teaching can be a combination of science and art?
- If so, describe what that looks like.

have a variety of strengths, skill levels, and labels: four are considered second language learners (ESL), one has a cognitive disability, three have a learning disability (LD)—two in reading and one in writing (Carmen)—two are considered gifted and talented (TAG), and two are identified as having behavior disorders (BD). One male student is openly gay. This classroom is also diverse in terms of race, social class, and ethnicity.

Lesson Plan Topic: Practicing Perspective

Lesson Length: 55 minutes

Content Objective: Students will learn the term *perspective* and how it applies to the characters of Enrique and his mother in the text: *Enrique's Journey.*

Language Objective: Students will define the term *perspective* in written form and be able to express what it means in their own words (*Element C: Differentiation by Student Learning Profile—Addressing the Needs of English Language Learners Through Language Objectives*).

Rationale: In many content areas, perspectives of different actors are important to address. Students need to see why decisions are made and that they may or may not agree with the perspective of the decision maker. As it is often in the news, students have been asking about illegal immigration and the anti-immigration bills. They also note a sentiment toward anti-bilingualism in the media as more "English Only" instruction bills have been introduced in other states. Additionally, you have noticed that your class is having difficulty relating to one another's perspectives. This lesson, therefore, could strengthen the overall classroom community as well as individual empathy (*Element C: Differentiation by Student Readiness—Addressing the Needs of Your Classroom Community*).

Materials: *Enrique's Journey* by Sonia Narario. This could be used in multiple subject areas (*Element E: Multicultural Text*).

Anticipatory Set—Journal Prompt (10 minutes): Have you ever had a major disagreement with your friend or parent? Supporting questions: What was it about? What were you trying to say? What was your friend/parent trying to say (*Element C: Differentiation by Student Learning Profile*)? The supporting questions are to help all students contribute responses in a variety of ways.

Class will share examples out loud in groups of four (*Element F: Flexible Grouping—Small Groups*).

Activities (35 minutes): Students will continue reading *Enrique's Journey* as a large group (*Element C: Differentiation by Content*). Have the student with a learning disability in reading who struggles with comprehension of large amounts of text read only selected excerpts instead of the whole book (*Element C: Differentiation by Process*). Have another student with learning disabilities in reading—who has high level of comprehension but difficulty in decoding—use a digital audio format, or listen along with the student with a cognitive disability when the teacher reads to a small group. At times this group could also have students who just prefer to hear reading out loud, in order to avoid permanent ability grouping.

Class will come back as a large group to brainstorm what the term *perspective* means. Once they decide on a definition, all will write this definition in their personal dictionaries (*Element B: Universal Design—Equitable Use*).

Students will be given 20 minutes to create a project displaying their understanding of perspective on their own (*some examples of Element C: Differentiation by Product*). For example, one may want to write about the perspective of Enrique's mother in taking care of his family. The student who is openly gay may address how gangs harassed Enrique and relate it to his own experience with the hall monitor. The student with a behavioral disorder may do a role-play of how Enrique feels while riding on top of the train (*Element D: Multiple Intelligences*).

Students will be told they will have more time to finish their project tomorrow.

Students will critique social inequities: Why is immigration necessary? What factors contribute to illegal immigration? Do children in the United States have to take these types of risks? How does this story affect your perspective on the issue of illegal immigration?

Large Group Check-in: "Based upon your conversations, what are some new thoughts you've had about this topic?"

Assessment—Exit Slip (5 minutes): Students will record a definition of perspective and hand it in to the teacher on the way out. This can be in writing and/or in the form of drawing, bulleted information, or an oral expression of knowledge.

Closure (5 minutes): To close the lesson, the teacher will return to the content and language objectives for the day, checking in with students to ensure these objectives have been met.

Activity 8.9: Meeting Individual Students' Needs

Imagine you are Carmen or Pei as this class is occurring.

- In what ways has the teacher made sure you have access to the lesson?
- What may be some other options that the teacher can utilize?

Additional Multiple Intelligence Activities to Consider

Linguistic intelligence: Teach perspective through letters back and forth from Enrique and his mother (or other characters in the book).

Logical-mathematical intelligence: Consider the physical aspects of riding on trains and the actual journey (number of miles, amount of money, time it takes), and create a map or diary including this information.

Bodily-kinesthetic intelligence: Role-play scenes from the book.

Musical intelligence: Write a song about Enrique's journey (include details from the book).

Interpersonal intelligence: Have a debate (e.g., Enrique vs. Mom or those for & against fencing the border). What is their stance? What is the reason for the stance they are taking? How are they feeling?

Intrapersonal intelligence: Journal prompts: Share (through writing, verbal, digital) a story about a time you had to take a risk.

Naturalist intelligence: What types of natural environments will Enrique encounter as he rides the trains north through South and Central America? What challenges does this pose for him?

In closing, we realize that our suggestions are not always fail safe, perfect, or guaranteed. However, we do believe that they can help educators develop into lifelong creative thinkers who always strive in the direction of "let's try" and "can do."

GROUND TRUTH: THE PRACTITIONER'S VOICE

Kristen L. Pavelec
Teacher, Middletown, New Jersey

Two years ago I worked with a cooperating teacher to differentiate an 8th-grade assignment to meet the diverse population of students in the room. This inclusive language arts classroom had students from all walks of life with varying abilities, interests, and needs. The unit was titled "Do the Right Thing" and asked students to consider this theme while learning about the civil rights movement and the Holocaust. Using a problem-based learning model, students were asked to research a historical figure from this era, describe his or her time period, and provide insight about this traumatic time through this person's point of view.

The content area teacher and I provided students with the choice of whom they would research, what time period they would focus on, and how they would present their information. Students were also given the choice of forming a group for this project. I worked with the content area teacher to create lessons that appealed to various types of learners by utilizing video, audio, and text during the instructional period. After the day's lesson, students were given time to work with their peer groups on their assignment. During this time the teacher and I would confer with individuals about their topic and what steps they set up to complete the day's task. I was thrilled to notice students making fitting choices based on their needs. For example, Brian, a gregarious student with severe ADHD, selected an oral presentation with a group because it allowed him to move around and talk to his peers. He used video archives and live interviews for his research. On the other hand, Evan, a student struggling with a severe speech impediment, chose to work alone and design a website. He used Google Sites, which he learned about in his computer class.

Unfortunately, I also noticed that differentiating in this way can also provide an opening for less-motivated students in a classroom to take advantage of a situation. For example, James was a member of the group with Brian. James was considered a Title I student, receiving intervention services. He scored below proficient on his state tests for the previous year, habitually did not complete his homework, and was not motivated to improve his grade. Allowing James to work in a group gave him the opportunity to hide behind his group members and avoid doing his share of the assignment. In addition, James avoids writing in general, as he needs support in this area; selecting an oral presentation provided James with a chance to side-step writing during this task. Additionally, while Evan was relieved to work on his own, we realized that because of this option he missed out on a valuable opportunity to work on his social skills with his classmates.

Differentiating is a powerful and necessary tool in an inclusive classroom. Teachers who differentiate help their students feel safe and encouraged in their classroom. However, it is important to be aware of how differentiating without support, guidance, and assessment can adversely impact less-motivated students. As a teacher, it is important to know your students and possibly eliminate some of the choices, depending upon the desired skills being taught to a particular student. Finally, when working in an inclusive setting, a classroom culture should be created so that students understand that everyone gets what he or she needs in order to learn and grow as a student.

REFERENCES

Burgstahler, S., & Cory, R. (2008). *Universal design in higher education: From principles to practice.* Cambridge, MA: Harvard Education Press.

Council for Exceptional Children. (1999). Universal design: Ensuring access to the general education curriculum. *Research Connections in Special Education, 5*(2). Retrieved from http://www.hoagiesgifted.org/eric/osep/recon5/rc5sec1.html

Florence, N. (2010). *Multiculturalism 101.* New York: McGraw-Hill.

Gardner, H. (1983). *Frames of mind: The theory of multiple intelligences.* New York: Basic Books.

Gay, G. (2003). *Becoming multicultural educators: Personal journey toward professional agency.* San Francisco, CA: Jossey-Bass

Gutierrez, K. D., & Rogoff, B. (2003). Cultural ways of learning: Individual traits or repertoires. *Educational Researcher 32,* 9–25.

Kagan, S., & Kagan, M. (1998). *Multiple intelligences: The complete MI book.* San Clemente, CA: Kagan.

Mace, R. L., Hardie, G. J., & Place, J. P. (1991). Accessible environments: Toward universal design. In W. E. Preiser, J. C. Vischer, & E. T. White (Eds.), *Design intervention: Toward a more humane architecture* (pp. 156–188). New York: Reinhold.

Miller, A. (1952) *The crucible.* London: Penguin.

Moll, L. C., Amanti, C., Neff, D., & Gonzalez, N. (1992). Funds of knowledge for teaching: Using a qualitative approach to connect homes and classrooms. *Theory into Practice, 31*(1), 132–141.

Rose, D. H., & Meyer, A. (Eds.). (2008). *A practical reader in universal design for learning.* Cambridge, MA: Harvard Education Press.

Tomlinson, C. A. (1999). *The differentiated classroom: Responding to the needs of all learners.* Alexandria, VA: ASCD.

Tomlinson, C. A. (2001). *How to differentiate instruction in mixed ability classrooms.* Alexandria, VA: ASCD.

Valle, J. W., & Connor, D. J. (2010). *Rethinking disability: A disability studies approach to inclusive practices.* New York: McGraw-Hill.

CHAPTER 9

Considering Behavior as Meaningful Communication

Robin M. Smith

> Treat every person as if they were a dignitary from another country who doesn't speak your language very well.
>
> —Eugene Marcus

Key Principle 9: *All behavior is a form of communication, including that which is labeled as "problem behavior." Educators who understand the underlying message of the behavior (often an important need of the student) can create more effective instructional and environmental interventions (Donnellan et al., 1984).*

The subtext of Key Principle 9 reveals that if we look at behavior as a language we will perceive it as meaningful, and therefore we must assume competence. Otherwise, we are easily prone to attempting to diagnose and suppress certain behaviors. Without accepting behavior as meaningful language (presumed competence), we are left with the conclusion that behaviors we do not understand are either meaningless or malevolent.

Assuming competence makes us more likely to look for different interpretations of people's behavior. When we assume competence, we can better see the whole person with strengths, interests, talents, and other ways that he or she is unique and integral to the fabric of the community. We assess behavioral (language) challenges on a competence-oriented basis. We look for meaning in behavior we do not (yet) understand. We become language/behavior detectives.

The implications of this apparently simple principle are broad. At first we might wonder if the person can do what others can do and often the answer is either obscure or a resounding "No!" Then what? My own growth in this area came in fits and starts over time.

My first "aha!" moment was when I participated in an advocacy group in the late 1980s to get lifts on transit buses. Several of my fellow advocates had spent most of their lives in institutions and had gotten out through various advocacy efforts to live independent lives. They communicated with machines such as the Liberator, by typing, or by labored speech. Many of us used wheelchairs. My new friends had been, in effect, jailed by others' attitudes toward their disabilities. I remember Ken, who drove his wheelchair with his right foot, the only body part he could control. His speech took considerable getting used to as he took time to form each word as best he could. When we mounted a public protest against an inaccessible major fast food downtown restaurant, the leaders made him the go-to spokesman to the press. Aha! Even though I thought of myself as appreciating and respecting Ken, I thought, "Why didn't I think of that?"

Then, as a graduate student, I set about getting to know a student with Down syndrome who was fully included in high school. Gerard spoke in short sentences, and a few of the teachers told me that he was only there to learn social skills. However, the teachers who treated him as a real student found he was learning along with his class with differentiated instruction. I also noticed, as I came to learn how he responded, that he was following the lectures and answering rhetorical yes/no questions correctly. When he said, "I don't know," it didn't mean he was lazy (the opinion of his special education teacher, who had not learned how to interpret his behavior); it meant instead that he felt that an answer was socially required but he couldn't find the words in time. Aha! I realized that students with intellectual disabilities who communicated through atypical behaviors had a right to intellectual stimulation, and that some teachers were misinterpreting Gerard's behavior and missing the fact that he was actually learning.

> **Think About This:** "Being there to learn social skills" is a common misconception about inclusion of students with significant disabilities. As we've seen in Chapter 6, increased learning of *academic* skills is an important benefit of effective inclusion of students with significant disabilities.

With these realizations that students are both competent and fully engaged, I took a second look at how to understand behavior in this new strength-based light. I began to look at different aspects of understanding and supporting students as *corollaries* to the principle of behavior as communication that we should avoid misunderstanding—and misinterpreting. Rather, we need to expand our approaches to understanding and support, which we will do in the following explorations of the eight corollaries.

UNDERSTANDING THE MEANING OF BEHAVIOR

Corollary 1: Language Is Powerful

We must be careful about how we talk to and about students and speak in ways that foster their intellectual and social participation. The ways we perceive, speak to, and speak about students are likely to *predict* their participation.

The easiest way to think about this is to contrast competence-oriented and deficit-oriented perspectives toward students (Smith, 1999). Competence-oriented teachers tend to do the following:

- Address students directly
- Call on them during class discussions
- Check up on them during seat work as much as on the other students and demand they stay on task in the same tone used with other students ("Get to work, you know this.")
- Include them in group work
- Assign them classroom jobs

However, deficit-oriented teachers tend to do the following:

- Ignore students
- Rarely call on them
- Accept non-participation
- Take over their assignment, leaving them out of the process

Corollary 2: Assuming Competence Includes Having High Expectations

Assume that all students have and seek meaningful goals. This assumption is true regardless of the severity of a disability, the proficiency of an English language learner, the living or economic situation of a student, and/or the struggles the student brings to school from home or community. We need to think about our students in a meaningful context; we should be thinking about students' goals, in a larger context than getting better at an isolated social, functional, or academic skill. This corollary mandates *the least dangerous assumption* (Donnellan, 1984)—it is less dangerous to assume competence than not. For example, if I assume you cannot and never will read, then I will not expose you to print and you definitely won't read. On the contrary, I have known people with severe developmental disabilities who were "discovered" reading (see Kliewer & Biklen, 2001) and Spanish-speaking migrant students who got all A's in Mexico but were

Activity 9.1: Teacher Talk

- Observe how you and other educators talk to and about students. Take notes, including direct quotes, and indicate if the talk is deficit- or competence-oriented.
- Can you add new categories?
- Bring examples to class, and discuss how to transform deficit-oriented talk into competence-oriented talk.
- Write statements you have heard spoken to or about students, and indicate if each statement is C-O (competence-oriented) or D-O (deficit-oriented).

then placed in segregated classes for students with intellectual disabilities in the United States. If you assume incompetence, then a student is never exposed to possibilities. When you assume the behaviors are incompetent and meaningless, you miss that the student knows when he or she is not respected. If you assume competence, the student can, and is likely to, take advantage of opportunities to learn, whether you can detect it or not.

Corollary 3: Interpreting Behavior As Meaningful Communication

All behavior is a form of communication, including that which is labeled as "problem behavior." Educators who understand the underlying message can create more effective instructional and environmental supports (Donnellan, Mirenda, Mesaros, & Fassbender, 1984).

Review the quote from Eugene Marcus at the chapter opening. If your student does not speak or express his or her needs and wants in a way you understand, then you must put on your detective hat and learn the student's "behavioral language"—a substitute for the student's unspoken or inarticulate words.

A given behavior can have many interpretations, but it means something specific to the student. If a student puts her head down when everyone else is working on an assignment, does it mean boredom? Disinterest? Lack of sleep? Not feeling well? Despair? Not understanding the directions or the work? The way in which the behavior is interpreted will have a profound effect on the teacher's future reactions and decisions.

Think About This: Watch a powerful video by Amanda Baggs in which she explains the meaning of what others see as meaningless autistic behavior: http://www.youtube.com/watch?v=JnylM1hI2jc

Delete negative problem-based terms from your vocabulary such as *resistant, non-compliant, unmotivated, maladaptive, inappropriate,* and *normal.* These interpretations are in the eye of the beholder; they are not useful for thinking about meaningful support. Instead, determine what the student *is* doing, and then be descriptive. A good description must precede an interpretation of possible reasons for a behavior; a negative label is not functional. For example, consider the following questions:

- A student pushes his neighbor right before his turn to read out loud (*descriptive*) and says "no." Is the student "defiant" (*interpretive*) or standing up for himself against humiliation of showing his struggles with reading (*possible reason*)?
- A student taps and chats during a vocabulary drill (*descriptive*). Is the student "disruptive" (*interpretive*) or is the lesson so boring (or difficult to follow) that the student does something disruptive for entertainment or in order to be exiled to a more interesting environment (*possible reason*)?

Here are some other questions to ask when trying to interpret what behaviors are communicating:

- Is the student bouncing, tangled up in his chair, or otherwise moving in a distracting fashion as "a ploy for attention" (*interpretive*) or due to a physical need or urge to move due to physical discomfort (*possible reason*)?
- Is the student behavior of putting his hands over his ears "meaningless" or is it an attempt to distract herself from another physical discomfort (such as how much her skin hurts)?
- Is a student's behavior "deviant" (*interpretive*) or is it the best the student can muster given what he has learned and practiced?
- What about other motivators we know about and often name or misname?

Corollary 4: Behavior Is Related to Quality of Life

The student's quality of life both in and out of school is an important factor in behavior. Think about the context of the student's response and assess his or her passions and feelings associated with flourishing. Notice the relationship between quality of life, motivation, and behavior.

Quality of life is the ultimate intrinsic motivator. Look for indicators of self-determination and full citizenship in the classroom community. Self-determination, for the purposes of this chapter, is a student's ability and opportunity to make choices and set goals and to identify, enlist, and use resources and support to achieve them. Self-determination also has a variety of related applications ranging from curriculum and curriculum design to policy considerations (Turnbull & Turnbull, 2006). (For further information explore TASH.org.) Full citizenship precludes isolation, marginalization, and assumptions supporting exclusion. In other words, the student has a voice that is heard and has equal opportunity to act and flourish. (See Chapter 11 for more information on self-determination and self-advocacy.)

The "Circle of Courage" is an approach first used for educating youth at risk and incarcerated youth among the Lakota Nation. It is based on a wheel representing four needs/values: mastery, belonging, independence, and generosity (Brendtro, Brokenleg, & Van Bockern, 2002). I have used the acronym for these values, MBIG, as an easily remembered assessment tool to think about student needs. There may, of course, be other needs, but the following starter list of questions helps us put needs in a larger context and expand our thinking about how to support students; these motivators may overlap.

Need for experiencing mastery/competence

- Does the student get to express knowledge or share expertise in class?
- Does the student get to experience (and show, if desired) accomplishment?
- Is the student aware of the power of her or his own attention?
- Does the student have support and opportunities for success in areas of difficulty?

Need for belonging/significance

- Does the student experience positive give and take in peer relationships?
- Does the student experience giving and receiving respect and friendship?
- Does the student experience having fun with others by laughing with them?
- Does the student experience safety and skills to express feelings, wants, and needs? (Is there a need for direct instruction in how to do this?)
- Does the student know how to identify and express his or her own feelings?

Need for independence/power/autonomy

- Does the student have choices that are not forced choices?
- Does the student have opportunities to take initiative?
- Does the student have opportunities for creativity?

Need to express generosity/virtue

- Does the student get to help others or to make his or her mark?
- Does the student have opportunities for service and leadership?

The Circle of Courage values are presented as a circle, and posing related questions can help us determine where the circle is broken. It has changed the ways I teach positive behavioral support and changed how educators think about students when they are assessing the purpose of challenging behaviors during a functional behavioral analysis (FBA).

A typical FBA might find that a student is making loud noises in class to get attention, drawing notice away from the fact that he or she struggles with reading and writing (avoidance). A typical teacher response might be to brush off the need for attention and offer rewards for staying on task.

A middle school teacher benefited from thinking about a student, Matt, in terms of where the Circle of Courage was broken. Matt's intrusive and persistent attention-getting tactics yielded isolation from peers and teacher rejection. Yet he was seeking belonging. Mastery was an obvious issue as he struggled with English language arts activities, and he wanted to do the work, but he had no support at home and had alienated his teachers. He was waiting to be old enough to drop out. The special education teacher, knowing about his good qualities, invited Matt to become a teaching assistant—to take attendance, write the daily work on the board, and pass out papers. If he did the job and his class work, he could "be teacher" on Fridays to share his passion, dirt bikes. The TA and teaching jobs sparked Matt's spirit of generosity; he did better in class, and his fellow dirt bike enthusiasts discovered he was a "neat kid" and became his after-school friends. His other teachers noticed the change in his attitude in class, too.

SUPPORTING POSITIVE SOLUTIONS

Corollary 5: A Positive Solution to Unwanted Behavior Is More Than Non-Occurrence

Although it seems obvious that we want the wiggly student to be still, the impulsive talking out and clowning to stop, and the self-injurious behavior to cease, will we settle for just that if the student still hates school but "behaves" while being shut down and uninvolved or experiencing physical stress? The solution may be more likely found in engagement, social and academic skill building, and stress reduction. The solution will be found in resources the student already has and skills that he or she can learn. A colleague taught me a way to think about some of the popular but inappropriate goals educators set for students; it is called "the dead person's test." In essence, if a dead person can do it, it's not a great behavioral goal—for example, sitting still, not talking, not hitting, not throwing objects, not swearing, and so forth (Sapon-Shevin, 2012, personal communication).

Figure 9.1 provides a look at solution-focused assessment. In this figure, we can see how replacing labels and vague interpretations with observable descriptions and real motivations makes a difference in how we assess and plan supports for the student.

Figure 9.1 Assessment and Responses to Challenging Behaviors

Challenging Behavior	Problem-Focused Assessment & Response	Solution-Focused Assessment & Response (MBIG)	Differences
Matt is frequently off task, initiates unwanted conversation with classmates. Expresses interest in socializing and dirt bikes during instructional time.	Labels: LD, oppositional, lazy, and unmotivated Offer consequences and rewards, ignore him as long as he isn't too disruptive.	Mastery: Struggles with reading and writing. Belonging: Feels isolated and lonely. Independence: Has little opportunity for meaningful choices. Independence: Needs a place to shine and make his mark. Generosity: Wants to share his expertise. Focus on strengths: Good sense of humor; passionate about dirt bikes and construction; likes people; wants support. Offer and coach: Create classroom job with leadership role. Teaching opportunity: Help with academic struggles.	Problem focus limits responses to single skills & issues; solution focus opens possibilities not obviously related to the problem. Student builds meaningful relationships with peers and educators and learning. Solutions are in context. Positive school behaviors are a side effect of improved quality of life.

Activity 9.2: Solution Finding and Assessment

Using Figure 9.1 as a model, create your own example of responding to a student's challenging behaviors with solution-focused assessment.

Corollary 6: A Competence-Oriented Behavior Assessment Yields a Competence-Oriented Solution

A competence-oriented attitude during assessment predetermines our interpretation of motivation. Extrinsic rewards to attempt to solve problem behavior are typically deficit oriented and problem centered. They are a product of superficial understanding of what behavior communicates. Extrinsic rewards, such as points, prizes, and privileges, turn behaviors into commodities for sale, and more often than not, devalue the hoped-for behavior (Kohn, 1993, 1996). In addition, Kohn (1993) cites many studies where extrinsic rewards stifled creativity and productivity.

Extrinsic punishments, often misnamed "consequences," turn negative behaviors into crimes, emphasize the student-teacher power differential, and also devalue the preferred behavior. If a person does not grasp the inherent reasons to practice desired behaviors beyond that of avoiding punishment, behavior modification will be ineffective.

Meaning, autonomy, and purpose (MAP) are three universal intrinsic motivators identified by Pink (2009), who also cites examples of how rewards inhibit creativity. Pink allows that rewards can be useful for tasks where thinking and creativity are not needed, such as assembly-line work or other repetitive or simple tasks. However, intrinsic motivations apply in schools and business. Along with MBIG, MAP is a memorable assessment tool to fill gaps when considering quality of life and motivation.

Corollary 7: Race, Class, Gender, Sexual Orientation, and Culture Influence Behaviors

Educators who recognize sociocultural influences on behaviors and understand how race, class, gender and gender orientation, and culture influence behaviors are less likely to misinterpret them and more likely to engage in behavioral management strategies that are respectful. As discussed in Chapters 2 and 7, consider the implications of your own assumptions, not only about behavior but also your interpretation of behaviors not common to your own culture of origin. Be alert to concepts such as code switching, when we need to code switch as educators, and

Activity 9.3: Motivation History

Think of times when you felt motivated in these ways:

- highly motivated to do something you desired
- motivated to do something you didn't want to do

Contrast and compare the differences in feelings during and afterward:

- What made you keep going? Or want to stop?
- How can you relate your experiences to the motivations mentioned in this chapter (Circle of Courage and meaning, autonomy, and purpose)?
- Now think about the experiences of your students as you seek to learn their motivations.

when to teach the concept of code switching to students. Code switching is a sociocultural linguistic term that refers to switching between a variety of languages, dialects, or vocabulary (e.g., insider/outsider, home/work) to depending on the context (Nilep, 2006). Code-switching awareness here means we need to be aware of the settings where our customs change to fit in; we develop multiple repertoires. We not only need to acquire cultural knowledge across cultures but learn how to translate it into action. For example, we may speak differently at home and at work. As educators we may use words to express frustration or anger in private that we would never say in front of our students. We would never use our street words at work or during a ceremony or with friends in formal settings.

> [We should] advocate the need to understand how socialization patterns stemming from race, ethnicity, and socioeconomic status, among other factors, demarcate boundaries of acceptable conduct in addition to informing behavioral interpretations . . . and construct [our] practice as an extension of students' home lives with their values, traditions and practices. (Monroe, 2005, p.154)

Thus student behaviors are often inappropriately labeled as disruptive or aggressive and referred for disciplinary action. African American students have been suspended for insubordination when they thought they were being direct, for fighting when they were "messing around" or "ribbing" with real friends (Weinstein, et.al. 2004).

If a student is breaking the rules or not following directions, it may be about cultural differences rather than something going on with their inner life. Different cultures within and without the United States have different rules about showing respect, eye contact, personal space, interrupting, tone of voice, participation in discussion, disagreeing in class, asking questions, leadership styles, and so on. If you can't learn about these distinctions from a student, who may be inarticulate about these culture differences, see what you can learn from the parents and other resources. And above all, inspect your own beliefs and assumptions about proper behavior so that you'll be more likely to remember to find out what is really going on with your culturally and linguistically diverse students.

Corollary 8: If the Intervention "Doesn't Feel Right," It Probably Isn't

Think about whether you would want a proposed intervention done to you (or to a vulnerable person you love). If not, then you should not tolerate it for others. Follow their lead in devising support.

For example, I don't like being talked down to if I do not understand something, so why talk down to a young person or someone learning my language? Less-complicated communication does not mean less-competent communication. I would not want anyone to humiliate me or inflict pain, and we should not tolerate such behavior done to or among others. "Do no harm" applies universally. In terms of what I may view as positive, I might love hugs and physical contact, whereas other people may not like that at all or even find physical contact painful due to sensory issues. I may be a visual learner but my students may be tactile-kinesthetic learners, so it pays to learn the preferences and strengths of others we seek to relate to and support.

Aversive treatment is still widely used in schools and institutions (e.g., Pilkington, 2012). However, a wide range of non-aversive methods are more effective in managing dangerous or disruptive behaviors (see TASH.org). Aversive treatment such as isolation, shock, pepper spray, and restraints are not only unethical but violate the Geneva Convention against torture, and they have led to student injury and death in both public and private schools (Walsh, 2012).

Practicing perspective shifting can open your mind to ideas you might have overlooked (Smith, 2009). (See also the lesson plan on perspective in Chapter 8.) Sometimes, it makes sense to share your new understanding or your first-person statement with a student with behavioral differences. One

> **? Think About This:**
> Suppression of challenging behavior has often been practiced in education. However, even when these efforts are successful in suppressing the original behavior, other (sometimes worse) behaviors are likely to pop up in their place. Remember that challenging behaviors express students' unmet needs.

Activity 9.4: Assuming Competence

1. Make a 60-second commercial urging adults to assume competence. This should include visuals, a skit, and a jingle or song. Also, make commercials from some of the corollaries in this chapter.
2. Turn the core concepts of this chapter into a rap, a play, a cartoon, or a video; include examples.
3. Read the online essay "Presuming Competence" by Amy Sequenza, in which she eloquently shares her perspective of what it was like when people did and did not presume competence and the effects of these attitudes on her behavior (http://ollibean.com/2012/04/19/presuming-competence/?result=search).
4. Intrapersonal reflection: Recall a time when you were presumed competent and a time when you were presumed incompetent, and share the effect on you in any of the following ways: write in a journal; talk with a friend; or create a drawing, skit, song, or poem.
5. Read autobiographies by people with disabilities.
6. Perspective shifting: Walk in your students' shoes. Think about a student who is isolated or who has a challenging behavior. Write a first-person statement (around 100 words) as if you were the student saying what school (or another situation) is like for you. What are you (as the student) thinking, for example, about what you do and others' response to you? Then think about the basis for your statement and what the student is teaching you so far.

such student was pleased that he felt finally understood, and he said, "Now I like school." Others have listened to their teacher's insights about themselves and added what they would like help with (e.g., "controlling my temper"). A teacher, Ms. Hu, put herself in the shoes of a student whom teachers yelled at a lot for hitting other students, interrupting and disrupting class, and throwing tantrums. She wrote the following statement from his perspective:

I love to be the funny person in class, and I love for people to look at me. My friends don't like to be around me because I'm loud and sometimes I hit them; this makes me very sad because I don't mean to be loud and hit. My teachers yell at me a whole lot and that makes me upset. I don't mean to make them mad; I just can't help it. I love music! I sing my favorite songs all day, and it makes me happy. I can do my work easier if I sing. I really wish my teachers would let me play with my cars instead of doing my writing; I really don't like writing. Maybe, if I throw myself on the floor and make a lot of noise, my teachers won't make me do my writing work. Writing is so hard! (Sam, according to his kindergarten teacher, Ms. Hu)

Ms. Hu said that when she read this statement to Sam, he felt understood and hugged her. She felt he was misunderstood, and his needs for attention and understanding and belonging were central. He responded to having classroom jobs, participating in class community-builders (Sapon-Shevin, 2010), and teaching the other kids weekly lessons on making food or crafts or about animals. They loved his efforts and praised him for his knowledge. Ms. Hu also arranged for other supports and stress-reduction lessons. The result was an increase in Sam's feeling of belonging as he felt safer in class and his expression of generosity generated friendships and compliments.

We have been exploring aspects of the principle that behavior is meaningful communication. Use the corollaries and suggestions to bridge the gap when your interpretation of the behavior seems to differ from what it means to the student. A student with behavior challenges may be inarticulate, but you must consult the student first—and if you still don't know what is going on, put on your detective hat, get help, and return to this chapter and the others for your box of tools. The Related Resources (www.tcpress.com) provide you with supplements to the activities as well as resources created by people with significant disabilities and others that will give you insights into the diverse behaviors and motivations of people we encounter.

GROUND TRUTH: THE PRACTITIONER'S VOICE

Pam Nester
Teacher—Special Education/Inclusion, Pine Bush, New York

Marcus was a student who had transferred mid-year to our urban school in upstate New York. The principal had called me into the office to "warn" me about the new student I was receiving, whose aggressive and disruptive behavior had caused him to be expelled from a Bronx public school. I saw very quickly from the negative reactions of my students that walking in someone else's shoes is not something that is necessarily an innate behavior. The very next day I arranged to have Marcus out of the classroom. I explained to my students about walking in someone else's shoes and had them write a first-person statement about Marcus. (This also was an excellent ELA lesson for my students!)

When Marcus returned to the classroom, we shared some of the writing samples with him. Marcus cried, and tried to hide it. He told us that he wanted friends, and to fit in, but he had difficulty sitting and tended to get in trouble "all the time." He said he had tried to make it all a joke so that everyone would laugh and like him anyway. Together, the class made a plan for Marcus, and whenever he would start to act out one of the students would make the statement, "Marcus, when you ......, I can't get my work done. What other choice can you make?" Marcus had shared that he loved to dance hip-hop. At the end of every successful week, he would give the class a dance lesson or demonstration. You truly have never seen anything until you've seen Marcus do the "Harlem Shake"!

I ran into Marcus a few months ago when he spotted me at an intersection. He told me he had gone through a very rough time, had gotten mixed up with the wrong people, and had gotten into drugs and dropped out of school. He explained that my whole class had remained friends all through high school and when he dropped out they came and found him. They told him to think, "What would Ms. Nester do?" every time he was tempted, and then to reach out to one of them instead.

Using extrinsic motivation such as reward systems takes less time and effort on our part. Doing things the right way and assuming competence takes more effort and more of an investment in ourselves. This experience erased any lingering doubts I may have had about this approach.

REFERENCES

Brendtro, L., Brokenleg, M., & Van Bockern, S. (2002). *Reclaiming youth at risk: Our hope for the future* (2nd ed.). Bloomington, IN: Solution Tree Press.

Donnellan, A. M. (1984). The criterion of the least dangerous assumption. *Behavioral Disorders, 9*(2), 141–150.

Donnellan, A. M., Mirenda, P. L., Mesaros, R. A., & Fassbender, L. L. (1984). Analyzing the communicative functions of aberrant behavior. *Journal of the Association for Persons with Severe Handicaps, 3*, 201-212.

Kliewer, C., & Biklen, D. (2001). School's not really a place for reading: A research synthesis of the literate lives of students with severe disabilities. *Journal of The Association for People with Severe Handicaps, 26*(1), 1–12.

Kohn, A. (1993). *Punished by rewards: The trouble with gold stars, incentive plans, A's, praise, and other bribes.* New York: Houghton Mifflin.

Kohn, A. (1996). *Beyond discipline: From compliance to community.* Alexandria, VA: Association for Supervision & Curriculum Development.

Monroe, C. R. (2005). The cultural context of 'disruptive behaviour': an overview of research considerations for school educators. *Improving Schools, 8*(2), 153–159.

Nilep, C. (2006). "Code switching" in sociocultural linguistics. *Colorado Research in Linguistics, 19*, 1–22.

Pilkington, E. (2012). UN calls for investigation of US school's shock treatments of autistic children. *The Guardian.* Retrieved fromhttp://www.guardian.co.uk/society/2012/jun/02/un-investigation-shock-treatments-autism

Pink, D. H. (2009). *Drive: The surprising truth about what motivates us.* New York: Riverhead Press.

Sapon-Shevin, M. (2010). *Because we can change the world: A practical guide to building cooperative, inclusive communities* (2nd ed.). Thousand Oaks, CA: Corwin.

Smith, R. M. (1999). Academic engagement of students with significant disabilities and educators' perceptions of competence. *The Professional Educator, 22*(1), 17–31.

Smith, R. M. (2009). Fostering belonging when and where it counts: Let students shine. *TASH Connections, 35*(1), 26–29.

Turnbull, A. P., & Turnbull, R. (2006). Self-determination: Is a rose by any other name still a rose? *Research and Practice for Persons with Severe Disabilities, 31*(1), 1–6.

Walsh, M. (2012, February 21) Justices decline school district's appeal in 'isolation room' case. *Education Week.* Retrieved from http://blogs.edweek.org/edweek/school_law/2012/02/justices_decline_school_distri.html

Weinstein, C. S., Tomlinson-Clarke, S., & Curran, M. (2004). Towards a conception of culturally responsive classroom management. *Journal of Teacher Education, 55*(1), 25–38.

CHAPTER 10

We Are What We Assess: How Schools Construct and Shape Identity and Performance

Elizabeth B. Kozleski
Laura Atkinson

Key Principle 10: *Assessment methods and results are impacted by the expectations and level of respect we have for students. Unbiased and culturally sensitive processes enhance and assist in identifying students' strengths along with their needs.*

Imagine a richly detailed picture with a bold and slightly menacing snake in the foreground, rows of brightly colored flowers, small houses in the distance, and a deep blue sky. This was the picture that Nathan painted as a 7-year-old in his first quarter of 1st grade. Nathan had already been noticed, not for his extraordinary drawing skills but for his problematic behavior and academic performance in kindergarten. Nathan began his elementary career with his kindergarten teacher referring him to special education. The kindergarten teacher based her decision to evaluate Nathan for special education on his preschool experience. Nathan's preschool teacher provided documentation that substantiated her concerns about him. She provided work examples that bolstered her claim that Nathan was developmentally delayed. In response, the kindergarten teacher initiated testing for Nathan. After months of assessment, multidisciplinary meetings, and data analysis, Nathan qualified for special education services. The team determined that Nathan had a specific learning disability and behavioral issues. Nathan spent his kindergarten year splitting his time between general and special education classrooms.

When I (Laura) was preparing my 1st-grade classroom for the start of a new year, I reviewed my class roster and noticed that Nathan was on my list. I knew of Nathan since his kindergarten teacher had warned the 1st-grade team about him and encouraged us to set up a Behavior Intervention Plan (BIP) on the first day. She also told us that Nathan's academic performance was very low. It was a month into Nathan's 1st-grade year when students received a project to complete during literature circle time. The students had to create a picture, choosing from a variety of material, and then share their creation with the group and tell a story about it. Nathan was determined to finish his painting, so he worked on it while the rest of the class had center time. When it was time to share our pictures and stories, Nathan raised his hand and asked if he could go first. The teaching assistant that worked with Nathan in the general education classroom asked him if he wanted her to stand by him in the front of class as he presented. Nathan replied, "No." When Nathan stood up and showed the class his picture, the students were captivated—just as I was. One student yelled out, "Wow! How did he learn how to draw like that?" As Nathan was telling the story of his picture, the whole class was mesmerized and did not say a word. Nathan was articulate and animated when he started talking about the snake. I was so impressed with Nathan's presentation that I saved

> **Think About This:** If you are a teacher in the upper grades, what analogies can you draw between this example and teaching older students?

his picture to share with the school staff. Once I shared Nathan's work with his IEP team, most of the team members were amazed that Nathan created such a beautiful piece of art. The special education teacher said that Nathan had never expressed interest in art to her. Nathan's former kindergarten teacher said that Nathan hadn't spent much time at the art center because he was always finishing his assignments at his seat, so he didn't have the free time to go to the centers.

HOW DIFFERENCES INFLUENCE ASSESSMENT

This story underscores so many of the misconceptions and misperceptions about teaching and learning in classrooms with a range of diverse learners. What do we mean when we talk about diversity? As Martha Minow (1990) has so elegantly reminded us, when we use notions like *diverse* or *different*, they require naming what the sameness is that we are comparing difference to. Who gets to name what the *normal* or *like us* space is? If we were in Mumbai, India; Peoria, Kansas; or Biloxi, Mississippi, diverse and different would depend on whether we were talking about language, religion, skin color, ethnicity, cultural histories, abilities, and practices. So when educators and parents talk about diverse learners, they need to be conscious of how difference is being named and by whom. Particularly, when educators are responsible for assessing students, they must be conscious of their own notions of what normal is. Many of the assessments that educators use also embed particular notions of normal. This chapter helps to unpack some of the issues that surround assessment and reminds us that the practice of assessment carries a great deal of responsibility to ensure that children are not misidentified or misunderstood because of the personal histories of educators and the institutional contexts in which they practice.

Nathan's cultural history and that of his family may be very different from that of his classroom teacher. So, how the person with institutional authority (probably his teacher) perceived him in his kindergarten class might easily say as much about the cultural and intellectual history of the teacher and the contexts and experiences she has had as it does about Nathan. Both Nathan and his teachers live in a social context in the United States that has deeply embedded notions of what and who counts in its public institutions and communities. Thus, labels of "difficult to teach," interventions that require specific adult-driven activities, and suspicions about what a student is able to do can plague students and families.

Students, particularly young ones, have no way of knowing whether what happens to them in school is useful or not for their own learning. Rarely do they have the ability to explain to their parents what is happening to them. Therefore, families have to rely on adult communication to catch the nuances of classroom activity. If families assume that schools are making decisions in their children's best interest without knowing that they need to question and get involved, then many subtle decisions can be made that impact how children are perceived. Let's begin this chapter by reminding ourselves of the importance of Key Principles 3 and 4 as they connect to how and why we assess in classrooms and what we need to be mindful of in how we understand and interpret what is assessed (see Figure 10.1)

Key Principle 3 reminds us that differences are part of each of our identities (see Chapter 3). We have multiple identities that are formed and reformed by the experiences and responses that we encounter in our everyday lives. Students integrate broader community values in how they think about themselves. So when they find themselves in a situation in which they are expected to perform and where an adult is providing evaluative feedback such as, "Yes, that's right!" or "Good job!," they already have an internalized notion of themselves as a learner. Claude Steele and his colleagues (2004) have demonstrated how these internalized notions, called "stereotype threat," impede and intrude in children's performances, putting students who belong to historically marginalized groups, such as African Americans, children with dis/abilities, and English learners,

Figure 10.1. Key Principles 3 and 4

3. Traditionally marginalized differences (including but not limited to disabilities, cultural/linguistic/racial background, gender, sexual orientation, and class) are best understood and responded to within a broader construct of diversity; each of us has multiple identities that can be represented or viewed in different ways.
4. Marginalized differences are socially constructed; how we respond to individual differences is impacted by factors such as history, culture/geography, race, gender, and socioeconomic status.

---

at risk in assessment situations. They often perform based on what they think they are supposed to be capable of accomplishing, rather than what they are able to do.

Key Principle 4 (see Chapter 4) reminds us that our everyday actions are mediated by the communities that we are part of. Thus, children bring their social histories and experiences with them into a schooling context that has institutional histories. Both of these contexts are in play as children and educators build their own community that is influenced and mediated by invisible histories. Learning is a collective production in which individual capacities are influenced, buffeted, and mediated by the opportunities, actions, and responses of the communities in which learners find themselves. Accomplishment is a product of this sociocultural space. When we assess, our interpretations of performance must be tempered by this notion of learning as a sociocultural phenomenon. This important idea frees educators to focus on the design, supports, and access to learning, instead of trying to fix students.

FOUR DISCOURSES OF ASSESSMENT

Four discourses are interwoven in this chapter to uncover and explore the ways in which assessment practices serve to catalog and disadvantage specific groups of students: the discourses of power, fairness, difference, and measurement. Together these discourses frame the ways that learners experience and access opportunities to learn, grow, and develop in formal and informal learning settings.

The Discourse of Power

Despite Fullan's (1997) observations that all education reforms will fail until educators, parents, and students are meaningfully engaged, active partners in school improvement efforts, issues of power, privilege,

Activity 10.1: The Fairness Map

What do power, fairness, difference, and measurement have to do with what educators do in the classroom?

Make some notes as you continue reading.

Organize the notes into "buckets" that each represent one of these four big ideas.

Consider what you can do in the classroom to address power, fairness, difference, and measurement.

standards, equity, access, and participation remain at the margins of education discourse. "Scientifically based research" (SBR) is mentioned well over 100 times in current education legislation. SBR is defined as including experimental or quasi-experimental studies, with a preference for randomized controlled trials (No Child Left Behind, 2002). The focus on science and particular kinds of methodologies serves notice that other, more practice-informed ways of knowing and understanding may not be as valued in decision-making processes. This is concerning, since U.S. schools struggle to educate new generations of students who bring with them the accumulated histories of far-flung cultures (the global diaspora), marginalized cultures that exist at the fringes of schooling and local communities (American Indian cultures), and the cultures of Latino/a and Black Americans that are systematically caricatured in the media and in texts like *A Framework for Understanding Poverty* (Payne, 1998, 2005).

For educators who want to innovate and personalize their instruction to meet students' needs, documenting student work and connecting outcomes like end-of-unit performances with specific kinds of teaching design is important. Being careful to connect assessments that you make of your students' skills to the choice of instructional and feedback processes will go a long way to ensuring that your classroom practices meet the standards that your district and school are being held to (see Activity 10.2).

Unfortunately, by standardizing what is to be tested, state departments of education have transferred the power for determining what is to be learned from local and contextualized practice to distal authority that has the consequence of dis-empowering practitioners. It also makes alternative perspectives difficult to develop and engage since numbers and statistics become more important than the interpretation of performance by skilled educators. Nathan's teachers were tricked by this very thing. They originally saw Nathan through his poor performance on standardized assessments. His behavior was linked to the failure that he constantly experienced in school. Once they were able to see what he was capable

Activity 10.2: Matching Student Understanding and Feedback Formats

You notice that some students are experiencing difficulty using paraphrasing to remember core information from their readings on the American President Abraham Lincoln. You work separately in a power-strategy session to break down the steps for paraphrasing (read; ask questions to identify the main idea and details; paraphrase, putting the ideas into your own words). Students learn to paraphrase sentence by sentence, or paragraph by paragraph. They practice the strategy daily until they can apply the skill across several different texts. You provide feedback to improve their paraphrasing by

1. mimicking students' incorrect paraphrases;
2. telling students when their paraphrases are incorrect; or
3. paraphrasing their mistakes and asking peers to rephrase main ideas.

Select one of these three options and explain your choice.

of producing, they began to plot a curriculum experience that capitalized on his strengths, using his interest in and artistic abilities to explore topics that interested him but expanded his understanding of the world around him. Nathan began to blossom once he had the opportunity to show what he could do. He was able to try more difficult tasks and ask for help when he needed it.

> **Think About This:** State-mandated, high-stakes, standardized testing is a powerful force in today's educational culture. But teachers need not relinquish control over their informal assessments and, perhaps most important, their own interactions with students.

Imagine what would have happened if educators had begun by asking Nathan what he liked to do and then asking him to show them what he could do. They could have explored both his learning strengths and abilities as well as understood how he coped with risk and mistakes. That would have helped them develop a learning plan that focused on his strengths but also expanded the kinds of learning challenges that Nathan would be willing to tackle.

The Discourse of Fairness

Fairness in testing begins with the notion of whether opportunities to learn the concepts, language, and relationships that form the constructs to be assessed on a test have been made available. Fair in this sense means that assessments measure what individuals have experienced. Yet, some assessments are meant to filter who can have access to particular kinds of learning experiences. For instance, many schools allow only students who have already had access to foundational information to participate in an advanced placement course. But how fair is that when only some students have had those advantages while other students, year after year, fail to qualify because they did not attend schools where the content was readily accessible? What are the conditions of fairness? For students who get saddled with disability labels, access to general education content is often problematic because assumptions are made about

> **Think About This**: For a graphic enactment of privilege (and unfairness), see this activity on the Level Playing Field: https://people.creighton.edu/~idc24708/Genes/Diversity/Privilege%20Exercise.htm

how much they can learn and what they should learn based on predictions of what their perceived disability means. This chapter questions the fairness of the pathways through the educational institution, the cultural values that are embedded within schooling, and the degree to which assimilation is forced through valuing some ways of knowing over others, some ways of inquiry over others, and some ways of expression over others. Originally Nathan's schooling experience was marred by a lack of fairness. Instead of finding out what Nathan could do, he was asked to conform to particular ways of knowing that matched what he would be tested on; then, he was seen as coming up short rather than seeing that the system failed to ask the right questions.

The Discourse of Difference

Cole and Bruner (1972) first introduced the notion of difference as a way of digging out from under notions of deficit thinking in which the learning challenges faced by children in schools were thought to reside within the child, home life, or family. This notion of within-child deficits permeates much of what passes as preventive or intervention practice in schools. That is, children who fall behind the typical curricula are given boosters to help them catch up to their peers. Little thought is given to critiquing what is embedded within the curriculum that values some ways of thinking and knowing over others. For example, students who produce three writing assignments that meet the standards may be rewarded over the student who spends time on a single burst of inspiration and creativity. The structures of schooling themselves that are organized around standardized developmental growth, access to resources distributed on the basis of demonstrated ability, and specific kinds of pedagogies favor students whose cultural practices match the cultural nature of schooling in the United States. The discourse of difference urges us to consider the idea of difference as a comparative concept in which what is considered normal must also be contested as communities and social contexts evolve.

The Discourse of Measurement

Underlying all forms of assessment is that specific instruments can capture *accurate* snapshots of a learner in progress and tie these snapshots to student capacity, classroom curriculum, pedagogy, teacher efficacy, and school practices, depending on the tool and the intended unit of analysis. Gauging performance against sets of benchmarks has value for developing pathways into the future. Yet the assessment industry has torpedoed this notion of the inextricable connection between learning and assessing by focusing on static, knowledge-based, culturally limited forms of testing what children know and can do. The outcomes of these assessments are used to distinguish good and bad teaching, effective and ineffective schools and districts. Lost is the notion that assessment should help guide how the conditions for learning are organized and contextualized to help learners develop. Nasir, Rosebery, Warren, and Lee (2006) describe how children learn outside of school. The authors provide an example of children learning to play dominoes. This process involves learning, assessment, and feedback in a nonlinear, sometimes overlapping manner; more important, the assessment that occurs is not used to label kids' ability. In this chapter we explore the discourse of measurement from a sociocultural perspective to help you consider the role and place of assessment in a comprehensive and responsive educational system.

Summary

Together the discourses of power, fairness, difference, and measurement offer insight into the intractable nature of disproportionality in schools where race, class, gender, and ability are used to sort and categorize students. For the system to move forward we need a *discourse of equity*. Thus, educators might ask themselves and their colleagues about the function of the kinds of assessments that their students take to demonstrate what they've learned at the end of each year. Questioning assessment practices and looking at the outcomes of decisions made through assessment are critical. Educators may discover, in the process, that a disproportionate number of students of color or students who are English learners are being identified as having learning problems. If this is the case, examine where the problem solving process begins. Ensure that teachers and school leaders examine their curricula and instructional designs to make changes that create ramps of support into a redesigned curricula that is relevant and connected to the contexts of the students.

STRUCTURE AND PURPOSES OF ASSESSMENT

Assessment may be defined as any systematic method of obtaining evidence from tests, examinations, questionnaires, surveys, and collateral sources in order to draw inferences about characteristics of people, objects, or programs for a specific purpose. A central function of assessment for educators is to help them understand who learners are, what resources they and their families bring to the process of learning, and how educators might begin to design environments that support student learning. So many factors impact how students engage what is to be learned, how they persist in learning over time, and how much of what they experience in schools becomes part of their continually changing understanding of the world around them and their space in it. To start with, there was a time in which knowledge was considered to be something that people had or they didn't have. For instance, a student might know how to combine two quantities and have a way to represent the new combined quantity. They might be able to say that if Jane and Dick each brought two apples to the picnic, they would have four apples all together. That way of thinking about knowledge as a process of accumulating facts is still present in schools and represents some of the constructs that undergird test development. Educators need to understand that tests are flawed in a number of ways that make the use of test scores problematic as a key source of evidence for educational decision making.

From Testing to Assessment

Testing is a way of finding out what comprises a student's accumulated knowledge in particular areas. It often assumes that individuals have knowledge that is distinct from the contexts in which it might be used and the social settings in which the knowledge is produced. You may have taken an exam as you finished high school in the United States called the Scholastic Aptitude Test (SAT) or an Advanced Placement Test in a particular subject or the American College Test (ACT). All these tests are designed to determine knowledge accumulated across various disciplines like English, math, and social studies. In some cases, they are also designed to test procedural knowledge like how to go about designing a science experiment or conditional knowledge that requires making fine-grained distinctions between procedures and knowledge arenas to choose the best solution to a problem. These are very brief descriptions of tests that have been carefully designed over long periods of time and continually evaluated and improved. The important point for this discussion is that these tests provide summative accounts, based on particular assumptions, of what students getting ready to go to college know and are able to do academically. But many students do poorly on these exams and still perform well in college and beyond because the tests lack the capacity to account for individual personal and language histories, and fail to account for individual habits of learning and performance. Yet, done well, an assessment can help educators make informed design decisions about how to help a student learn.

Nathan's story at the beginning of this chapter offers an important illustration of this point. Nathan's teachers found a way to tap into his creativity and imagination to gain insight into how Nathan understands the world. What Nathan created offered a window through which to view his abilities. What turned the drawing into an assessment was the careful interpretation of what the drawing represented. It is this interpretation in which educators bring their knowledge of development, learning, and context into play that produces an assessment that can be used in finely detailed designs for learning.

While testing is one way that students are assessed, it is only one part of a broad, comprehensive, and continuous process. And as educational research expands, the usefulness of grades as a way of measuring student progress is increasingly called into question. But, like many of the activities that are played out in schools on a regular basis, grading is part of an institutional history in which students are repeatedly sorted and categorized. Because this way of cataloging which students perform well on particular kinds of testing has been part of the way that families were told how well their students were doing in school, families, as well as school personnel, have held

> **Think About This**: Be alert to systems of differentiation (like Response to Intervention) that sound like they are meeting students' individual needs but can actually function as tracking systems and lead to the re-institutionalization of more segregated educational environments for certain students.

onto grading well beyond its usefulness as a way of assessing how well the design of learning works for individual students.

Notice the switch in the last paragraph from what students know to how well the design of learning meets the needs of learners. This underlying principle that *schools* and *teachers* in *collaboration* with families, school districts, and the policies that govern them are responsible for designing learning environments that work for students is a major shift in how we understand the work of teachers and other school practitioners. This shift is not complete in many schools. Much of what passes as acceptable practice in our accountability system is still grounded in sorting and classifying. As a school practitioner yourself, you will want to be mindful of the transformations in research, scholarship, and many practice environments that have occurred, while understanding that these transformations are still under way in many other places.

A Shared Understanding of Assessment Concepts and Practices

As a classroom teacher, you'll be engaged in assessment throughout the school year. This section offers an overview of the classroom assessment landscape covering both formal and informal assessment. Many schools are using a tiered system for thinking about teaching and learning in the social, emotional, physical, linguistic, and academic arenas. At the foundational level, there is a core curriculum that students are expected to gain mastery over. Most students in schools fall into this foundational level in which they are able to progress, develop skills and understanding, and over time, build a repertoire of tools for learning and developing. Every school will have a small number of students who need extra support in a particular area to boost their skills. Students may need some specialized support to ensure that they get a handle on how to express their emotions, deal with grief, understand math concepts, develop a stronger set of reading strategies, or some other kind of specialized support. Another very small group of students may need more sustained support throughout their day to help them navigate the demands of learning in the complex social and academic settings of school. How students are assessed and what the assessments accomplish vary among these three tiers of support. Students in multi-tiered systems of support participate in what might be called a *universal screening process* to understand what skills, knowledge, and learning approaches they bring to school. Ongoing assessment of progress in the curriculum helps educators to fine-tune their teaching approaches. In the next section, we explore approaches to monitoring student progress through a number of assessment processes.

CLASSROOM ASSESSMENT FOR STUDENT PROGRESS

Formal assessments have data drawn from tests referred to as standardized measures. These measures have been tested before on students and have statistics that support conclusions such as the student is reading below average for his or her age. The data are mathematically computed and summarized. Scores such as percentiles, stanines, or standard scores are most commonly derived from this type of assessment.

Informal assessments are not data driven but rather content and per-formance driven. For example, running records are informal assessments because they indicate how well a student is reading a specific book. Scores such as 10 correct out of 15, percentage of words read correctly, and most rubric scores are obtained from this type of assessment.

Formal or standardized measures should be used to assess overall achievement, to compare a student's performance with others at their age or grade, or to identify comparable strengths and weaknesses with peers. Informal assessments, sometimes referred to as criterion-referenced measures or performance-based measures, should be used to inform instruction.

Assessment for Learning

What educators need to know is how their students learn. When they know this, they can alter the pace of introducing material, choose how to introduce new material, and gauge how much information to provide before letting the students practice working with new concepts, vocabu-lary, and ways of thinking or problem solving. When designing learning is the focus of assessment rather than sorting and categorizing students, it changes how educators think about what and when to assess. For instance, Nathan's teachers might begin introducing a new book by drawing a pic-ture in which they reveal, as they draw, increasingly detailed information about the chief protagonists of the story. By capturing Nathan's attention through drawing, they acknowledge his learning space, but they also help all the students engage with the characters in the new story. This kind of preparation helps students learn to predict and anticipate what they might encounter when they read. The teacher might use this time to intro-duce unusual vocabulary, connect students with the context in which the story is set, and help them read for meaning and understanding. Using drawing is a strategic move for Nathan, but the strategies the teacher uses scaffold all the students.

As you design learning in each of the content areas you are respon-sible for, remember to design for the end in mind. Think about what you want students to be able to do, to accomplish, and how they will demon-strate what they have learned. These outcomes will help guide you as you plan a unit of study. And they will guide you to think about what you need to know about your students and what you might assess to better design the learning process.

You will want to think about what social arrangements in the class will support how the students work together to master the content and their learning strategies. After all, learning is a social process in which stu-dents learn as much from one another's planning, working, and assessing what they've accomplished as they do from what the teacher does. Understanding how your students handle working alongside one another and knowing the skills they need to observe, question, and provide feedback are critical for a successful, actively engaged class. This area is also important to assess.

Observation will be an important part of what you do in the classroom; particularly notice the following:

- Who is able to pause and take someone else's perspective?
- Who wants to be the center of the attention? Why?
- What strategies do the students need to develop to alter their approaches to learning together?

These questions will need continual reflection as you try to organize processes for how students work together.

Performance Assessment

Performance assessment is based on the notion that educators have a more complete understanding of how students understand a problem, the approach to solving it, and the elements of a polished performance when what they are asked to demonstrate is based on an authentic performance of a skill. So, giving a reading of a well-known poem that involves both knowing the words, phrases, and sentences, as well as how to pronounce them and their meaning, so that a public reading conveys the emotion and intent of the poet is an example of a performance. Being given a problem to solve such as how to build a model of a swing set can use what a student or a team of students understands about geometry and physics. These kinds of performance assessment tap into deep-level knowledge that answering multiple-choice items on a written test does not. History, science, language arts, and mathematics can all be assessed using performance assessment. A compilation of this kind of assessment through video and audio recordings, as well as other artifacts of performances, can be assembled into a portfolio. Students can use their portfolios to tell the story of their learning progress through a curriculum.

Progress Monitoring Through Dynamic and Authentic Assessment

Students travel a learning path as they progress through units of study. Educators need to track how students are progressing to determine what supports they may need to provide to ensure that robust learning occurs. Checking daily with students to find out what they are learning and what they need to work on next is a good practice because it helps students to develop their own internal processes to monitor their work. Many units of study require an amalgam of learning processes. Some parts are technical. For instance, to paint with acrylics requires a different kind of brush, pressure on the canvas, and paint stroke. These are technical skills associated with the kind of paint that the painter uses. Reading an author like Judy Blume requires a different pace and attention to language than reading Charles Dickens. Judy Blume writes about contemporary issues that preteens face in language that mirrors the experiences of White middle-class girls in the United States. Charles Dickens used the language of 19th-century England when he wrote *Great Expectations*. Reading about Pip and Miss Havisham requires significant cultural translation even for proficient readers. In both cases, students need to develop and use a set of technical reading skills that enable them to slow down or speed up to make meaning, understand metaphors, and piece together the story that is being told and its symbolic significance. Progress monitoring means that educators are paying attention to how students are developing the technical skills to master a particular task or unit of study.

Similarly, reading, painting, experimenting, and solving math problems requires attention to the context of what students are being asked to do as well as to the critical dimensions. Learning where and when to apply particular skills and understanding who is benefiting from what is being learned and why are also parts of the learning space. All of these require that educators attend to how and what students are learning along the way. It is in progress monitoring that teachers receive the feedback they need to modify, adapt, and transform what they have designed to better support their students' learning.

To be effective at progress monitoring, educators need to ensure that they have carefully planned their units of study:

1. Know what is to be accomplished at the end;
2. Identify the curricular outcomes including the technical, contextual, and critical;
3. List the skills that will need to be learned to meet the outcomes;
4. Construct the tasks that students will perform to demonstrate their understanding and learning;
5. Know what skills must be displayed through performance.

This approach to the assessment of learning is termed *formative*. It helps form educators' understandings of who their students are and how they can best support their learning. Careful attention to formative assessment produces a richly layered learning environment in classrooms in which the learning needs of all students are accounted for in the way that material and concepts are introduced and supported.

Activity 10.3: Dynamic Assessment in the Classroom

Keisha Tyson is a 6th-grade teacher in an urban city school system with 128 elementary schools K–6. She's been a 6th-grade teacher for 7 years. This year she has 28 6th-graders, including 10 students on Individual Education Plans (IEPs). Of the students on IEPs, three of them have significant disabilities that include labels of autism, intellectual, and sensory impairments. The 6th-graders stay with Ms. Tyson for all their core subjects: reading, math, social studies, and science.

Ms. Tyson is planning a lesson on classes of animals that will include mammals, birds, fish, reptiles, and amphibians. Students will categorize, classify, and record information about each class of animal. Students will learn to identity animals by the classes that they belong to and be able to identify characteristics and animals in each class by the end of the unit.

They will each pick a profession that will be informed by this information. Students will be responsible for learning how to classify and sort animals. Teams of four students will each receive a shoebox of animals, a memo detailing their job, and a calendar for determining how they will break the task down into parts so that it can be accomplished by the due date.

Design the progress monitoring system for this unit. How will you, as the teacher, understand how each student is progressing in this task?

Family Involvement in Assessment

Families are a vital source of information about how students are performing outside of school. Families can help school professionals translate students' behaviors so that the meaning behind patterns of behavior can be uncovered. Involving parents and students in understanding student progress and determining what is to be learned is an important element in developing lifelong learners. Students can lead their own family conferences in which parents and educators become the audience for what a student knows and determining the way forward. If there is cause to refer a student for special testing, families must be notified and give their permission before any formal data gathering or testing can occur.

Reliable and Valid Measurement

Educators must ensure that the tools used for assessment are reliable and valid. That means that even for teacher-made assessments that use a rubric to describe what the teacher is measuring, care must be taken that the rubric provides a consistent measure across student work. In addition, assessments, both formal and informal, must measure what the test is designed to test. If a test is created to measure math knowledge, it must provide that information for every learner, not change its purpose depending on the student. Think about an English learner taking a math test. If the reading level on the test is demanding, it may be testing the student's knowledge of the language, not knowledge of mathematics. Be sure to use assessments with Anne Donnellan's (1984) principle of the least dangerous assumption in mind: Interpretations of evidence should be made with the intent to cause the least danger to the student.

Modification of Testing Practices

Some students may be able to demonstrate their grasp of content and procedural knowledge more effectively when certain kinds of accommodations are made. For instance, English learners may need a glossary that explains specific words on a test. Recent research suggests that translating text items verbatim from English into the student's language of origin does not seem to improve student performance when students have been taught the subject area in English (Abedi, Hofstetter, & Lord, 2004). It is the language of instruction that seems most relevant, not the student's first language. English reading proficiency and length of time in the United States seem to affect how students perform in the language of instruction as well. When test items are designed to minimize the use of low-frequency vocabulary and complex language structures that are not related to content knowledge being assessed, students who are English learners seem to do well and English-proficient students are not affected. All students could benefit from a content-specific glossary that defines terms to ensure that students understand what is being asked.

CONCLUSION

Consider how asessment impacts how you think about instructional design in your classroom. Pay attention to the kinds of questions and expectations that are embedded in assessments that you are asked to give. Covert assumptions about what children should know at particular stages in their lives are embedded within much of our assessment tools. More devastating, children whose performance suffers because of the culture and context of their lives may be seen as at risk. Students whose approaches to learning require different sets of scaffolds and feedback can also be viewed as deficient, based on standardized notions of what counts as learning. Remember Nathan's story. It should remind you to be vigilant about how difference is conceptualized and embedded into the notion of assessment. How you approach the matter of measuring and judging human performance has consequences for your students and their families. Be mindful of the ways in which the interpretation of assessment data can inform your work, hone your skills, and improve your students' outcomes. This chapter helps to unpack some of the issues that surround assessment and reminds us that the practice of assessment carries a great deal of responsibility to ensure that children are not misidentified or misunderstood because of the differences between their personal life histories and those of educators and the institutional contexts in which they practice.

ACKNOWLEDGMENT

The authors acknowledge the support of the Urban Professional Learning Schools Initiative under the Office of Special Education Program grant #H325T070009. Funding agency endorsement of the ideas expressed in this manuscript should not be inferred.

GROUND TRUTH: THE PRACTITIONER'S VOICE

Cean R. Colcord
Special Education Teacher, Phoenix, Arizona

I have worked with many Nathans in my years as a special educator. I agree with the chapter authors that it is important to get to know students individually. For this reason, I use baseline, authentic, and informal assessments to check, monitor, and record the progress of each of my students. Assessing each child in a fair and equitable manner helps me and other teachers design individualized lessons that improve outcomes for all students.

By finding out our students' interests, we, as teachers, can craft lessons that engage and integrate our students' funds of knowledge into our daily classroom practices. In addition to individual student interviews, I meet with my students' families several times a year to review their children's progress both inside and outside of the classroom. Working as a team, we share information with one another to improve school success.

In addition to getting to know our students and their families, it is also important that our assessments are designed based on what we are teaching our students in the classroom. In my state, all 3rd-grade students are required to take the statewide standardized reading test that measures their vocabulary and reading comprehension ability. On one such test, there was a question about an aardvark. Although our class had studied and learned about aardvarks over the course of the year, our textbook did not refer to this animal as an aardvark, but instead referred to it as an anteater. Therefore, few of the students were prepared to answer the questions that followed the short story about aardvarks because they had never heard of an aardvark and many had difficulty even pronouncing the word. Some of the students were able to determine that the story was about an anteater after reading through the text about the animal's diet and habitat. Unfortunately, only a few made this connection. Most were unable to make the connection between the school's curriculum and curriculum selected by the company hired to create the assessment. The students got caught in the middle, and their learning accomplishments took second place to the knowledge that was valued on the test.

REFERENCES

Abedi, J., Hofstetter, C. H., & Lord, C. (2004). Assessment accommodations for English language learners: Implications for policy-based empirical research. *Review of Educational Research, 74*, 1–28.

Cole, M., & Bruner, J. S. (1972). Preliminaries to a theory of cultural differences. In I. J. Gordon (Ed.), *Early childhood education: Yearbook of the National Society for the Study of Education*, (Vol. 71, pt. 2, pp. 161–179). Chicago, IL: University of Chicago Press.

Donnellan, A. M. (1984). The criterion of the least dangerous assumption. *Behavior Disorders, 9*, 141–150.

Fullan, M. (1997). *The challenge of school change: A collection of articles.* Arlington, Heights, IL: IRI/Skylight Training and Publishing.

Minow, M. (1990). *Making all the difference: Inclusion, exclusion, and American law.* Ithaca, NY: Cornell University Press.

Nasir, N., Rosebery, A., Warren, B., & Lee., C. (2006). Learning as a cultural process: Achieving equity through diversity. In R. K. Sawyer (Ed.), *Cambridge handbook of the learning sciences* (pp. 489–504). Cambridge, England: Cambridge University Press.

No Child Left Behind Act of 2001, Pub. L. No. 107-110, 115 Stat. 14.

Payne, R. K. (1998/2005). *A framework for understanding poverty* (4th ed.). Highlands, TX: RFT Publishing.

Steele, C., Perry, T., & Hilliard, A., III (2004). *Young, gifted, and Black: Promoting high achievement among African American students.* Boston: Beacon Press.

CHAPTER 11

Fostering Self-Determination Through Culturally Responsive Teaching

JoDell R. Heroux
Susan J. Peters
Maryl A. Randel

Key Principle 11: *Self-determination is the right of every person to direct his or her own life; effective educators help each student identify and move toward his or her personal vision. Educators can help discover each student's vision through close observation of and interaction with that student and and his or her family, rejecting the notion that some students are incapable of academic achievement, self-determination, sexuality, integrated employment, or post-secondary education (cf. TASH 2000a, TASH 2000b). Each student must have a rich repertoire of experiences to draw upon in developing his or her vision and the appropriate supports to communicate and grow toward this vision.*

Today's classrooms are incredibly diverse in their academic, cultural, and economic composition, increasing the importance of providing opportunities for students to develop an awareness of themselves as individuals, as learners, as students, and as members of a community. Self-awareness is a key component of self-determination and is essential for all students— minority, gay, straight, male, female, disabled, gifted, economically dis/ advantaged, and so forth. All students must be aware of their strengths and limitations, preferences and desires, needs, and choices in order to make informed decisions and set attainable goals.

Much of the research on self-determination focuses on individuals with disabilities due in large part to the federal emphasis on and funding to promote self-determination as a component of the education of youth with disabilities. However, we believe self-determination is crucial for all students, particularly those students routinely marginalized by the ableist, heteronormative, "middle class, Euro-centric frameworks that shape school practices" (Gay, 2000, p. 21). In other words, we marginalize students in big and small ways every day, for example, when we assume that a student

Think About This: Students considered gifted also benefit from attention to self-determination, especially those who may have had less access to a rich repertoire of well-supported experiences to draw upon in developing a personal life vision and the appropriate supports to communicate and grow toward that vision.

with a disability is not capable of participating in classroom activities; when we construct the curriculum around norms of traditional families and mainstream cultural ideals; and when we schedule parent meetings during the workday and accuse parents who don't come of not caring enough to attend.

We begin this chapter with JoDell's account of her experience with facilitating student self-determination. Then the next section will provide a working definition of self-determination and describe the key components of self-determination as outlined by prominent researchers in the field. The third section will provide educators with tools for teaching the component skills of self-determination through Geneva Gay's Culturally Responsive Teaching (CRT) framework (Gay, 2000).

WHY IS SELF-DETERMINATION IMPORTANT?

I (JoDell) learned the importance of self-determination while I was teaching 7th-grade math in a resource room. I had been an elementary teacher for 13 years prior to this assignment and was extremely confident, some might say arrogant, about my instructional abilities. I had spent the summer preparing to teach middle school math by reviewing Individualized Education Plans (IEP) and developing lessons based on my students' needs. I began the school year focusing on core mathematical concepts of calculation, and much to my dismay, the students were less than en-

Think About This: Self-determination (or the lack thereof) can be linked to broader patterns of *adultism*, which refers to the systematic oppression of young people—which exists within and outside of schools.

thusiastic. Disruptive behaviors skyrocketed, and I spent less time playing instructor and more time playing referee. What went wrong? Lessons were well planned, areas of instructional need were identified and interventions

Activity 11.1: Self-Reflection

Think about your time as a student:

- Did you ever encounter a similar situation—a time when someone else made a decision for you?
- What was it?
- What role did you play?
- What feelings did it elicit?
- What were the benefits and/or drawbacks of this situation?

implemented—why weren't my students engaged? In desperation and exhaustion, I broke down and asked my 11 students why they weren't interested in doing math. After several moments of complete and utter silence, one student, Bobby, said, "I don't like this math, it's boring." He went on to say that he didn't want to do *this kind* of math. He wanted to do 7th-grade math in a 7th-grade class with a 7th-grade math teacher. Stunned, I asked the rest of the class; they unanimously agreed with Bobby, expressing their frustration at being segregated and their humiliation at being placed in a special education classroom.

At this point, I realized that the disruptive behavior was their way of telling me that they were angry, frustrated, and humiliated. As a class we talked about some of our options and discussed how we could present our proposal to the principal. It took some time, several meetings, and some willing participants but we were finally able to join a 7th-grade math class for the remainder of the school year and co-teaching became a frequent practice in the middle school.

This experience will always stand out as one of the most pivotal moments of my career. I was no longer the "all-knowing" professional who managed students but rather the facilitator who recognized the power of listening to the interests and desires of students and who supported them through their educational journey. Our success also hinged on collective action to change the system from one of exclusion to an inclusive environment. Together, our voices provided the power to improve educational opportunities for ourselves, others, and our school community.

THE FOUNDATIONS OF SELF-DETERMINATION

Although numerous definitions exist, we will define self-determination as an expression of personal agency, understanding one's own strengths, limitations, needs, and preferences well enough to evaluate options and goals and determine a clear vision for the future (Cobb, Lehmann, Newman-Gonchar, & Alwell, 2009). Setting goals, decision making, and problem-solving skills are essential for all individuals who desire greater autonomy. To be self-determined is to be empowered, empowered to make one's own decisions in all aspects of life. Empowered, self-determined individuals not only take responsibility for their own personal development, but the development of the world around them. The more empowered individuals are, the more committed they may become to social action; the more people feel they have power to influence what happens to them, the more they may use that power for the benefit of others and their community (Phares, 1976, as cited in Paxton, 2006). Additionally, people who are more self-determined have more positive employment and independent living outcomes and report that they have a higher quality of life (Palmer & Wehmeyer, 2010).

Self-determination, first, foremost, and always, is about the *self*. However, the *self* exists within a nest of relationships among family and friends, school, and society (see Figure 11.1). Self-determination manifests itself within the context of these nested relations. Our society places great importance on independence and autonomy, yet many other societies recognize the importance of social relations, networking, and institutional supports. The old adage that "no person is an island" is a good one to remember and apply when thinking about self-determination.

Research shows that increasing levels of self-determination give rise to greater integration of the students' own sense of purpose, interest, and desire that may be required of them from outside forces (Toshalis & Nakkula, 2012). Additionally, they suggest that student-centered classrooms

Figure 11.1 Circle of Self-Determination

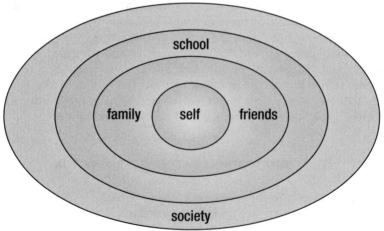

that capitalize on the power of self-determination can substantially increase achievement and motivation for all students. Wehmeyer and Schalock (2001) identify four essential characteristics of self-determined behavior (see Figure 11.2). We will describe each characteristic and how it relates to self-determined behavior.

Autonomy

A behavior is considered autonomous if a person acts according to his or her own preferences, interests, and/or abilities without undue external influence or interference (Wehmeyer & Schalock, 2001). An essential feature of autonomy is choice. All students need opportunities to make choices, to determine preferences and develop interests. However, with the increasing academic demands placed on students and teachers in public schools, these opportunities are limited. In many states, secondary students' programs are essentially pre-determined based on the state's graduation requirements, which have become increasingly narrow due to standards-based reform efforts. Strict requirements can significantly reduce student opportunities for choice within their academic programs, failing to take into consideration students' post-graduation goals and alternative coursework that might be required to achieve those goals.

Figure 11.2. Four Essential Characteristics of Self-Determined Behavior

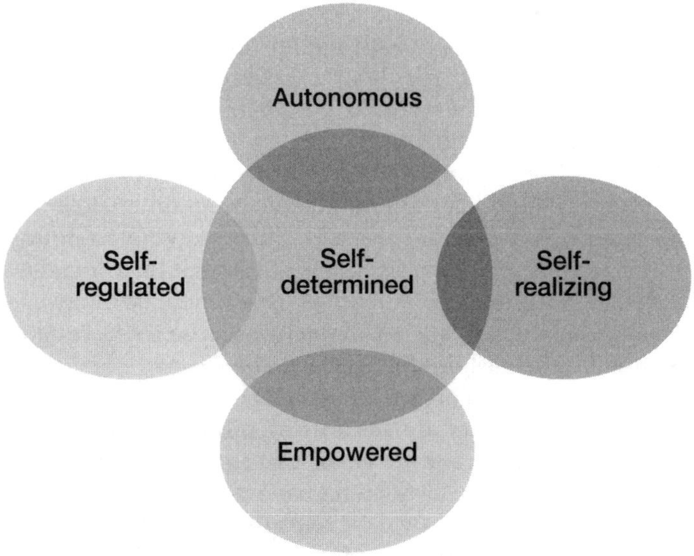

Note. Figure is based on information from Wehmeyer and Schalock, 2001.

Educational reform movements were initiated to increase academic performance across the nation. These reforms focus primarily on improving academic achievement; however, as Gay (2000) suggests, these reforms also need to be diversified according to the social variance of students, attending deliberately and conscientiously to such factors as ethnicity, culture, gender, social class, historical experiences, and linguistic capabilities.

Brittany, an 11th-grade student with learning disabilities, shares her experience with curricular restrictions:

> I told my special education teacher that I wanted to take a yearbook class. I really wanted to learn how to take pictures and go to all the school activities. I told her that if I was on yearbook, I would make sure that there were pictures of other students in the yearbook instead of just the popular kids. My special education teacher told me that I couldn't take yearbook; that I didn't have room in my program. So, I went to the yearbook teacher and asked her if she would let me take the class, and she said the class was full and there wasn't room for a junior. The first day of school my junior year, I went to the yearbook class, and there were tons of empty desks. When I asked the teacher if I could transfer into the class, she still said she didn't have room. I was so mad. It was unfair.

This student expressed autonomy by asserting her presence and making her needs known (Martin & Marshall, 1995, p. 147); yet she was denied based on the academic constraints of her program and non-supportive educators.

The goal of No Child Left Behind (2002) was to close the achievement gap for subgroups of students by raising academic standards and ensuring access to highly qualified teachers. Brittany's access to a highly qualified teacher in this situation did little in the way of ensuring her academic success. The rigidity of her academic program made it impossible for her to pursue *her* academic interests. Students who are routinely denied access to educational opportunities that spark their interest will become increasingly disengaged and often leave school. We may eventually close the achievement gap, but it will not be because we have actually improved student outcomes. It will appear to be closed because subgroups of students may no longer attend traditional schools. Many charter schools around the country are advertising more engaging curriculums, more effective educators, and more inclusive school cultures, which are particularly attractive to students who have not been successful in traditional schools. The last several years have also seen a rise in public virtual schools, touting individualized curriculums with flexible schedules. Students like Brittany may find their niche outside of traditional schools.

Activity 11.2: My Role in the Learning Process

Describe a time when you, as a student, demonstrated one or more of the self-regulatory skills described in this section:

- What outcomes did you experience as a result?
- How did you become aware of the strategy you used?
- How would/could you embed one or more of these skills in your teaching?

Self-Regulation

Zimmerman (2002) describes self-regulation as self-generated thoughts, feelings, and behaviors that are oriented to attaining goals. Self-regulated learners are proactive in their efforts to learn, are aware of their strengths and limitations, are guided by personally set goals and task-related strategies, monitor their behavior, and self-reflect on their effectiveness (Zimmerman, 2002). Students who effectively regulate their own learning increase self-satisfaction as they progress toward their personal goals and generally feel successful. Self-regulation is an important component of self-determination because it fosters life-long learning skills, making attainment of post-secondary goals much more attainable.

For many students, self-regulation comes quite naturally and appears effortless. Yet for some students, it may require explicit instruction and repeated practice. Again, restructuring the physical and social context requires institutional supports and collective efforts to change the system within which one struggles to self-regulate.

I (Maryl) recall a former student, Ronnie, who couldn't wait for 4th grade to begin because he would get his own locker with a combination lock. For Ronnie, this meant he was no longer a little kid; rather, he was on his way to becoming a young man, a young man with his own locker, his own lock, and his own combination. However, he didn't realize how difficult it would be!

All of his classmates learned to open a combination lock after a few days, and he was ready to give up, convinced he would never learn. I told him that he could also use a lock with a key, but he didn't want to. Ronnie was determined to learn how to use his combination lock. He asked for help, and he and I came up with a plan. The first night he memorized the combination. The next day I wrote out directions and showed him how to open it. Ronnie practiced at lunch and after school. The following day he came in to school frustrated—he was still struggling. I helped him to troubleshoot, and by the end of the day he was able to open the lock independently. He took it home that night and continued to practice, and finally, the following day he was able to put the lock on his locker.

Ronnie had solved his problem by asking for help, and together we made a plan. He spent time working toward his goal, and finally it was realized. This experience allowed Ronnie to recognize that he was capable of overcoming obstacles and that his own effort could lead to successful results.

Empowerment

At the core of empowerment is the understanding that individuals are truly empowered the moment they recognize the inherent authority they possess to control their own lives (Jones, 2006). People who act in a psychologically empowered way do so on the basis of beliefs that they have control over circumstances important to them, possess the skills necessary to achieve desired outcomes, and expect the identified outcomes to result if they choose to apply those skills (Wehmeyer & Schalock, 2001). Educators must intentionally address issues of empowerment for marginalized students. To achieve psychological empowerment, individuals must have access to environments that provide choice, aid in building self-confidence, and provide opportunities for successful attainment of goals.

> **? Think About This:** The concept of empowerment is complex because of the ways in which it maintains that the power remains in the hands of the person who is giving power to another. Consider this famous quote from Abolitionist Frederick Douglass: "Power concedes nothing without a demand. It never did and it never will."

But how do educators prepare empowered students when so much of the educational decision making is out of their control? Wehmeyer, Palmer, Agran, Mithaug, and Martin (2000) suggest that a critical element in teaching self-determination is teaching students to take greater control over their own learning, shifting from teacher-directed and teacher-driven instructional models to student-directed teaching models. According to Toshalis and Nakkula (2012), a more student-centered approach would include learning what motivates individual students to achieve in a particular class and then enlisting their help in identifying other factors that might elevate their motivation.

When students feel like they can do what is being asked with some facility (competence), when they feel like they have some control over how an activity is conducted (autonomy), and when they feel meaningfully connected to those around them while doing it (relatedness),

Activity 11.3: What's Your Self-Awareness?

With a partner or in a small group, consider the following questions:

1. What are your strengths and limitations? How did you come to recognize them? What role did educators, parents, or community members play?
2. How were your experiences similar or different from your partner's or those in your group?

students are understood to be self-determined (Toshalis & Nakkula, 2012, p. 9).

By considering student interests and including them in goal setting, progress monitoring, and self-reflection, educators can increase opportunities for student-centered learning.

Self-Realization

Self-determined individuals are self-realizing; they use a comprehensive and reasonably accurate knowledge of themselves and their strengths and limitations and act to capitalize on this knowledge (Wehmeyer & Schalock, 2001). To develop an awareness of one's strengths and limitations requires frequent opportunities to participate in activities in a variety of settings. It also requires an awareness of the various identities individuals embody (racial, ethnic, sexual orientation, gender, socioeconomic status, and so forth) and how they influence their perceptions of themselves in both academic and social spheres. Self-awareness is an important first step to empowering individuals to pursue the necessary resources and supports to become part of their community.

The gay, lesbian, bisexual, and transgender (GLBT) student population experiences similar issues with regard to self-awareness. In school settings, sexual orientation issues frequently go unaddressed by educators, leaving students feeling invisible and unimportant. GLBT students of all racial and ethnic backgrounds miss or drop out of school because of a lack of safety or respect for their gender or sexual identity. The number of such students is hard to measure due to absence of, and difficulty in obtaining, reliable data (Kim, 2009). Though the inclusion of GLBT people or issues in the classroom curricula has been shown to improve youths' feelings of safety and belonging, the vast majority of American schools do not include GLBT related materials in classroom instruction (Kim, 2009). The National Education Association's *Report on the Status of Gay, Lesbian, Bisexual and Transgender People in Education: Stepping Out of the Closet, into the Light* (Kim, 2009) shares one student's profile:

It was in middle school that kids started to ask Abi if she was gay. Everyone seemed so eager to label her because her hair was very short and she wore neutral or boy's clothes. "I guess I didn't conform to the feminine stereotype, but I really didn't know what I was. When my mom asked me if I was a lesbian, I said, 'No,' and I was telling the truth." Then the rumors started to fly around school that Abi and a girl with whom she liked to talk were in love. Abi found the rumors very embarrassing. She continued going to school and doing well academically. But she felt increasingly uncomfortable—so uncomfortable in fact that when it came time to attend high school, she did not go to the local high school. Instead Abi, the academically inclined student who is determined to go to college, enrolled in a technical high school in another town. "I needed a fresh start—I needed to get away from the rumors." She adds: "My middle school experience bummed me out for sure, but it was not nearly as bad as some other kids went through. I know kids who have had 'dyke' spray-painted on their lockers, kids who had their noses broken, kids who became suicidal." Abi's high school is half-academics, half-shop. And it turns out she likes shop (manufacturing technology), and she likes having a part-time job outside of school where she can earn some money. Her best friend at school is a gay boy who is a senior. And her favorite teacher is a history teacher who, at the beginning of the year, tells the students he will not tolerate the harassment or bullying of any student for any reason, including their sexual orientation or gender identity/expression. Sixteen years old and a junior, Abi is feeling "strong and independent and very cool." She has hooked up with an organization called "True Colors," which supports GLBT teenagers in New England, and she has come out on her Facebook page. "I said I am transgender and it felt great. Then of course I freaked out about what might happen to me. But nothing really did. One boy at school came up to me and said what's transgender, and I told him to look it up on Wikipedia." (p. 10)

Abi's story is a powerful example of the role educators play in providing safe spaces for minority students to develop knowledge of themselves, their strengths and limitations, and their needs and desires, which are crucial in developing the self-awareness necessary for becoming self-determined individuals.

TEACHING SELF-DETERMINATION

Though many educators feel constrained by current educational reform efforts that have heightened curricular expectations, Wehmeyer et al. (2004) suggest that standards-based reform may actually provide opportunities for infusing instruction in self-determination and increasing student involvement in the general curriculum. The vast majority of state-adopted standards expect students to learn and apply effective problem-solving, decision-making, and goal-setting processes. Educators can promote progress in the general curriculum by teaching standards-based content and knowledge related to the component elements of self-determined behavior. Teaching young people self-regulation, self-management, problem-solving, goal-setting, and decision-making strategies provides effective ways to enable students to engage deeply with and progress through the general curriculum. While many educators value self-determination, they typically do not incorporate it in their classroom instruction (Thoma, Nathanson, Baker, & Tamura, 2002; Wehmeyer, Agran, & Hughes, 2000). Brittany's experience teaches us that we need to work on changing the system in tandem with teaching autonomy in order to achieve our goals. Self-determination must provide the catalyst for change at both the individual (autonomous) and institutional level in order to be effective.

To develop self-realizing behaviors in all students requires educators to recognize, honor, and incorporate the personal characteristics of students into their teaching strategies (Gay, 2000). Toshalis and Nakkula (2012) address the need for educators to understand the social worlds students come from, and how those worlds influence efforts in the classroom. By doing this, educators are increasing the opportunities for all students to develop self-awareness, a building block of self-determination. Along with understanding where students are coming from, educators need to examine their biases related to those social worlds. An awareness of the biases we hold helps us to move beyond mere tolerance to genuine acceptance, which allows us to support students in their development of self-awareness and self-determination. Gay (2000) reminds us that culture is at the heart of all we do in the name of education, whether that is curriculum, instruction, administration, or performance assessment.

Today's classrooms are dynamic and diverse, posing challenges for educators who use traditional teaching strategies without cultural consideration and responsiveness. We believe that Culturally Responsive Teaching (Gay, 2000) provides a useful framework for promoting self-determination in all students because it "is empowering, it enables students to be better human beings and more successful learners. Empowerment translates into academic competence, personal confidence,

 Activity 11.4: What Are Your Beliefs?

For more about examining personal biases, try the Commonly Held Beliefs Survey found at http://www.tolerance.org/tdsi/cb_intro. Take a closer look at one of the 13 commonly held beliefs, and answer the questions that follow it.

courage, and the will to act" (p. 32). These qualities are inherent in the four essential characteristics of self-determined behavior identified by Wehmeyer and Schalock (2001): autonomy, self-regulation, empowerment, and self-realization, as presented earlier in the chapter.

Culturally Responsive Teaching to Promote Self-Determination

> If you can show me how I can cling to that which is real to me, while teaching me a way into the larger society, then and only then will I drop my defenses and hostility, and I will sing your praises and help you to make the desert bear fruit.

—Ralph Ellison

According to Gay (2000), there are four critical aspects of CRT: caring, communication, curriculum, and instruction. We will address the components of CRT in this section and the next.

Caring. The kind of caring essential for CRT includes teacher attitudes, expectations, and behaviors about students' human value, intellectual capability, and performance responsibilities (Gay, 2000). If positive and negative teacher attitudes and expectations profoundly affect student achievement, as the research conducted by Good and Brophy (1994) suggests, it is important to engage educators in activities that promote critical reflection on personal beliefs, attitudes, and assumptions. (See Activity 11.A: Circles of My Multicultural Self, Related Resources for Chapter 11, www.tcpress.com.) Gay (2000) points out that students who are perceived positively are advantaged in instructional interactions and those who are viewed negatively are disadvantaged, often to the extent of total exclusion from participation in academic interactions.

Educators can demonstrate caring in a variety of ways, from greeting individual students as they enter the classroom, to inquiring about students' interests and activities, to conferencing with individual students to develop short- and long-term academic and social goals. Checking in with students on an individual basis to discuss their academic progress or identify areas

 Activity 11.5: Creating a Culture of Caring

Watch Sonia Nieto's online video "Showing Caring While Having High Expectations" (http://www.tolerance.org/tdsi/asset/showing-caring-while-having-high-expecta). Then, brainstorm a list of things a teacher can do to promote and maintain a caring culture in the classroom.

of need shows students that you care about their learning. This can also demonstrate that you believe in their ability to meet academic standards and that you acknowledge and support their efforts. To maintain a caring relationship requires educators to follow up with students and monitor their progress frequently. This is a cyclical process rather than a one-shot deal. Sincere and genuine caring is demonstrated when educators continue to engage students in evaluating their academic and social progress.

Communication. Since communication is essential to both teaching and learning, it needs to be a central part of instructional reform in order to improve the school performance of underachieving students (Gay, 2000). If educators are to better serve school achievement of diverse students and increase self-determination by implementing CRT, they must learn how to communicate differently with them (Gay, 2000). Villegas and Lucas (2002) describe culturally responsive educators as those who take the time to learn about their students. Developing engaging, interactive lessons that motivate diverse learners requires effective communication with students and families. Effective communication at the individual level can support student autonomy and improve learning outcomes (Reeve, Ryan, Deci, & Jang, 2008). Educators can initiate informal conversations with students and families to learn about wants, needs, goals, and experiences outside of school. For students who are nonverbal, it may be useful to communicate with family and friends or conduct observations in social settings to learn more about the students' interests. (See also Activity 11.B: Student Interest Inventory, Related Resources for Chapter 11, www.tcpress.com).

> **Think About This:** The barriers to self-determination are massive: Schools as institutions are unlikely to embrace student empowerment if it really challenges the authority and practices of those in power.

Educators who know about their students' hobbies and favorite activities, as well as what they excel at outside of school, can systematically tie the children's interests, concerns, and strengths into their teaching, enhancing their students' motivation to learn (Ladson-Billings, 1994). This also provides valuable information that can be used to assist students in developing and meeting post-secondary goals. For example, asking students about the extracurricular activities they participate in demonstrates

> **Think About This:** Some students need exposure to a wider range of well-supported experiences to determine what their interests are. Their known interests and current level of participation in extracurricular activities may be limited by factors such as low expectations and financial, social, language, and/or cultural barriers.

interest in them beyond the classroom, while simultaneously providing a foundation for developing educational goals that build on their interests. Additionally, linking a student's interest in a particular sport or hobby to an academic task piques their interest and maintains their engagement with the content. For example, using scores from recent basketball games to teach a lesson on mean, median, and mode would be more engaging for students than using a list of arbitrary numbers copied from a textbook.

Incorporating Self-Determination in Curriculum and Instruction

Culturally Responsive Teaching leads naturally to a focus on integrating academic content and self-determination to support the success of all students. Students with strong self-determination are more likely to be intrinsically motivated, engage in school, experience academic success, achieve their goals, experience satisfaction with their lives, have positive adult lives, and have improved levels of well-being overall, which includes obtaining successful employment (Ryan & Deci, 2000; Wehmeyer & Schalock , 2001). Additionally, evidence suggests that self-determination skills and academic skills can easily be integrated into current classroom instruction (Konrad, Walker, Fowler, Test, & Wood, 2008; Wehmeyer, Field, Doren, Jones, & Mason, 2004). Educators may not even be aware that curricular materials and instructional methods for teaching self-determination are available (Grigal, Neubert, Moon, & Graham, 2003) or may feel that there is not time for explicit instruction because of increased accountability and standards-based reform. Though it may not be possible to implement a specific self-determination curriculum/program, educators can build self-determination skills through their current curriculum by shifting from teacher-centered to more student-centered instructional approaches. Providing increased opportunities for student choice, student goal setting, progress monitoring, and student self-reflection will aid in building the self-awareness, self-regulation, autonomy, and empowerment necessary to become self-determined individuals.

In reality, self-determination may already be part of your content-area standards. Many states have adopted the Common Core State Standards (NGACBP, 2010). Two of the mathematical practice standards in the Common Core State Standards are specifically focused on self-determination skills. The first states that students should "Make sense of problems and persevere in solving them" (p. 10). Another states that students should "Use appropriate tools strategically" (p. 10). Problem solving and decision making are important components of self-determination. Students are expected to demonstrate this type of problem solving across content areas. They are expected to develop goals, monitor progress, and evaluate results—a characteristic of self-regulating/self-determined individuals.

It is, however, important to recognize that standards alone do not determine the curriculum or instructional methods. What does your curriculum consist of? Who is represented in it—and more important, who is not? "Curriculum content should be seen as a tool to help students assert and accentuate their present and future powers, capabilities, attitudes, and experiences" (Gay, 2000, p. 111). Will your students encounter stories and contributions from diverse individuals and authors in your classroom? One way to empower students is to make sure that they are *represented* in the curriculum. Textbooks and literature frequently underrepresent marginalized groups such as GLBT, non-native English speakers, racially/ethnically diverse people, and persons with disabilities. Can your students see themselves in your curriculum? If not, one way to support and motivate them is to supplement your current curriculum with alternative texts that approach content and cover standards in a more supportive way. This ensures that curriculum will be meaningful to them, resulting in increased engagement and student achievement. (For examples of infusing self-determination strategies into existing lessons, see Activity 11.C: Infusing Self-Determination into the Lesson, as well as Additional Resources for Educators, Related Resources for Chapter 11, www.tcpress.com. See also http://www.imdetermined.org/life_lines/.)

In order for self-determination as a democratic outcome to be realized, it must be person centered and person directed, so that we don't unintentionally restrict student agency through our curricular decisions and teacher-centered instructional practices (Peterson, 2009). This goal of ensuring that self-determination is a part of the curriculum is extremely important and can be done in conjunction with current standards and without modifying current curriculum.

CONCLUSION

In this chapter, we have explored the concepts of self-determination and have emphasized how important self-determination is for students to achieve their goals in the classroom and beyond the classroom. We recognize that for students to achieve self-determination, educators face many obstacles. We have shared our personal and professional experiences and struggles in hopes that some of these will resonate with you. Culturally Responsive Teaching and the worldview that accompanies CRT are hard work, but they have significant payoffs, as you see students grow and develop, express their hopes and dreams, and become self-determined individuals who believe they can succeed in life and change the world into a better, more accepting place.

GROUND TRUTH: THE PRACTITIONER'S VOICE

Julie Croy
Middle School Science Teacher

I had never given much thought to teaching self-determination skills to middle school students. I was a firm believer that the teacher was responsible for delivering the curriculum and the students were responsible for learning it. I provided a variety of ways for students to practice learning the material but used a standard format for assessing their understanding. Then, I spent a semester co-teaching with a special education teacher who showed me how to differentiate assessments to better evaluate my student's learning. Together, we developed three to four different testing formats and allowed our students to choose which format they preferred. Providing *all* students—not just students with disabilities—the opportunity to choose resulted in increased test scores, decreased test anxiety, and greater responsibility for their own learning. This experience helped me realize that one way to increase student engagement and motivation was to allow them opportunities to choose. Gradually, I began to provide differentiated assignments and projects as well as assessments. My students began to see science as something worth learning and expressed more positive attitudes toward it.

REFERENCES

Cobb, B., Lehmann, J., Newman-Gonchar, R., & Alwell, M. (2009). Self-determination for students with disabilities: A narrative metasynthesis. *Career Development for Exceptional Individuals, 32,* 108–114.

Gay, G. (2000). *Culturally responsive teaching.* New York: Teachers College Press.

Good, T. L., & Brophy, J. E. (1994). *Looking in classrooms.* New York: HarperCollins Publishers

Grigal, M., Neubert, D. A., Moon, M. S., & Graham, S. (2003). Self-determination for students with disabilities: Views of parents and teachers. *Exceptional Children, 70*(1), 97–113.

Jones, M. (2006, September/October). Teaching self-determination: Empowered teachers, empowered students. *Teaching Exceptional Children, 39,* 12+. Retrieved from Questia database: http://www.questia.com/PM.qst?a=5035135496

Kim, R. (2009). *A report on the status of gay, lesbian, bisexual and transgender people in education: Stepping out of the closet, into the light.* Washington, DC: National Education Association.

Konrad, M., Walker, A. R., Fowler, C. H., Test, D. W., & Wood, W. M. (2008). A model for aligning self-determination and general education curriculum standards. *Teaching Exceptional Children, 40*(3), 53–64.

Ladson-Billings, G. (1994). *The dreamkeepers: Successful teachers of African American children.* San Francisco: Jossey-Bass.

Martin J. E., & Marshall, L. H. (1995). ChoiceMaker: A comprehensive self-determination transition program. *Intervention in School & Clinic, 30*, 147–156.

National Governors Association Center for Best Practices, Council of Chief State School Officers. (2010). *Common core state standards.* Washington, DC: Author.

Palmer, S., & Wehmeyer, M. L. (2010). What is self-determination and why is it important? *National Gateway to Self Determination Project.* Kansas City: University of Missouri.

Paxton, P. (2006, November). Building empowered students: The perennial challenge for university teachers. Originally published in the Proceedings of the EDU-COM 2006 International (Project) conference.

Peterson, A. J. (2009). Shana's story: The struggles, quandaries and pitfalls surrounding self-determination. *Disability Studies Quarterly, 29*(2). Retrieved from http://www.dsq- sds.org/article/view/922/1097

Reeve, J., Ryan, R., Deci, E. L., & Jang, H. (2008). Understanding and promoting autonomous self-regulation: A self-determination theory perspective. In D. H. Schunk & B. J. Zimmerman (Eds.) *Motivation and self-regulated learning: Theory, research, and applications* (pp. 223–244). New York: Taylor & Francis, Inc.

Ryan, R. M., & Deci, E. L. (2000). Self-determination theory and the facilitation of intrinsic motivation, social development, and well-being. *American Psychologist, 55,* 68–78.

TASH (2000a). *Resolution on choice.* Retrieved from http://www.tash.org/IRR/resolutions/res02choice.htm

TASH (2000b). *Resolution on services and supports in the community.* Retrieved from http://www.tash.org/IRR/resolutions/res02supports.htm

Thoma, C. A., Nathanson, R., Baker, S. R., & Tamura, R. (2002). Self-determination: What do special educators know and where do they learn it? *Remedial and Special Education, 23,* 242–247.

Toshalis, E., & Nakkula, M. J. (2012). Motivation, engagement, and student voice. *Education Digest, 78*(1), 29-35.

Villegas, A. M., & Lucas, T. (2002). Preparing culturally responsive teachers: Rethinking the classroom. *Journal of Teacher Education, 53*(1), 20–32.

Wehmeyer, M. L., Agran, M., & Hughes, C. A. (2000). A national survey of teachers' promotion of self-determination and student-directed learning. *Journal of Special Education, 34,* 58–68.

Wehmeyer, M. L., Field, S., Doren, B., Jones, B., & Mason, C. (2004). Self-determination and student involvement in standards-based reform. *Exceptional Children, 70*(4), 413–425.

Wehmeyer, M. L., Palmer, S. B., Agran, M., Mithaug, D. E., & Martin, J. E. (2000). Promoting causal agency: The self-determined learning model of instruction. *Exceptional Children, 66*(4), 439. Retrieved from Questia database: http://www.questia.com/PM.qst?a=o&d=5001765986

Wehmeyer, M. L., & Schalock R. L. (2001). Self-determination and quality of life: Implications for special education services and supports. *Focus on Exceptional Children, 33,* 1–16.

Zimmerman, B. J. (2002). Becoming a self-regulated learner: An overview. *Theory into Practice, 41,* 64–70.

CHAPTER 12

Advocating for Successful School Change

Valerie Owen, Kathleen Kotel,
Julie Ramirez, Virginia Zeitlin,
Elizabeth Z. Dejewski, & David Feingold

One of the chief joys of my life has been to watch the sweep forward
from the idea of education as a forward acquisition of material facts and
philosophical theories, to the more vital work of creative activity and
significance of community responsibilities.

—Elizabeth Harrison (American educator and founder of National Louis
University), 1930

Key Principle 12: *Effective education requires repertoires of advocacy to facilitate*
successful school change, including understanding factors that facilitate or hinder
change efforts.

Earl Warren, Chief Justice of the Supreme Court from 1953–1969, said,
"Everything I did in my life that was worthwhile I caught hell for."
Chief Justice Warren presided over important rulings in civil rights (e.g.,
Brown vs. the Board of Education), police powers (e.g., the *Miranda* case),
and separation of church and state (e.g., the outlawing of school prayer).
The rulings and interpretations of the U.S. Constitution by his court
changed the direction of the country and safeguarded voice and vote
for minority and poor Americans as well as upheld the importance of
freedom of speech. In the United States, there is a belief and value that
if people understand the structure of government they can overcome
discrimination and have influence on the power of government (Peters
& Chimedza, 2000). It is through legislation that those individuals in the
margins of society obtain access to power. Yet, we know laws are not

enough to change attitudes. We cannot legislate away negative attitudes or the resulting discrimination.

When one thinks about effective education and school change, it is usually in the terms of legislated reform; in other words, more testing, national standards, charter schools, value-added teaching, evidence-based practices, or closing the achievement gap. What we know about school reform is usually from the news headlines, or if we are practicing teachers, administrators, or other school personnel, from the added responsibilities placed on us because of new mandates. The dominant school reform narrative and discourse in today's media privilege the voices of politicians and those in the think tanks but rarely include the voices of educators, parents, and students, those on the front lines. When educators' voices are included in the discourse, they are usually interpreted in a tone that suggests they are barriers to reform rather than professionals with wisdom and fresh ideas. Students and parents are portrayed as incompetent or in need of our pity. Their voices are marginalized by those in power.

Such legislated and mandated educational reform, even if well intentioned to remedy inequities, is often a poor way to change attitudes and may result in a grudging skin-deep compliance with those legal mandates as well as other acts of resistance (Peters & Chimedza, 2000). As a result, school-reform efforts may not result in meaningful school change as all stakeholders are not working together; yet changes are happening so quickly that, as one school administrator remarked, "It feels like we are building an airplane while flying."

In practice, this understanding of school change results in a focus on measuring performance of students, educators, and schools and on ranking them based on their scores. Yet, in a review of research as well as analysis of individual state data, Nichols, Glass, and Berliner (2006) found that there exist little to no data demonstrating that high-stakes testing works to promote achievement. Furthermore, a number of other studies have found that the current practice of using high-stakes testing has resulted in an increased rate of minority students dropping out of school (e.g., Clarke, Haney, & Madaus, 2000; Heubert & Hauser, 1999; Orfield, Losen, Wald, & Swanson, 2004). High-stakes testing and a focus on narrow standards present an even greater dilemma, however. Heshusius (2004) describes quite eloquently how measuring and ranking obscure and prevent rather than honor diversity:

> A particularly sad dilemma involved is that the perceived obligation to measure, and thus rank, often flies in the face of the rhetoric everywhere in education, also within traditional special education, of "honoring diversity." Diversity and ranking are singularly incompatible. You *cannot* measure and rank diversity; doing so flattens and thus kills it. Diversity is flattened and

disappears in the very act of being measured and ranked. When those referred to as "diverse" in ability (by those who probably consider themselves as belonging to the norm, or at least to know the norm) are measured against a desired goal or standard, the goals and standards are always less diverse than diversity itself, and thus reduce diversity to the limited diversity *allowed* by the standards and measurement devices. (pp. 213–214; emphasis in original)

In other words, designers and proponents of this method of school change assume the superiority of majority culture. An alternative perspective is that effective schools are ones where diversity is valued, assumptions about the superiority of people without disabilities and members of the majority are challenged, and members of the marginalized groups make important contributions to their schools and communities (Peters & Chimedza, 2000).

Real school change requires a change in belief and attitude. Changing beliefs and attitudes requires critical analysis of current practices with the goals of acceptance of diversity and inclusion at the forefront. All stakeholders must take risks, engage in true collaboration, privilege the voice of those who are marginalized, and most important, be open to change. This chapter takes a closer look at how one goes about school reform beyond simply passing legislation and mandates, testing, evidence-based

 Activity 12.1: Charter Schools and Diversity

There have been efforts across the country and in the U.S. Department of Education to increase the number of charter schools and promote school choice as a primary component of school reform. Read *Schools Without Diversity: Education Management Organizations, Charter Schools, and the Demographic Stratification of the American School System* by Miron, Urschel, Mathis, and Tornquist (2010, http://nepc.colorado.edu/publication/schools-without-diversity). That report provides a comparison and analysis of enrollment of minority students in charter schools as compared to public schools in their neighborhoods and presents an alternative perspective.

- What could be some of the reasons people support charter schools as a means of school reform?
- Do you agree or disagree that they can be effective as a means to address the access to effective education for diverse student populations?
- Why or why not?

practice, and core curriculum standards. Advocating for successful school change challenges the assumptions of the dominant, values diversity, and requires the risk of speaking up.

A SOCIAL JUSTICE ADVOCACY IMPERATIVE

Social injustice for students with disabilities and students from other marginalized groups has been extensively documented. There are inequities in the following:

- curriculum and instructional practices (Ferri & Connor, 2005; Haberman, 1991)
- facilities (Kozol, 1991)
- teacher quality (Darling-Hammond, 2004; U.S. Department of Education, 2012)
- graduation and drop-out rates (National Center for Education Statistics, 2012)
- discipline (U.S. Department of Education, 2012)

Given this context, it becomes clear that advocacy must be a political process and educators, parents, and students need to be a part of that process. Although institutionalized social justice must be obtained through litigation and legislation, we have a personal responsibility to work toward social justice. An effective advocate for social justice can see injustice, envisions him- or herself in a position to make a difference, and has professional and personal skills and persistence to make it happen. Yet to fight injustices, both individual and collective actions are necessary (House & Martin, 1998). Effective educators fulfill many advocacy roles. In fact, it can be argued that we have an imperative to be advocates for excellence in education that values diversity and effective school change. (To analyze your school structures, see Activity 12.A: Understanding Barriers to and Opportunities for School Change, Related Resources for Chapter 12, www.tcpress.com.)

DEVELOPING AN ADVOCACY DISPOSITION
AND SPEAKING TRUTH TO POWER

Education, especially education of students who are marginalized by school and society, is fraught with barriers to change. There is too often a culture in many schools that forces educators, especially new ones, to conform. Sadly, new ideas can be seen as challenges to the comfort of the

Activity 12.2: Expressions of Exclusion Through Art

Maria loves art. She is a young woman with autism who attends a transition program. Because of budget cuts she was not allowed to attend a local community college to study art. When asked to describe what makes her happy, she draws a picture of her dog, Fluffy.

Late at night she would ask her mother, "Mom, what's wrong with me?" Societal ignorance and educational misguided perception of her in/abilities, made Maria feel lonely. Like her peers, she wanted to fit in. She wanted to get nice clothes, especially shoes.

These pictures tell a story of Maria, in ways that words cannot. Answer these questions:

- What do Maria's pictures mean to you?
- What are the implications for advocacy?
- What are the implications for educators?

status quo. Additionally, there are often low expectations for students. There are unintended consequences of laws designed to protect rights that result in labeling, exclusion, and marginalization. It is easy to feel discouraged or to be overwhelmed by a school's culture. One can rationalize that it "was like this when I got here," "we've always done it that way," or "it is out of my realm of control" and conclude that there is little that can be done to make a difference. Effective educators, however, believe they have the responsibility and power to make a difference. This is an advocacy disposition. Fiedler (2000) defined an advocacy disposition as a reflection of the values and attitudes toward commitment, sense of responsibility, and ethical behavior on behalf of students and their families. While political bureaucracies and educational institutions may, at times, seem impenetrable and impervious to change, they simply are made up of people who are carrying out the goals of the bureaucracy or institution (Weber, 1904/1949). If our beliefs and values are inconsistent with those goals, we must engage in collaborative and individual activities to make a difference in the lives of our students.

Risks of Speaking Up

There are risks, however: "What if advocating or speaking up means I may lose my job or worse?" Frith (1981) describes the dilemma in which an educator finds him- or herself if he or she "must decide whether to actively defend a child's rights when doing so would contradict the stated or implied directives of the professional's employing agency" (p. 487). Yet, as Fiedler (2000) concluded, "when the interests of the child and employer conflict, a true professional advocate must place a primary loyalty with the child" (p. 30). That requires that as an educator you are very clear about your beliefs and values and can articulate them. Interestingly, Chief Justice Warren's court also decided *Pickering v. Board of Education* (1968), which overturned a ruling by the Illinois Supreme Court and held that "absent proof of false statements knowingly or recklessly made by him, a teacher's exercise of his right to speak on issues of public importance may not furnish the basis for his dismissal from public employment." This means that because of the First Amendment of the U.S. Constitution, an educator has a right to speak up about issues of public importance and cannot legally be dismissed for doing so.

Advocacy Strategies

In spite of the legal protections, many educators are terrified to speak up, often with good reason. They can be told directly or indirectly not to speak to parents and ostracized, or worse, if they do. It is important,

therefore, especially in the early years of your career, to position yourself
so that you can have impact in the decision making in other ways.

One such advocacy strategy is to volunteer to serve on the committees that make curriculum decisions and recommendations. As a member
of selection committees you can ask questions and make comments that
can result in conscientization and transformative experiences as the underlying assumptions about inclusive practices become visible to others.
These questions can also result in pushback from others, and one should
be prepared for that. This is a time when an educator's confidence might
be challenged, as not all will share his or her beliefs and values, but the
process is important and can plant seeds of change for the future. It can be
a teachable moment, but it also may take many such moments for change
to happen. An effective educator is articulate and persistent, keeps the
ideal at the forefront, but also picks battles wisely. Effective educators
model advocacy and inclusiveness by successfully integrating individuals with disabilities and other marginalized differences into general education classrooms and the community.

School administrators can be powerful change agents when it comes
to building more inclusive schools. Administrators have budgets and
achievement scores to contend with that cannot be ignored, yet through
collaboration a bridge can be formed that allows all concerns to be expressed and ideas shared. An administrator in an elementary school with
a 95.8% Hispanic population recognized that 50% of the students were in
resource, self-contained, and ESL classrooms and that the needs of these
students could be met in the general education classes. She believed all
students need differentiated instruction and that she could facilitate that.
Through collaboration with the teachers and her administrative support
with scheduling and professional development, students experienced academic success and the effects of an equitable school environment.

Another administrator relates a story of how a parent who had recently moved to her district was so grateful that her son had been accepted and
included in the general education program. As the administrator stated,
"Truth is, it's very simple things that contribute to successful inclusion—
of course attitude and leading with one's heart cannot be understated."

Similarly, a middle school teacher in the suburbs of Chicago who teaches students with significant intellectual disabilities in a mostly self-contained class was asked by an administrator to map out what she would be
teaching over the year. Her plan included access to the general educational
curriculum and inclusive opportunities for her students. She worked col-
laboratively with general education teachers. As a result, her students attended classes and after-school clubs with their peers, but the results were
insufficient in that they were not making progress in the general education curriculum. She used that experience as an opportunity to create a

modified social studies curriculum that paralleled the general education curriculum. As evidence of her learning, one student wrote a four-word sentence on the interactive whiteboard while discussing citizenship, "I am a citizen." She then corrected herself and wrote, "We are citizens."

This teacher's work is an example of the reality of individual change and reflects the importance of persistence and confidence to continue advocacy efforts toward more inclusive practices, as change can take time. It also shows that change in a single classroom is insufficient. Systemic change is needed.

ADVOCACY THROUGH COLLABORATION

Advocacy for systematic school change requires the understanding of the different perspectives of parents, teachers, administrators and other school personnel, community members, and the students, and what's at stake for each. Effective educators work with the larger community to build coalitions across groups through ongoing discussions of social justice and other shared issues and values (Sapon-Shevin & Zollers, 1999). The building of coalitions across groups requires one to keep the focus of school reform at the forefront, while delicately balancing all perspectives.

The middle school teacher in the previous example, who advocated for inclusive education, spoke at the first faculty meeting of the year to request collaborative partners. After the meeting, she received four notes from interested teachers. The teachers met and the doors for building a

 Activity 12.3: Who Might Benefit from Inclusion?

Think about who might resist inclusion and why. Using the list of stakeholders below, from their point of view, list the possible reasons for resistance:

- administration
- general education teachers
- special education teachers and therapists
- parents
- students

Now think of the counterarguments that would advocate for inclusion.

Unexamined beliefs and assumptions need critical analysis. Think about how not including a student will affect him or her in the long run. As you complete this activity, refer to Chapter 6 for more information.

coalition and collaboration were opened. Educators were able to share their concerns in a trusting environment. A coalition team was formed. Sadly, three of the four teachers retired, yet the teacher continued to model inclusive practice. Slowly, change is happening. Additionally, more students are learning about acceptance of diversity. More administrators understand the importance of school reform in terms of inclusive practices. As she stated, "Some years are better than others." But she keeps the dialogue going and the desire at the forefront.

Building Coalitions

When working toward school reform in terms of inclusive practices, it is important to understand how different groups form coalitions through collaboration. Collaboration allows for understanding of different perspectives. Collaboration requires thoughtful questioning and listening of all parties. For example, Zeitlin (2012) found that parents do not perceive themselves as equal partners in the special education process. Many described feeling as if they lack needed knowledge, authority, and power to gain access to opportunity and supports for their children. Parents shared that they are eager for open, trusting exploratory dialogue when they attend IEP or planning meetings on behalf of their children. The parents in her study wanted embracing conversations, not those adversarial in nature. They talked of meetings that were collaborative and casual, with a team approach that reached out to make connections among participants. Kotel (2011) similarly found that mothers engage in a continual thinking, feeling, and acting process when advocating for their children with disabilities. In other words, the process of collaboration must allow time for reflection and reaction to the feelings, thoughts, and actions of all involved including educators, administrators, and community members.

> **? Think About This:**
> Coalition-building is an essential strategy to help protect untenured educators trying to advocate for school change. See Chapter 5 for more analysis of why coalition-building and shared advocacy are both desirable and challenging.

What parents expressed in both of these studies is what is at the heart of meaningful collaboration. All members want to be heard, need to actively engage in conversation without being bogged down with professional jargon, require time to process all the information, and build coalitions that respect the voices and desires of all in order to achieve school reform. Effective educators also understand resistance as expected and multidimensional; they identify and act upon potential teachable moments (Darder, Baltodano, & Torres, 2009; Sapon-Shevin,

2008). The teachable moments are opportunities for effective educators, parents, students, and community members to push forth the focus of school reform.

Recognizing All Voices

Advocacy for school reform is a step-by-step, give-and-take situation requiring effective educators to collaborate with all stakeholders.

Parents. A parent advocating for a more inclusive placement for her child was up against a rigid, unchallenged belief system in a former school district, but through a truly collaborative experience in a new district the self-contained classroom placement for her child was changed. At a meeting, she had expressed her belief that her child, who has an intellectual disability, would benefit from a more inclusive placement. The teachers and administrators were receptive to her request. The meeting was successful because the atmosphere was welcoming, all voices were heard, ideas were shared, and the conversation was relaxed without the typical educational jargon. The trust between team members grew, and the outcome not only resulted in the child being placed in a general education classroom, but the experience became a teachable moment that inspired changes in how one thinks about inclusion. When the parent shared her thoughts on how important it was for not only her child to be included with her peers but for other students to learn from her, the staff realized the school community goes beyond the classroom.

Students. Another characteristic of an effective educator is that he or she recognizes and privileges the knowledge derived from the lived experience of his or her students. Meaningful school change must include the voice of those most affected by the "underlying ableist assumptions that produce and reproduce structures of domination which disadvantage students with disabilities" (Bell, 1997, p. 11) as well as other marginalized groups. There is a great slogan of disability rights activists, "Nothing about us without us!" In fact, all students have knowledge about how they learn best or their barriers to learning. Honoring the voices of students empowers them and helps make visible the effects on them of secrets, power, discrimination, and marginalization.

Students are rarely included in any discussions regarding their education, but when they are, they are highly critical of the labels they receive as well as the procedures and mechanisms used to place them into special programs. We all know that students are mystified by this process of being labeled and placed in separate classrooms and programs. They share feelings of being powerless over educational decisions and of being pushed

Activity 12.4:. Art as an Expression of Marginalization

Look at this picture:

Artwork by David Feingold

- What do you see?
- Can you read the words "wheelchairs only"?
- Does the picture evoke any feelings?
- What does it say about stereotypes?
- Can you make any connections with other marginalized groups of students?
- What do you think the artist was saying through his picture?
- Would it make any difference knowing the artist is disabled?

There are many ways to build bridges between art and advocacy. (See also Activity 12.B, Advocacy Art Activities to Promote Social Justice, Related Resources for Chapter 12, www.tcpress.com.).

and pulled between general education and separate programs. Effective educators listen to the voices of their students. They frame differences in student learning as a natural part of learning, rather than focusing on perceived deficits. If students feel a particular service or placement is stigmatizing or isolating, they will not benefit from it. They will resist. Listening and honoring those voices empowers them.

Community Groups. Ideas for collaborative school reform can come from the community as well. Many local businesses cooperating with work-study programs and transition programs have a perspective that can help guide instruction. As long as the doors for collaboration are open, school reform is possible.

Summary

To review, some strategies to consider for effective collaboration include the following:

- a positive attitude toward the collaborative process
- a welcoming atmosphere that invites and expects involvement from all
- an awareness of frustration and emotions surrounding the issue
- an effort to minimize jargon and power plays
- a commitment to implementing contributions from all

Understanding the perspective and resistance of administrators, teachers, therapists, parents, and students is the beginning of how to create a shared value of acceptance and diversity. One cannot share a value without understanding the other's perspective. Ongoing collaboration, recognizing resistance, and acting on teachable moments are crucial for school reform.

 Activity 12.5: Poetry and Diversity

Review the poems on diversity from the following link: http://www. worldunityinc.org/winning_poems_for_the_diversity.htm
 Answer the following questions:

- What do these students have to say about marginalization?
- Diversity?
- Acceptance?
- What does advocacy look like for them?

CONCLUSION

School reform requires more than legislation and mandates. Testing, core teaching standards, and evidence-based practices do not create school change that supports diversity. Real school change comes from a change in attitudes and beliefs. Effective educators advocate for school change that embraces inclusion and diversity, and critically analyze curriculum and teaching practice. Sometimes that means taking risks. They reflect on the social issue of diversity. They engage in critical collaboration and take advantage of teachable moments. They privilege the voices of those who are marginalized and encourage the perspectives of all to be heard. They understand the influence social media has on society. Effective educators understand that advocacy is more than lofty discussions about the importance of acceptance and diversity; they create action and model advocacy. Critical analysis and collaboration are what will create true school change.

GROUND TRUTH: A PARENT'S VOICE

Michele,
Matt's Mother, Illinois

As the mother of four children, one of whom has Down syndrome, I have experienced many highs and lows pertaining to acceptance of diversity and inclusion in schools and the community. As I write this, it dawns on me that more of the highs have come with the community opportunities compared to our school district. Those involved in organizing the community opportunities understand the value of all individuals, not just those who excel at a particular activity. They have open hearts, open minds, and a willingness to step out into the unknown.

With regard to education, my son has experienced inclusion very successfully in elementary school due to a principal who believed all students should be valued and respected in school and in the community in general. She had the leadership skills to empower educators in her school to carry out that vision, which included optimizing and individualizing their education plans.

However, middle school has been a very different experience. There is no vision or belief system for inclusion, as that was not even presented as an option. Thus far in middle school any inclusive opportunities have been the result of parents who have gone before us. A path has been started but it is certainly parent driven. I believe there are some educators in our district who understand true collaboration and may be willing to take risks for the marginalized; however, they seem to be few and far between. I do know that by law I am an equal member of the team and of course as one of his parents I know him best, but it still feels risky advocating for changes to the usual way things are done when the belief system for inclusion is not shared. Although I am educated, I am not an educator. Will they view me as trying to tell them what to do? Will they placate me with words but no actions? Will my son get less attention or be treated poorly?

I am often overwhelmed when I try to figure out how to navigate the system. I imagine my son may feel the same due to his disability, yet he perseveres and takes pride in his accomplishments regardless of how schools measure those accomplishments. My son does that on a daily basis, so how could I not show that same courage to advocate for changes that will value diversity and inclusiveness?

REFERENCES

Bell, L. A. (1997). Theoretical foundations of social justice education. In L. Adams, L. A. Bell, & P. Griffin (Eds,), *Teaching for diversity and social justice: A sourcebook* (pp. 3–15). New York: Routledge.

Clarke, M., Haney, W., & Madaus, G. (2000). *High stakes testing and high school completion.* Boston: Boston College, Lynch School of Education, National Board on Educational Testing and Public Policy.

Darder, A., Baltodano, M., & Torres, R. (2009). *The critical pedagogy reader* (2nd ed.). New York: Routledge.

Darling-Hammond, L. (2004). Inequity and the right to learn: Access to qualified teachers in California public schools. *Teachers College Record, 106*(10), 1936–1966.

Ferri, B. A., & Connor, D. J. (2005). In the shadow of *Brown*: Special education and overrepresentation of students of color. *Remedial and Special Education, 26*, 93–100.

Fiedler, C. (2000). *Making a difference: Advocacy competencies for special education professionals.* Boston, MA: Allyn & Bacon.

Frith, G. H. (1981). "Advocate" vs. "Professional Employee": A question of priorities for special educators. *Exceptional Children, 47*(7), 486–492

Haberman, M. (1991). The pedagogy of poverty versus good teaching. *Kappan, 73*, 290–294.

Harrison, E. (1930). *Sketches along life's road.* Boston: The Stratford Company.

Heshusius, L. (2004). From creative discontent toward epistemological freedom in special education: Reflections on a 25-year journey. In D. O. Gallagher, L. Heshusius, R. P. Iano, & T. M. Skrtic (Eds.), *Challenging orthodoxy in special education: Dissenting voices* (pp. 169–230). Denver, CO: Love Publishing.

Heubert, J. P., & Hauser, R. M., Eds. (1999). *High stakes: Testing for tracking, promotion, and graduation.* Washington, DC: National Academy Press.

House, R., & Martin, P. (1998). Advocating for better futures for all students: A new vision for school counselors. *Education, 119*, 284–291.

Kotel, K. (2011). *Mothering children with Down syndrome: Same vision, different perspectives, working together.* (Unpublished doctoral dissertation). National Louis University, Chicago, IL.

Kozol, J. (1991). *Savage inequities: Children in America's schools.* New York, NY: Crown Publishers

Miron, G., Urschel, J., Mathis, W., & Tornquist, E. (2010). *Schools without diversity: education management organizations, charter schools, and the demographic stratification of the American school system.* Boulder, CO: Education and the Public Interest Center & Education Policy and Research Unit. Retrieved from http://nepc.colorado.edu/publication/schools-without-diversity

National Center for Education Statistics. (2012). Trends in high school dropout and completion rates in the United States: 1972-2009. Retrieved from http://nces.ed.gov/pubs2012/2012006.pdf.

Nichols, S. L., Glass, G. V., & Berliner, D. C. (2006). High-stakes testing and student achievement: Does accountability pressure increase student learning? *Education Policy Analysis Archives, 14*(1), 1–172. Retrieved from http://epaa.asu.edu/epaa/v14n1/

Orfield, G., Losen, D., Wald, J., & Swanson, C. B. (2004). *Losing our future: How minority youth are being left behind by the graduation rate crisis.* Cambridge, MA: The Civil Rights Project at Harvard University.

Pickering v. Board of Education. (1968). 391 U.S. 563.

Peters, S., & Chimedza, R. (2000). Conscientization and the cultural politics of education: A radical minority perspective. *Comparative Education Review, 44*(3), 245–271.

Sapon-Shevin, M. (2008). Teachable moments for social justice. *Independent School, 67*(3), 44–47.

Sapon-Shevin, M., & Zollers, N. (1999). Multicultural and disability agendas in teacher education: Preparing teachers for diversity. *International Journal of Leadership in Education, 2*(3), 165–190.

U.S. Department of Education. (2012). *New data from U.S. Department of Education highlights educational inequities around teacher experience, discipline and high school rigor.* Retrieved from: http://www.ed.gov/news/press-releases/new-data-us-department-education-highlights-educational-inequities-around-teache

Weber, M. (1949). *The methodology of the social sciences* (E. A. Shils & H. A. Finch., Trans.). New York, NY: Free Press. (Originally published 1904)

Zeitlin, V. (2012). *Rethinking the IEP process: The parent voice and considerations for change* (Unpublished doctoral dissertation). National Louis University, Chicago, IL.

Examining Perspectives on Inclusive Education

Diana Lawrence-Brown
Mara Sapon-Shevin

All that is needed for the triumph of evil is for good people to do nothing.

—Edmond Burke (1729–1797)

Some will have reached this point in the book energized, inspired, and ready to go! Others may be thinking, "This sounds very nice, but it's much too radical. It's pie-in-the-sky; it'll never happen. What are these people thinking?" We hope this final chapter will be helpful to both groups and to those in between.

If you are skeptical, you are not alone in wondering if what we are proposing is really possible. So much of the way we do schooling is so entrenched. Many schools educate in such similar ways that it can be hard to imagine that it could be otherwise. We hope that this book has made it clear that changing education is a huge task, complex and deeply embedded in conventional ways of seeing and talking about differences, equity, and change. In the sections to come, you'll find a dialogue about inclusive schooling, starting off with the doubts of an established special educator.

EXPRESSING RESERVATIONS ABOUT INCLUSIVE SCHOOLING

To begin the dialogue, Dr. Kate Garnett, professor of special education at Hunter College, explains her reservations about inclusive schooling (see Figure C.1). Using the instructions in the text that directly follows the figure, read and respond to this critique.

Figure C.1. Responding to "Let's Not Call the Whole Thing Off . . ." (Dr. Kate Garnett)

	Response
No, no, sorry, but no amount of good ideas or marginality rhetoric regarding what should be can make general education classrooms nearly adequate or appropriate for all kids with disabilities at all stages of their schooling. The authors' rather rigid stance about what's good (and, therefore, bad) intrudes upon their otherwise clear-headed, kid-oriented portraits of how to make classrooms more hospitable and teaching more broadly effective. The text offers practical means for teachers to repossess their teaching and do right by the kids in their care—planning for different starting places, opening options for multiple modes of expression, and bringing out the grain of kids' diverse talents.	__ I agree __ I'm not sure __ I disagree Comments:
Yes, yes, yes to all of that, but... • Why insist upon the same arrangement for every kid, at every stage of schooling—that is, general education integration with typical peers in all aspects of instruction? Why this inflexible prescription?	__ I agree __ I'm not sure __ I disagree Comments:
» Is flexibility employing strong inclusive practices really such magic—even when employed uncommonly well? Are the parameters of a 30-kid, grade-level, general education classroom infinitely flexible? » Is time limitlessly malleable in the school day for widely diverse purposes? Sorry, no: inclusive practices are potent, not all-powerful; laudable, valuable, and worth pursuing, but not sufficient unto the task.	__ I agree __ I'm not sure __ I disagree Comments:
Why privilege "access-to-the-curriculum" as the end-goal, with its two common denominators: engaging grade-level content in classrooms and participation of typical age-level peers? While a worthy goal among goals, access-to-the-curriculum is a narrow viewpoint within the wide expanse of an appropriate education. For example, other life-important goals took prominence for my friends Molly, Julian, and Jamal during several of their 12+ years of schooling—goals requiring intensive use of time, a distinctive setting (with space of their own, limited group-size, and more-like peers), and specially-designed instruction. . . . Molly's three-year respite in a special class allowed re-entry in 6th grade without the daily stomachaches and tears. . . . While Julian's mother had sought solutions since 1st grade, not until middle school did Julian get an evaluation (norm-referenced is not an evil concept) which revealed gifted learning prowess alongside processing weakness and which finally triggered intensive reading work (remediation is not a dirty word). . . . Jamal shifted to a life skills program starting in 9th grade, enabling independence in his young adulthood.	__ I agree __ I'm not sure __ I disagree Comments:

- It escapes me: How were these bad moves for these kids? Was the notion of a cascade-of-services really such a rotten idea, harmful to both kid and society?

___ I agree
___ I'm not sure
___ I disagree
Comments:

- And, why, given its many valuable accomplishments in the lives of children and families, is special education tarred here as the problem and set up as a whipping boy? Have we not contributed significantly to general educational practices, as well as to the welfare of kids with special needs? Have we not persisted in reminding the larger enterprise about the dignity and value of individual differences?

___ I agree
___ I'm not sure
___ I disagree
Comments:

- Have my years of probing and discerning what's with particular kids with learning disabilities actually resulted in a deficit lens that has increased their problems? Many, many kids (and their parents) have responded with gratitude and a melting relief at finally being seen. Before their disability was brought into focus and shared, they were battered by misrepresentations born of ignorance.

___ I agree
___ I'm not sure
___ I disagree
Comments:

Yes, definitely yes, classrooms can (and should) flex their ways of operating. Yes, we need to keep the pressure on to broaden and refine schools' instructional palette, keep the good ideas flowing, promote skilled teaching and responsive classrooms, but… not sacrifice our kids' learning needs on the altar of an all-inclusive ideal.

___ I agree
___ I'm not sure
___ I disagree
Comments:

Can you hear my being torn between two goods, pained by the pitting of inclusive practices against other worthy, and important, special educational responses to significant individual differences? And, in the pit of my stomach, I am afraid that demonizing special education has us heading precipitously towards its demise, leaving the larger enterprise (e.g., schooling and society) much impoverished, and once again challenging those stalwart families who did it the first time to do it all over again.

___ I agree
___ I'm not sure
___ I disagree
Comments:

P.S. Help me understand why none of the 50+ inclusive classes I have visited in the past three years was providing electronic read-aloud text of any kind for its students—truly perplexing. Clearly, there's a long row-to-hoe for general education classrooms to get where they can go—let us work toward that, among other solutions.

___ I agree
___ I'm not sure
___ I disagree
Comments:

Kate's comments help us look at how hard it will be to change education and what some of the resistance might look like. And even if you are not one who shares this "too radical, pie-in-the-sky" viewpoint, you should be prepared for such a response from some others if you proceed down the path that we propose.

First, read Kate's comments in column 1 of Figure C.1 (don't worry about the right-hand column with your response just yet). Although she focuses on students with disabilities, some of the challenges she raises about the nature (and intractability) of general education are relevant across a wide range of diverse students. See if you can apply a basic message of the book, Dan Wilkins's phrase "same struggle, different difference," to extend her critique to education of students with other marginalized differences as well.

Next is your opportunity to respond to the critique, a chance for you to weigh in with your own perspectives. Go back and consider each point again. This time, please indicate your general feelings about each point by checking one of the three options in column two of Figure C.1. Use the "Comments" space to explain your thinking. You may also find it helpful to go back and review previous chapters pertinent to the issues under discussion.

The author of the critique in Figure C.1 clearly sees some of the same rigidities and restrictions of general education that we do—as it is currently enacted. Students who are different are not always well accepted, and their needs are often unmet in typical classrooms. She wonders why we think that inclusive classrooms in which there is a strong community, where curriculum and pedagogy are differentiated and responsive and educators are adequately supported, are a possibility. She wonders if special education is always a problem and what we will lose if we conceptualize it that way.

SUMMING UP THE CASE FOR INCLUSIVE EDUCATION

Now it's our chance to respond to the skeptics and naysayers about inclusive education, including Kate and many others we have met and interacted with. The following points sum up our approach to inclusive education, as presented throughout this book:

- *Inclusive education is possible*—with *the appropriate supports.* Let's be clear; we are *not* talking about "calling the whole thing off," if "the whole thing" is special *services.* But we believe that the right amount of clear-headed, kid-oriented ideas, *and accompanying supports* for students and educators, can make inclusive general education classrooms at *least* as adequate, appropriate, hospitable, and effective as segregated classrooms for all kids (even those without disabilities) at all stages of their schooling. Necessary supports *include* special services (e.g., special and gifted education, bilingual, remedial) provided using a collaborative, push-in model based in the general education classroom.

- *We cannot assume that education is better in special classes and worse in general education without evidence* (see Chapter 6). Nor can we assume that simply placing marginalized students in general education will automatically create the needed changes to make that setting appropriately inclusive. All of this will take hard work. Segregated classrooms have no special ability to produce educators who repossess their teaching and do right by the kids in their care—planning for different starting places, opening options for multiple modes of expression, and bringing out the grain of kids' diverse talents. None of that requires (or is more likely in) a segregated program. In fact, some of those changes are more difficult in segregated settings because of the lack of appropriate peer models.

- *We have to look at children and their characteristics differently.* Of course, figuring out "what's with" not just particular kids, but every kid, is a necessary part of effective teaching (see Chapters 3, 7–10). And yes, every student also deserves to *finally be seen*; no student should be battered by misrepresentations born of ignorance of dis/ability or any other traditionally marginalized differences. But understanding learning differences also doesn't require segregated programs.

- *Equity and social justice* don't *mean treating everyone the same.* We are most assuredly *not* insisting upon the same arrangement for every kid, at every stage of schooling. That's not at all the same as effective inclusion with typical peers in all aspects of instruction, which insists upon *responsive pedagogy* at every stage of schooling. We reject narrow interpretations of inclusion—simply throwing all kids back into a regular classroom without adequate supports and without huge changes in how we *do* curriculum, pedagogy, teacher education, and school culture. We reject the idea that it's the students who have to change or be fixed in order to be allowed into general education. We place the onus of change squarely on the educational system itself.

- *Collaboration among professionals and skill-sharing are essential to the success of inclusion.* Schools and programs that pigeonhole and segregate professionals ("You're a special educator"; "You're a school counselor"; "You're a Title One teacher") are problematic for many of the reasons we've named in this book. All individuals have multiple identities, and if we focus on the program and the professional associated with it, we will continue to have rigid, inflexible schools and programs that create false and unnecessary distinctions among learners and how we conceptualize their educations. Yes, definitely, general and special educators can (and should) flex their ways of operating, as should other school personnel. Yes, we need to keep the pressure on to broaden and refine schools' instructional palettes, keep the good ideas flowing, promote skilled teaching and responsive classrooms, and change what constitutes "general education."

- *Specialized services are not the problem—it's* where, by whom, *and* to whom *they are provided.* We still need specialized services—every professional can't know everything. We need people who understand speech and language development, queer youth, curriculum modification, anti-racist pedagogy, and on and on. Let's bring those with specialized knowledge bases and skills into inclusive classrooms (where others can benefit as well), and begin to dispense with the stigma created by exclusion (be that the gifted program, the resource room, or friendship groups for marginalized students). Specially designed instruction in important life goals (necessary for greater independence for students like Jamal, above, and Pei, Chapter 8) does require intensive time—and supports. However, this instruction is most effectively taught in natural settings (e.g., general education and community environments), *not* segregated life skills programs (for detailed implementation guidance, see Browder & Spooner, 2011; Ryndak & Alper, 2003; for outcomes research, see Chapter 6). And, let us not forget that, just as the push to *develop* special services was led by stalwart families, such families have also been leading the push to *locate* those services in inclusive classrooms.

- *Effective inclusion of students with traditionally marginalized differences can really happen.* We are certain about this because it is already happening in many places, and not always under ideal circumstances. For example, inclusion of students with disabilities (the most segregated group of marginalized students) has been steadily on the rise in the United States, from well under 40% of students with disabilities spending at least 80% of their day in general education settings in 1990 (Giangreco, Hurley, & Suter, 2009) to 61% of students with disabilities in 2011 (U.S. Office of Special Education Programs, 2012). Meaningful multicultural education is increasing as well, and is being incorporated into structures such as teacher certification requirements and accreditation standards. And all over the country, schools are undertaking anti-bullying efforts, spurred on to a great extent by concern for GLBT and other marginalized youth.

CHOOSING APATHY OR ACTIVISM

As Suzanne SooHoo (2004) eloquently warns in her article, "We Change the World by Doing Nothing," apathetic bystanders, as well as activists, have an impact on our schools and society. Or, in the words of songwriter Neil Peart (1980), "if you choose not to decide, you still have made a choice." SooHoo describes apathy not as mere failure to act but as indifference and denial amounting to complicity. However, she explains, often people are not so much uncaring as unequipped to act, unprepared to oppose dominant forces.

Educators at all levels have a responsibility to develop critical thinkers capable of acting on behalf of a just society. Students at all levels (including those in higher education) need the following (SooHoo, 2004):

 Activity C.1: Your Own Vision

Now it's your turn to think about all you've read. Respond to the following questions:

1. What aspects of the vision we've presented throughout the book—in terms of responses to differences, teaching, advocacy, etc.— are appealing to you? What parts particularly resonated with you? What would it be like if the world (and schools) came to be that way?
2. Are there aspects of the vision we've presented that seem impossible to you? Perhaps you're thinking that people will never accept transgender students or that individual needs can never be met in something called "the general education classroom." What do you think are the biggest obstacles to overcome in order to make this vision of equitable, inclusive education possible?
3. How do you connect our vision of equitable, socially just, inclusive education to the broader community and the world? What are the implications of this vision for how society would need to change? What are the ways in which current societal, economic, and political practices make this vision hard (Sapon-Shevin, 2007)? Think, perhaps, about how schools are financed in the United States and the implications of that formula for the goal of achieving equitable schooling. Or think about the ways in which women are portrayed in the media and how that affects the possibilities of enacting gender equity in schools and addressing sex-role socialization and its concurrent limitations.
4. What is your own vision for equitable, socially just education?

- the ability to question the status quo, asking "why this way?" and "who benefits?"
- a specific vision for social justice that incorporates alternatives that are both equitable and attainable
- to be able to explain their moral positions and "become proficient in naming, problem posing, critiquing, creating alternatives" (p. 208)
- to form coalitions with diverse colleagues who respect risk-taking and honest dialogue
- to be able to deconstruct power relations and processes, to "critically examine conflict and assess the economic, social, and political conditions that produce it" (p. 208)
- a realistic sense of barriers, to be able to strategically defy the stifling impact on progressive school change efforts of both apathy and active resistance
- to be able to create strategies for action toward greater equity, justice, and democracy

The task is big, and it is important—critical to our survival as a democratic society. Let us continue it now, together.

 Activity C.2: Your Action Plan

For your final activity of the book, use the list above to create your own action plan to help you move forward. You might want to consider these questions to start you on your way:

1. What are three areas about which you feel you need to learn more in order to create inclusive schools? How will you address your own personal learning agenda? Whom will you talk to? Where will you find resources? How will you make sure that the resources you find are accurate? Say, for example, that you've identified that you know almost nothing about Islam and that you feel hesitant that you could meet the educational and social needs of Muslim students in your class. How will you learn more about this area? What immediate steps could you take to increase your knowledge and comfort?
2. What are three concrete steps you could take *right now* to move yourself, your colleagues, your community, and your world toward a more inclusive reality? Who could support you in taking these steps? What will you do to maintain your focus and vision?

REFERENCES

Browder, D., & Spooner, F. (2011). *Teaching students with moderate and severe disabilities*). New York: Guilford.

Giangreco, M., Hurley, S., & Suter, J. (2009). Special education personnel utilization and general class placement of students with disabilities: Ranges and ratios. *Intellectual and Developmental Disabilities, 47*(1), 53–56.

Peart, N. (1980). Freewill [Recorded by Rush]. On *Permanent Waves* [Record]. Mercury.

Ryndak, D. & Alper, S. (2003). *Curriculum and instruction for students with significant disabilities in inclusive settings* (2nd ed.). Boston: Allyn & Bacon.

Sapon-Shevin, M. (2007). *Widening the circle: The power of inclusive classrooms.* Boston: Beacon Press.

SooHoo, S. (2004). We change the world by doing nothing. *Teacher Education Quarterly, 31*(1), 199–211.

U.S. Office of Special Education Programs. (2012). Table B3-2. Percent of all students ages 6 through 21 served under IDEA, Part B, by educational environment and state: Fall 2011. Retrieved from www.ideadata.org/arc_toc13.asp#partbLRE

About the Authors and Contributors

Diana Lawrence-Brown is associate professor of differentiated instruction at St. Bonaventure University and has more than 20 years of experience with a broad range of diverse learners in a wide variety of settings. Her work focuses on authentic and responsive pedagogy for the full range of diverse learners, specializing in assistive technologies, multilevel differentiated instruction, the history of inclusive education, understanding factors that facilitate educators' comfort with inclusion, and the critical analysis of education policy and practice, including how power is exercised in schools and who benefits.

Mara Sapon-Shevin is professor of inclusive education at Syracuse University. Her areas of interest include full inclusion, teaching for social justice, teacher education, and anti-oppressive education. Her recent books include *Widening the Circle: The Power of Inclusive Classrooms*, *Because We Can Change the World: A Practical Guide to Building Cooperative, Inclusive Classroom Communities*, and (with Nancy Schniedewind) *Educational Courage: Resisting the Ambush of Public Education*.

Subini A. Annamma is currently an assistant professor at Indiana University-Indianapolis. Previously, she was a special education teacher working with culturally and linguistically diverse students with emotional, behavioral, and learning disabilities. Subini's research interest include educational equity, racial identity development, and the disproportionate representation of culturally and linguistically diverse sudents in special education.

Laura Atkinson is a clinical instructor in the Mary Lou Fulton Teacher's College, Arizona State University (ASU) and a doctoral student in Curriculum and Instruction-Special Education. Laura was the coordinator of the Urban Professional Learning Schools Initiative (UPLSI) master's program at ASU. Laura received her MA in special education from the University of Wisconsin-Madison and spent over 10 years teaching in general and special education.

David J. Connor is an associate professor in the School of Education at Hunter College, City University of New York. Previous to this position, he worked in New York City schools for 18 years. David's research interests include effective classroom practices, inclusive education, the overrepresentation of children of color in special education, learning disabilities, and intersectional work with dis/ability, race, class, gender, sexuality, and nationality.

Elizabeth Z. Dejewski, MA, is a special education teacher and a doctoral student in the Disability and Equity in Education Program at National Louis University. She is a mother of two children with and without disability relentlessly pursuing issues of equality and integrity for all.

David Feingold, EdD, earned his doctorate in disability and equity in education from National Louis University. David was a school social worker for 15 years, advocating for and helping students with disabilities meet their social, emotional, and behavioral potential. David not only has multiple neurological disabilities, he is a prolific artist, whose unique work is represented in numerous online disability art websites and art shows.

Ana Maria García is chair of the Department of Sociology, Anthropology, and Criminal Justice and associate professor of women's studies and sociology at Arcadia University in Glenside, Pennsylvania. Professor García's courses and research revolve around understanding the dynamics and meanings of negotiating a subaltern identity in terms of gender, race, and sexuality.

Kathryn Henn-Reinke, PhD, is a professor of ESL/bilingual education at the University of Wisconsin, Oshkosh. She specializes in biliteracy and development of academic language with English learners. Several of her publications focus on biliteracy and development of multilingual language skills.

JoDell Heroux is a doctoral candidate in special education at Michigan State University. She is currently involved in piloting a hybrid format of internship teacher supervision. Her research interests include exploring beliefs about disability, inclusion, and special education, and how knowledge of competing paradigms of disability influences teacher practice.

Kathleen Kotel, EdD, earned her doctorate in disability and equity in education at National Louis University. Kathy is the mother of a child with a disability. Prior to raising her children, she taught middle school for 13 years. Kathy is an adjunct professor at NLU and continues to consult with schools and parents of children with disabilities.

Elizabeth B. Kozleski is chair and professor of special education at the University of Kansas. Her work focuses on theorizing systems change for equity, inclusive education, and professional learning for urban schools. Author of multiple books, chapters, and articles, she was awarded the UNESCO Chair in Inclusive International Research in 2005 and received the TED-Merrill award for her leadership in special education teacher education in 2011.

Valerie Owen, PhD, is professor emeritus at National Louis University and is the former director of the Disability and Equity in Education Doctoral Program. For over 30 years she has been an advocate for teachers and the students they teach and support.

Susan Peters is an associate professor emeritus from Michigan State University. As a Fulbright Scholar she undertook extensive fieldwork in Zimbabwe. Her work and publications have focused on international and comparative inclusive education. In addition to her scholarly work, Susan has been an advocate of disability rights for over 25 years and has held various leadership positions in disability rights organizations.

Julie Ramirez, MEd, is a special education teacher in the suburbs of Chicago and a candidate in the Disability and Equity of Education Program at National Louis University. For 16 years, she has taught and advocated for preteens with significant intellectual disabilities who do not have a voice for themselves.

Maryl A. Randel, MA, is a doctoral candidate in the Department of Special Education at Michigan State University. A former special educator and reading specialist, she works on improving access to high-quality literacy instruction for diverse youth in and out-of-school settings.

Janet Sauer is an assistant professor at the University of Colorado in Colorado Springs (UCCS), where she co-teaches with people with disabilities, their family members, and guests from other disciplines to illustrate the complex and interdisciplinary nature of disability. She has taught children in Africa, on a Navajo Reservation and in Boston, Ohio, and Iowa. In all of these places, she has worked toward building inclusive communities.

Stacey N. Skoning, PhD, is an associate professor and chair of the Department of Special Education at the University of Wisconsin Oshkosh. She has degrees in both general and special education. Dr. Skoning's current research focuses on developing teaching methods and strategies that better support all students within the general education setting, whether they have disabilities or gifts and talents.

Graciela Slesaransky-Poe, PhD, is associate professor of education at Arcadia University. She coordinates the programs on gender and sexuality in education. Her recent work has been published in *Sex Education*, *The Teacher Educator*, *Equity Alliance*, *Phi Delta Kappan*, and the *LGBT Youth Journal*.

Robin M. Smith, PhD, is an associate professor of special education at the State University of New York at New Paltz in the Department of Educational Studies/Special Education Program. Her research and teaching interests include integrating the principles of disability studies, inclusion, assuming competence, and social justice into daily life.

Virginia Zeitlin, EdD, received her doctorate from the Disability and Equity in Education Doctoral Program at National Louis University. She is an assistant superintendent of instructional services in suburban Chicago and is an adjunct professor at Dominican University in River Forest, Illinois. She has been working in the area of student support for over 30 years, with a particular interest in inclusion and parent-school collaboration.

Index